TRUTH IN VISUAL MEDIA

Aesthetics, Ethics and Politics

Edited by Marguerite La Caze
and Ted Nannicelli

EDINBURGH
University Press

Edinburgh University Press is one of the leading university presses in the UK.
We publish academic books and journals in our selected subject areas across the
humanities and social sciences, combining cutting-edge scholarship with high editorial
and production values to produce academic works of lasting importance. For more
information visit our website: edinburghuniversitypress.com

Edinburgh University Press Ltd
The Tun – Holyrood Road
12 (2f) Jackson's Entry
Edinburgh EH8 8PJ

Typeset in 10/12.5 pt Sabon
by IDSUK (DataConnection) Ltd

A CIP record for this book is available from the British Library

ISBN 978 1 4744 7446 7 (hardback)
ISBN 978 1 4744 7448 1 (webready PDF)
ISBN 978 1 4744 7449 8 (epub)

CONTENTS

FIGURES

NOTES ON CONTRIBUTORS

Susan Best is Professor of Art Theory and Deputy Director (Research and Postgraduate) at Queensland College of Art, Griffith University. She is a fellow of the Australian Academy of the Humanities. She is the author of *Visualizing Feeling: Affect and the Feminine Avant-garde* (2011), which won the Australian and New Zealand Art Association prize for best book in 2012. Her most recent book, *Reparative Aesthetics: Witnessing and Contemporary Art Photography* (2016), was joint winner of the Australian and New Zealand Art Association prize for best book in 2017.

Damian Cox is Associate Professor of Philosophy at Bond University. He teaches philosophy and film, ethics and political philosophy. He has co-authored three books: *Integrity and the Fragile Self*, *A Politics Most Unusual: Violence, Sovereignty and Democracy in the War on Terror* and *Thinking Through Film*. Current projects include work on 'affect mirrors' in the cinema.

Kris Fallon is an assistant professor in the Department of Cinema and Digital Media at University of California, Davis. His research focuses on non-fiction visual culture across a range of platforms, from still photography and documentary film to data visualisation and social media. His essays on digital technology and documentary have appeared in journals such as *Film Quarterly* and *Screen* and several edited anthologies including *Contemporary Documentary* and *Documentary across Disciplines*. He is currently completing a book entitled *Where Truth Lies: Digital Culture and Documentary Media After 9/11*.

Mette Hjort is Chair Professor of Humanities and Dean of Arts at Hong Kong Baptist University. Previously she was Professor of Film Studies at the University of Copenhagen, Professor II of Art and Media Studies at the Norwegian University of Science and Technology, Affiliate Professor of Scandinavian Studies at the University of Washington, Seattle, and Honorary Professor of Visual Studies at Lingnan University, where she previously served as Associate Vice President (Internationalization and Academic Quality Assurance). Selected publications include the influential monograph *Small Nation, Global Cinema* (2005) and, most recently, the edited volume *African Cinema and Human Rights* (with Eva Jørholt, 2019).

Amy L. Hubbell is Senior Lecturer in French at the University of Queensland where she researches francophone autobiographies of exile and trauma. She is author of *Remembering French Algeria: Pieds-Noirs, Identity and Exile* (2015) and *À la recherche d'un emploi: Business French in a Communicative Context* (2017), and co-editor of several journal volumes as well as *The Unspeakable: Representations of Trauma in Francophone Literature and Art* (2013) and *Textual and Visual Selves: Photography, Film and Comic Art in French Autobiography* (2011). She is currently working on her new project, 'Hoarding Memory: Covering the Wounds of the Algerian War'.

Marguerite La Caze is Associate Professor in Philosophy at the University of Queensland. She has research interests and publications in European and feminist philosophy in the fields of ethics, political philosophy and aesthetics, including philosophy and film. Her publications include *The Analytic Imaginary* (2002), *Integrity and the Fragile Self* (with Damian Cox and Michael Levine, 2003), *Wonder and Generosity: Their Role in Ethics and Politics* (2013) and *Ethical Restoration after Communal Violence: The Grieving and the Unrepentant* (2018). She is currently working on a project on film philosophy and non-violent resistance to authoritarian regimes.

Ted Nannicelli teaches at The University of Queensland. He is editor of *Projections: The Journal for Movies and Mind*. His most recent book is *Artistic Creation and Ethical Criticism* (2020).

Tom O'Regan was a key figure in the development of cultural and media studies in Australia. His positions included Professor of Media and Cultural Studies at the University of Queensland (2004–20), Director of the Australian Key Centre for Cultural and Media Policy (1999–2002, Griffith University) and Director of the Centre for Research in Culture and Communication (1996–8, Murdoch University). Tom co-founded the media and cultural studies journal *Continuum* (1987–95) and was Australia's UNESCO Professor of Communication from

2001 to 2003. He was elected a Fellow of Australian Academy of the Humanities in 2002.

Ellen Marie Saethre-McGuirk is Associate Professor at Nord University, Norway, and in 2018 was a Visiting Fellow at the Design Lab, Queensland University of Technology. Her research interests are at the crossing points between philosophical aesthetics, modern and contemporary art and design, and cultural pedagogy within the digital sphere. Her work explores areas of learning, creativity, and the creative act on and through the digital interface in relation to working with materials and the physical object. Her most recent work includes the exhibition 'Norwegian Sublime: Landscape photography in the age of the iPhone', shown at the Frank Moran Memorial Gallery in Brisbane.

Robert Sinnerbrink is Associate Professor in Philosophy and Australian Research Council Future Fellow at Macquarie University, Sydney. He is the author of *Cinematic Ethics: Exploring Ethical Experience through Film* (2016), *New Philosophies of Film: Thinking Images* (2011) and *Understanding Hegelianism* (2007/2014), and is a member of the editorial board of the journal *Film-Philosophy*. He has published numerous articles on the relationship between film and philosophy in journals such as the *Australasian Philosophical Review*, *Angelaki*, *Film-Philosophy*, *Necsus: European Journal of Media Studies*, *Projections: The Journal of Movies and Mind*, *Screen*, *Screening the Past* and *SubStance*. His book *Terrence Malick: Filmmaker and Philosopher* was published in 2019.

Grant Tavinor is Senior Lecturer at Lincoln University, Aotearoa/New Zealand. He is the author of *The Art of Videogames* (2009) and co-editor of *The Aesthetics of Videogames* (2018).

INTRODUCTION

Marguerite La Caze and Ted Nannicelli

In the era of fake news, truthiness, reality creation and widespread cynicism and disaffection about images and how they are presented, an examination of the role of visual media of all kinds and their relation to truth is timely. This collection traces continuities between the aesthetic, ethical, and political questions raised by traditional visual media and shows how new visual media have reshaped these questions and raised new ones for spectators, artists, and theorists, as well as different aesthetic affordances, ethical challenges, and political potential. The chapters investigate the interrelations between aesthetics, ethics, and politics in a variety of visual media forms ranging across art installations, Facebook Live, film and television, both narrative and documentary, Instagram, painting, photography, video games, and interactive documentaries. They explore how different ethical questions, political implications, and aesthetic pleasures arise and shape one another in particular ways in distinct visual media. The themes include the use of cinema as a medium for ethical and political thought, how documentary subjects and artworks both conceal and reveal truth, how art can work to enact and further reparation, new ethical questions arising from inter-active media, such as documentary, the role of images in responding to political events and trauma, and the particular manifestations of political relationships as a result of recent transformations in the production, distribution, and reception of various media forms.

Part One, 'Aesthetics', comprises chapters on painting, photography, and the use of photography in Instagram. Leading off the section, art historian and theorist Susan Best, in her chapter 'Repair and the Irreparable in Contemporary Aboriginal Art', examines two very different reparative approaches to representing Australia's shameful colonial histories by Indigenous artists working in a range of media, such as installation, machine technologies, painting, photography, printmaking, and video. The concept of 'reparative' refers to ethical and political repair of past wrongs. These concepts are discussed extensively in fields like law, philosophy, and political science, but Best's work in reparative aesthetics is opening up a new area of research (2016). These contrasting artistic approaches are either to hold and express both negative and positive feelings about the past together, or to represent the irreparable and the trauma of that history.

Best analyses contemporary Indigenous art that goes beyond the well-known approaches of postmodern political art that was prevalent in art from the 1970s to 1990s preoccupied with identity politics. In Best's view, a focus on identity politics tends to involve expressions of anger against discrimination. However, contemporary Indigenous artists concentrate in different ways on representing the harm of certain accounts of race and atrocities like massacres that occurred in the past. Best's chapter shows how these recent works are able to commemorate in a reparative fashion these historical atrocities. Utilising the work of queer theorist Eve Kosofsky Sedgwick (2003) and providing moving descriptions of the artworks, Best considers that one approach to reparative aesthetics is to articulate the ambivalent feelings towards an unassimilable past (Judy Watson and Robert Andrew) and another is to mark the nature of the irreparable harm that has been caused (Gordon Bennett and Vernon Ah Kee). They also both stress a need to witness the truth of our feelings and the truth about the violence of our colonial histories. Both approaches are invaluable in developing reparative art and Best's chapter develops further the possibilities of reparative aesthetics.

Amy L. Hubbell's chapter, 'Circulating Bodies: Retelling the Trauma of the Algerian War through Photography and Art', also considers questions of reparation and how art can contribute to or undermine such reparation. She specialises in autobiographies of exile and trauma in the francophone world (2015). Hubbell asks whether the images of trauma of the diaspora of former French citizens of Algeria, known collectively as the Pieds-Noirs, circulated on the internet and then reworked into paintings, has a mitigating effect on the trauma they experienced. In recent years, the Pied-Noirs have increasingly turned to the internet to reconnect with each other and their lost homeland by circulating images, primarily photographs, as well as texts from their former home. While the charming shots of Algeria that at first dominated community remembrance still circulate freely, over the past decade, traumatic images from the Algerian War for Independence have also multiplied on Pied-Noir listservs and websites. The images of mutilated corpses are shocking initially, but as they pile up, the viewer becomes more and more desensitised to their power. Once the viewer engages with the images, she eventually recognises that the same select bodies are continuously circulating but alongside a variety of political messages.

Hubbell explains that it is improbable that further images will join these collections; the often-repeated photos are now appearing in different formats such as paintings and installation art. Her chapter concentrates on the work of Nicole Guiraud, who survived the Milk Bar bombing in the Battle of Algiers, which happened when she was ten years old, in 1956. She uses traumatic images from the Algerian War (1954–62) in her work, of victims and survivors, including herself. What is significant about Guiraud's works, in painting and installation art, is how she transforms the experience of exile and trauma of the Pieds-Noirs through placing the well-known images in new configurations that alter their meaning and enable viewers to re-engage with the historical account. Hubbell's insightful chapter explores the phenomena of desensitisation of the circulated photographs and the resensitisation through Guiraud's powerful art for the viewer, so that we can recognise the true horror of what happened, thus to begin the process of reparation.

Ellen Marie Saethre-McGuirk is both theorist and practitioner of photography, and has exhibited her work taken on an iPhone (2018). Her fascinating chapter, 'An i for an Eye: The Collective Shaping of Experience in the Age of Machine-Mediated Art', interprets the photo-sharing platform Instagram as influencing and shaping participants' photographic choices and aesthetic experience, as lives are curated for and by the platform. At a time when smartphones are used globally for photography and the use of social media means that visual communication thoroughly permeates society, this chapter explores how our aesthetic vision and our aesthetic tastes are shaped by and through such machine-mediation. In this period of machine-mediated art, Saethre-McGuirk argues that increasingly we are framing and composing real life so that it is suitable for the platform experience. By cropping and editing the subjects we photograph and through the subjects we choose, we impart many of the aesthetic pleasures of our lives and physical presence to apps like Instagram that are two-dimensional and algorithm-controlled.

Saethre-McGuirk maintains that this mediation of our experience is really a dialectic, where our aesthetic experiences are not only shaped *for* the mediation by our phones, but are also retroactively shaped *by* machine-mediation and social media responses. She first reflects on how the food we eat has changed, and on how fashion photography is mediated and fashion itself is altered through Instagram. Then the chapter investigates how our aesthetic sense is conditioned in relation to landscape photography through using the platform. This conditioning plays out in several different ways, even though it is an aspect of contemporary culture that is surprisingly unobtrusive and understated.

Engaging with Susan Sontag's classic text *On Photography* ([1977] 2008) and Alva Noë's more recent work *Strange Tools: Art and Human Nature* (2015), Saethre-McGuirk contends that social network platforms such as Instagram have transformed not only our way of seeing, but our way of being and experiencing ourselves in fundamental respects. She sees the digital technology of Instagram as going much further than earlier photography in disrupting our engagement with and relationship to the world, and suggests that we need to consider how to reconnect with genuine experiences. Saethre-McGuirk's concern with the effects on our experience of a life dominated by an addiction to pretty images begins to raise significant ethical questions.

In Part Two, 'Ethics', some of these challenging questions are approached directly. One thread that emerges in this section is an emphasis upon the ways that artworks in traditional media are able to surmount a variety of ethical challenges and realise the potential for ethical and political achievement afforded by those media. It opens with Mette Hjort's chapter. Hjort works at the intersection of film, literary studies, media studies, philosophy, and theatre studies (2018). Her chapter, 'The Ethics of Filmmaking: How the Genetic History of Works Affects Their Value', considers the interconnections between ethical and aesthetic value. She asks how ethical value could imply aesthetic value and whether the media used and the context of production influence these values. Her focus is on short films and feature films. Hjort argues that the ethical aspects of production have definite repercussions for the aesthetic value of the film, engaging with Berys Gaut's 'ethicism' – a position which contends that ethical merits in a work always make it aesthetically better and ethical flaws always make it aesthetically worse (2007).

While Hjort takes this position to be preferable to other views on the relation between aesthetic and ethical values, she believes it needs to be extended by considering the conditions of production of film and the relationships between the actors, producers, and the director, for example, and by considering how individuals are vulnerable or harmed in the process. Her approach to developing this extension of the ethicist position is to concentrate on the 'genetic' histories of a range of films to provide an account of a continuum of ethical values that are aesthetically relevant as well as where on that continuum any particular work should be situated. Her cases for the two extremes of the most ethical to the least ethical are Erik Poppe's film concerning the massacre in Norway, *Utøya: July 22* (2018), and Lasse Nielsen's and Ernst Johansen's 1970s Danish youth films. Her incisive discussion exposes some of ways that an ethical approach to cinema can be achieved and the way that knowledge and understanding of the truth about unethical practices in filmmaking are obscured by an excessive focus on the art product. Hjort's chapter concludes with considerations of how the ethicist position she develops could be used to reform the way that films are made.

The theme of reparation appears again in a different form in the next chapter. How documentaries *The Act of Killing* (2012) and *The Look of Silence* (2014) contribute to an ethics of atonement through their approach, the participation of the perpetrators and survivors, and the impact of their screening, is the subject of Marguerite La Caze's chapter, 'The Look of Silence and the Ethics of Atonement'. Her work on ethical restoration informs her reading of these films (2018). In *The Act of Killing* Joshua Oppenheimer interviewed perpetrators from the political genocide in Indonesia in 1965–6 of hundreds of thousands of communists or suspected communists. One of his strategies was to film them re-enacting the killings in a variety of film genres, usually as the perpetrators they were, although sometimes as victims. They show few indications of feeling remorse, with one exception, and playing the role of victim seems to have an effect in evoking that response. Developing an idea of communal atonement first suggested by Linda Radzik (2009), the chapter considers how the documentary film can play a role in that atonement, partly by rendering explicit the true experience of the massacres and their aftermath. The film itself, La Caze contends, can be understood as an attempt at atonement or moral transformation that tries to make up for past wrongs, in spite of the attitudes of the perpetrators, and may even lead to real steps to atone, since millions of Indonesian viewers have seen the film and recognised the wrong of the genocide. *The Act of Killing* revealed the truth of the murders, the legal and social impunity of the killers, and the lack of atonement and redress after fifty years.

The second documentary in Oppenheimer's diptych, *The Look of Silence*, goes further in portraying confrontations between the survivors and the killers and with the descendants of the perpetrators. The film concentrates on Adi Rukun, a survivor born after the genocide, who is determined to find out the truth about his brother's murder by meeting with perpetrators at a number of levels of responsibility for the genocide. La Caze's chapter investigates the film's portrayal of Adi's search for atonement and how it relates to the possibility of communal atonement. One of the enigmas of atonement is how it can be carried out if the perpetrators are not remorseful and have no interest in atonement. La Caze argues that Oppenheimer's filming of the documentary, Adi's participation in it, and its global screenings contribute to communal atonement in spite of the killers' intransigence, beginning with the acknowledgement of what truly occurred.

In his chapter, 'Truth, Performance and the Close-Up: Paradoxical Candour in Errol Morris's "Interrotron" Interviews', Robert Sinnerbrink asks what happens when documentary films attempt to reveal the subjectivity of human subjects by focusing the cinematic gaze on them. Sinnerbrink works in the philosophy of film and brings his knowledge of filmic techniques and ethical experience to his intriguing discussion of this relatively neglected aspect of contemporary documentary filmmaking (2016). He observes how recent documentaries have utilised interviews and reconstructions of past events to expose the 'truth' about documentary subjects even though the subjects themselves try to hide, defend, or excuse their past deeds and views. The works Sinnerbrink finds relevant here are films by Werner Herzog, like *Grizzly Man* (2005); by Errol Morris, such as *The Fog of War* (2003), *Standard Operating Procedure* (2008), and *The Unknown Known* (2013); and by Joshua Oppenheimer – *The Act of Killing* (2012) and *The Look of Silence* (2014). What they share in common, he contends, is that they reveal what he describes as 'the paradox of candour'. The paradox consists in the mismatch between the subjects' attempts to hide themselves and the revelation through the documentary camera. In the works Sinnerbrink analyses, the subject accepts being filmed and tries to control their representation by the documentarian. However, he argues that against their intentions, the disguised 'truth' of the subject is revealed through nuances in their emotional and bodily appearance. Furthermore, on his view, documentary makers such as Morris and Oppenheimer deliberately use this interplay between what the subjects are attempting to display and what they unwittingly reveal. Sinnerbrink's chapter focuses on two of Errol Morris's 'Interrotron' political documentaries, *The Fog of War* and *The Unknown Known*, and using recent theories concerning facial expression and considering the roles that close-ups play in documentary, Sinnerbrink demonstrates that the exploitation of paradoxical candour can undermine the 'truth' that the subjects, Robert P. McNamara and Donald Rumsfeld, perform and can encourage reflection on the subjects' ethical and political roles in history.

The following chapter, by Damian Cox, explores ethical questions in relation to a fictionalised television series. His research is in ethics and on philosophy of film and television (Cox and Levine 2012). In his chapter '*Mindhunter*: The Possibility of Knowing Evil', Cox persuasively argues that the Netflix series *Mindhunter* (2017–), directed by David Fincher (episodes 1, 2, 9, and 10), portrays an ethical conundrum. He demonstrates how attempting to comprehend the true minds of serial killers results in a basic conflict between understanding them from the 'outside' and thus not gaining insight into how their minds work, and understanding them from the 'inside' and so risking moral corruption and mental breakdown. The series also faces the aesthetic issues of representing the minds of serial killers in ways that audiences can approach and find bearable. *Mindhunter* uses the strategy of having the main character, Holden Ford (Jonathan Groff), deal with the problem by imagining the perspectives of the serial killers. That way the spectators should not have to, and the long form of the series, if watched over time, enables the spectators to distance themselves. Across the ten episodes, *Mindhunter* gradually displays how, through empathising with the killers, Ford declines from his initial curiosity and excitement to a mental breakdown. The series also explores two different forms of understanding: identification and causal explanation, which is pursued by the psychologist Wendy Carr (Anna Torv), and *verstehen*, or perspectival understanding, which is Ford's goal.

Furthermore, Ford as protagonist becomes less attractive as the episodes go on and his perception of how serial killers' minds works increases. Cox argues that *Mindhunter*'s finale demonstrates the epistemic impossibility of understanding for both Carr and Ford, as neither of them finds out the truth behind the serial killers' actions, and the ethical dangers of attempting to understand serial killers from the 'inside'.

Finally, a rather different theme emerges in Part Three, 'Politics'. In contrast to an emphasis on the potential for ethical and political achievement or reparation, for example, the chapters in this section are more focused on registering ethical and political questions and concerns in relation to the emergence of new visual media with new affordances. As a transition between the sections, Ted Nannicelli's chapter, 'Interactive Documentary, Narrative Scepticism and the Values of Documentary Film', surveys recent debates about the relative epistemic and ethico-political merits of interactive documentary film versus traditional narrative documentary film. He describes how interactive documentaries, or i-docs, as they are often called, are a new sort of documentary that require the active participation of viewers in selecting, shaping, and organising content. The participatory nature of i-docs has inspired quite a bit of idealistic thinking about this new art form's capacity to further the projects of progressive activism and radical democracy. Nannicelli acknowledges the partial truth in this utopian thought, but also takes a more balanced approach by considering the ways that interactivity or a non-linear, 'database' structure might in fact amplify ethical and political challenges inherent to documentary.

Nannicelli also considers whether traditional linear narrative documentaries are somehow epistemically flawed or anti-progressive in a way that interactive documentaries are not, a narrative scepticism that his chapter contends is unwarranted. According to Nannicelli, we should assume neither that interactive documentary is epistemically or ethico-politically valuable solely by virtue of its technological affordances, nor that narrative documentary is epistemically or ethico-politically dubious solely by virtue of its narrative form.

Following this transition, Grant Tavinor's chapter on video games, 'Won't Somebody Please Think of the Children! On the Moralisation of Video Game Violence', considers the relationship between traditional ethical questions about screen media's harmful effects on audiences to considering the political context for concern about these kinds of harms. Tavinor's work concentrates on the relationship between the arts and video games (2009). His chapter concentrates on the moral and political features of the social reception of violent video games, rather than their content, the enjoyment of them, or their production, and his argument is a kind of 'hermeneutics of suspicion' approach to the claims about violent video games and the true motivations behind them. Tavinor takes his cue from Stanley Cohen's (2002) comments concerning a moral panic about Mods and Rockers more than fifty years ago to investigate contemporary concerns about how violent video games are seen by the public today. The discrepancy between the vehemence of condemnation of video games and the evidence for the link between video games and harm could suggest that we are witnessing a similar moral panic. Tavinor asks whether this is true and why violent video games are so consistently morally condemned as harmful to children and society in general, and more specifically, as leading to mass shootings. He contends that moralism about violent video games is in part related to the way political and public figures are able to leverage their strong reaction against them for political gain.

The diagnosis that Tavinor outlines pinpoints elements of class-based aesthetics in the moralism of the middle class about violent video games, and identifies the focus on children as a way of advocating for greater restrictions on playing these games. Furthermore, he warns that moralism about violent video games may be used to play the role of leading us to overlook other important social risks that are more likely to lead to violence such as mass shootings.

Rounding out the collection are two complementary chapters that explore visual data's and Facebook's implications for our ethico-political landscape – one by Tom O'Regan and one by Kris Fallon. Tom O'Regan was a pioneering scholar of cultural and media studies interested in audience measurement of broadcasting, cultural institutions, and production studies of film, new media, and television (2011). In his chapter, 'Re-reading *Personal Influence* in an Age of Social Media', O'Regan develops the suggestion that there are important similarities between Mark Zuckerberg's comments about Facebook and the work of Elihu Katz and Paul Lazarsfeld in their seminal study of communication and media studies, *Personal Influence* ([1955] 1964). This text concentrated on research on the 'role of people' in communication, and made a change relevant to our understanding of contemporary social media by regarding interpersonal communication as a medium of mass communication like print, oral, and visual media. O'Regan shows how there are both similarities and differences between interpersonal communication and mass media and most importantly, that when Katz and Lazarsfeld wrote, interpersonal communication was not available and studied like mass media. *Personal Influence* changed that by demonstrating the central characteristics and significance of interpersonal communication in sharing and interpreting media and social life with others. After more than fifty years passed, Facebook re-mediated and transformed interpersonal communication or 'word of mouth' communication into an accessible social medium. In his compelling chapter, O'Regan argues that Facebook attempted to overcome what was seen as a limitation of interpersonal communication in that advertisers, marketers, and media networks had very few ways to identify and control the way interpersonal networks operated. He outlines how social media has been able to address these limitations in traditional media by finding informal groups and influencers and making it possible to target them to shape their opinions, and how the work of *Personal Influence* has helped to make this possible.

Thus, O'Regan investigates the analogies and disanalogies between Katz and Lazarsfeld's research into interpersonal communication and Facebook's and Instagram's capacity to develop and utilise social media as a form of market research. He shows how central concepts from *Personal Influence* have been used within social media, as well as identifying the distinct features of current social media. He argues that one of the ways in which Katz and Lazarsfeld's research of audiences in the 1950s had a stronger commitment to truth than contemporary social media is that it made its research public and transparent. The research they carried out could be used by a range of advertisers and media providers and was described in their publications. However, the research provided by Zuckerberg's Facebook in the early twentieth century remained private, protected, and kept secret. Furthermore, O'Regan explains, Facebook has taken what were previously distinct roles of collecting data from users, providing media, and acting for advertisers and combined them in one operation. After fifty years, the apparent 'problems' of interpersonal communication were solved, but simultaneously a whole new set of problems that in fact undermine communication have been created. O'Regan's chapter suggests that revisiting *Personal Influence* would enable us to comprehend and analyse these new problems.

The final chapter is by Kris Fallon, who works on documentary practices in a range of forms, including film and photography, and the focus here, data visualisation, and describes how what is perceived as truth keeps mutating (2019). His chapter, 'Principles of Exchange: Free Speech in the Era of Fake News', demonstrates how the practices and implications of mass media, including the spread of what is called 'fake news', have interacted with the deep fractures in the political structures of Western democracies, revealed by a number of contentious elections throughout the world. Fallon argues that questions of free speech and freedom of the press in this context need to be understood within the model of the 'marketplace of ideas'. His reasoning is that, although freedom of the press and freedom of speech tend to be regarded as inalienable rights at the foundation of most democratic systems, the actual protections they provide individuals and the role they play in politics are constantly changing. For most of the last hundred years, the metaphor of the 'marketplace of ideas' has given a framework for accepting these protections and a working model as to how they should be applied. A 'marketplace of ideas' is supposed to allow citizens in a democracy a range of ideas and views that afford the possibility of criticisms and of electoral choices.

However, in addition to the problems faced by democracies, Fallon contends that the accepted role of media and citizens has been overturned by new digital platforms that can act like mass media in spreading individual speech. His authoritative chapter investigates the interplay of new digital technologies and political ideals that are freedom of the press and free speech, showing how the debates around 'fake news' are symptomatic of a larger change in both cases. Despite criticisms of the 'marketplace of ideas' metaphor as limited or outdated in its application to contemporary life, Fallon argues that in fact it provides a precise description of the various economic, political, and technological contexts of all kinds where speech, whether true or false, professional and individual, and real and fake, takes place. Furthermore, he finds that the metaphor provides a normative aspiration that can be used to judge the extent to which there is a genuine marketplace of ideas in our polities.

All the chapters in this book show how age-old social and political conflicts are recast in new forms in new media. So while we must remember the earlier debates concerning the media and truth, we also need to be cognisant of the ways that technologies force us to rethink many of the terms of these debates. The truth that we think we have found is often complicated by another dimension as new technologies allow new ways to distort and manipulate the truth, as well as more ways to uncover these distortions and manipulations.

Finally, a brief personal note: the publication of this book is bittersweet because in the final stages of preparation, we lost our friend and colleague, Tom O'Regan. Tom not only contributed a chapter to the book; behind the scenes, he was the force that conceived of this project as a way of connecting colleagues across schools and faculties within our university who were all working at the intersection of aesthetics, ethics, and politics in visual arts. As he did countless other times, Tom laid the groundwork for a project only to step back behind the curtain once it was up and running. In this case, he secured the funding that made the project possible by establishing our presence as a distinct node within the Visual Politics research programme, supported by the University of Queensland's Faculty of Humanities and Social Sciences – actually writing a grant proposal for a project he wanted his colleagues to undertake (and which he knew they would not undertake without his insistence). We are grateful to the Faculty of Humanities and Social Sciences and especially grateful for the boundless enthusiasm and support of the Visual Politics overall project leader, Professor Roland Bleiker. But our greatest debt is to Tom O'Regan for his astonishing intellectual generosity and collegiality. We miss him dearly.

REFERENCES

Best, Susan. 2016. *Reparative Aesthetics: Witnessing in Contemporary Art Photography*. London: Bloomsbury.

Cohen, Stanley. 2002. *Folk Devils and Moral Panics*. 3rd edition. Oxford: Routledge.

Cox, Damian, and Michael Levine. 2012. *Thinking through Film: Doing Philosophy, Watching Movies*. Oxford: Wiley-Blackwell.

Fallon, Kris. 2019. *Where Truth Lies: Digital Culture and Documentary Media after 9/11*. Berkeley: University of California Press.

Gaut, Berys. 2007. *Art, Emotion and Ethics*. Oxford: Oxford University Press.

Hjort, Mette. 2018. 'Guilt-Based Filmmaking: Moral Failings, Muddled Activism, and the Documentary *Get a Life*.' *Journal of Aesthetics and Culture*, special issue, edited by Elisabeth Oxfeldt, 10.1: 6–13.

Hubbell, Amy L. 2015. *Remembering French Algeria: Pieds-Noirs, Identity, and Exile*. Lincoln, NE: University of Nebraska Press.

Katz, Elihu, and Paul Lazarsfeld. [1955] 1964. *Personal Influence: The Part Played by People in the Flow of Mass Communications*. New York: Free Press.

La Caze, Marguerite. 2018. *Ethical Restoration after Communal Violence: The Grieving and the Unrepentant*. Lanham, MD: Lexington Books.

Noë, Alva. 2015. *Strange Tools: Art and Human Nature*. New York: Hill and Wang.

O'Regan, Tom. 2011. 'Styles of National and Global Integration: Charting Media Transformation in Australian Cities.' *Studies in Australasian Cinema* 5.3: 223–38.

Radzik, Linda. 2009. *Making Amends: Atonement in Morality, Law, and Politics*. Oxford: Oxford University Press.

Saethre-McGuirk, Ellen Marie. 2018. *Norwegian Sublime: Landscape Photography in the Age of the iPhone*. Fran Moran Gallery, QUT. <https://blogg.nord.no/downunderbynord/wp-content/uploads/sites/5/2018/06/Research-portfolio-Norwegian-Sublime.pdf> (last accessed 16 March 2021).

Sedgwick, Eve Kosofsky. 2003. *Touching Feeling: Affect, Pedagogy, Performativity*. Durham, NC: Duke University Press.

Sinnerbrink, Robert. 2016. *Cinematic Ethics: Exploring Ethical Experience through Film*. London: Routledge.

Sontag, Susan. [1977] 2008. *On Photography*. London: Penguin

Tavinor, Grant. 2009. *The Art of Videogames*. Malden, MA: Wiley-Blackwell.

PART ONE

AESTHETICS

1. REPAIR AND THE IRREPARABLE IN CONTEMPORARY ABORIGINAL ART

Susan Best

This chapter examines the representation of trauma in Aboriginal art from South East Queensland, focusing in particular on art that directly or indirectly addresses Australia's shameful colonial histories. I analyse contemporary art that moves beyond the familiar repertoire of postmodern political art, which dominated identity politics art of the 1970s, 1980s, and 1990s. That language is effective for the registration of anger, but less effective in conveying the damage caused by annihilating narratives about race and historical atrocities such as massacres. I consider how the work of Brisbane-based Indigenous artists Judy Watson and Robert Andrew occupies the ambivalent space of reparative aesthetics articulated by queer theorist Eve Kosofsky Sedgwick. Sedgwick frames the reparative position as one that can hold in tension both negative and positive feelings; ambivalence speaks to this complexity rather than registering indecision or indifference. In contrast, the work of artists such as Gordon Bennett and Vernon Ah Kee underscores the irreparable and the deep marks of trauma. The chapter considers how these different strategies memorialise the traumatic effects of Australian colonial history.

Trauma

I want to begin with what I believe is one of the most searing, compelling, and devastating images of trauma in recent Australian art. The image, *unwritten 9* (2008), is from the series also titled 'unwritten' by Brisbane-based artist

Vernon Ah Kee. Ah Kee began this series in 2007. This particular version of 'unwritten' is a charcoal drawing on canvas, but there are also lithographs and other prints. The 'unwritten' images are visceral, yet not didactic. On first sight, the degradation of humanity is clear in the image – the title points to the process (the unwriting) that has caused that degradation – yet the originating force of that action is not given (although of course it can be inferred). Urban Indigenous art in Australia has consistently pointed to the ongoing effects of colonisation as the source of this unwriting.

All of the works in the series use straight lines like cuts or slashes to articulate a skull-like head. There is something deeply disturbing about the precision with which the image is constructed and the destruction of the head that results. The face collapses into blackness below the nose, and the sightless sockets are scary and inhuman. The disjuncture between the precise geometric mode of construction and the resulting image highlights the way in which seemingly neutral Western systems of representation can have violent and destructive effects.

There is insufficient particularity to call the head a portrait, but nonetheless that is the genre that makes most sense of the images. The 'unwritten' series are portraits of a deeply alien and alienated life form. The title 'unwritten' suggests something unpicked or taken apart – the destruction of being, or to use a stronger term, the annihilation of being. However, Ah Kee also talks about this series from the opposite perspective: he describes the heads as 'becoming' (quoted in Leonard 2009: 9). So while the title suggests an entity that is coming undone, his commentary suggests something created or in the process of being created. For Ah Kee, the series is about the complicated process by which colonial recognition obliterates Aboriginal humanity. The two movements that are usually opposed – undoing and creating – are in fact shown to be one and the same in a colonial framework.

Or more precisely, Ah Kee describes the 'unwritten' series as tracing the emergence of a severely limited Aboriginal subjectivity within that framework:

> They are primitive people becoming more human to the Western eye. As that happens white features are ascribed to them. And where white people see those features ascribed to them – like learning to dress and learning to talk – they are rewarded. So these faces have high cheekbones and long noses, characteristics of a very general white Anglo-Saxon face, but they don't have eyes, nostrils, ears, mouths. They are people who haven't been recognised as human and, at the same time, are starting to have this white ideal applied to them, just enough to give shape to their faces. The work is about becoming. (Quoted in Leonard 2009: 9)

The process of becoming that Ah Kee describes here would have been cloaked as a 'civilising' process – being recognised as human is to become like the

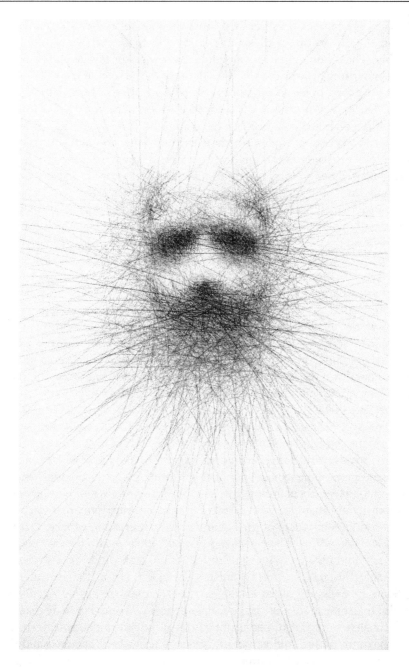

Figure 1.1   Vernon Ah Kee, *Unwritten #9* 2008, charcoal on canvas, 150 x 90 cm. Collection of the Art Gallery of New South Wales. Image courtesy the artist and Milani Gallery, Brisbane.

colonisers. The series thus partly adopts the gaze of the Western coloniser, showing the distortion and destruction wrought by oppressive colonial ways of seeing. The inhuman half-formed figure is the result of that way of seeing.

The unwriting process usually does not stay at the level of the skin and surface appearances. In his seminal book, *Black Skin, White Masks*, post-colonial theorist Frantz Fanon coined the term the 'epidermalisation of inferiority' to explain the psychological effects of the colonising process ([1952] 2008: 11). He uses this expression to describe how the outer inscription of black skin by colonial powers leads to the interiorisation of feelings of inferiority. By now, his argument about cultural inscription is very familiar to us: decades of work in feminist and post-colonial studies have made visible the oppressive and demeaning characterisations of women and non-Western others.

In identity politics art, which is one of the dominant forms of political art in the West from the 1970s onwards, there are innumerable images identifying the degradation of women and non-Western others. Such images frequently point out the typical patriarchal and colonial ways of seeing. The work of American feminist artist Barbara Kruger is emblematic of the genre. For example, her photomontage *Untitled (Your gaze hits the side of my face)* (1981), like many of Kruger's works, combines text and image to underscore the routine ways in which women are objectified. The black and white photograph of the head of a female mannequin is shown in profile and in sharp light. The text is delivered in a staccato manner down the left-hand side of the image, mostly one word at a time. It reads: 'Your / gaze / hits / the / side / of my / face'. Breaking up the sentence in this manner slows down the apprehension of its meaning, giving it additional punch as the final word is reached. The accusatory message addressed to the male gaze turns sight into an act of violence: the gaze 'hits' the side of my face. The work has the clarity of advertising copy, unambiguously conveying the unwanted intrusion of the male gaze on the female body. The substitution of a mannequin instead of a woman to take the ocular blow speaks to the further refusal of objectification.

Another emblematic series in this vein by African American artist Carrie Mae Weems examines instances of the dehumanising construction of race. Her series 'From Here I Saw What Happened and I Cried' (1995–6) also uses the combination of text and photographs. Some of the photographs in the series are drawn from archival sources, such as the images of slaves taken in 1850 in the American South by Swiss naturalist Louis Agassiz. The photographs by Agassiz were intended to demonstrate a theory of racial inferiority. Weems lays bare that intention through her use of text. For example, one image shows a nude African American woman in profile, and across the image that has been enlarged and tinted a rich red the text reads: 'You became a scientific profile'. The use of linguistic shifters, like 'I' and 'You', is a very effective way of bringing these images taken in the past into the present. Weems's text thereby seems to speak directly to the depicted woman, rather than to us. In that address, she serves her intention to give 'the subject another level of humanity and another level of dignity that was originally missing in the photograph' (2000). The image as a whole, however, remains largely closed off from that re-reading; the woman is pinned by the text and its main purpose is to uncover her reduction to a specimen. As Weems also states, her aim was to 'heighten a kind of critical awareness around the way in which these photographs were intended' (2000). In other words, the series exposes the racist attitudes of that time in European and American history. The title of the series, however, identifies Weems's current feelings: 'from here I saw what happened and I cried'. Her feelings of sorrow in the present may frame the series but those feelings are not conveyed by the objectifying image and text combination, which instead underscores the kind of shameful nineteenth-century racist attitudes with which an educated audience would be all too familiar.

These classic postmodern images, with their very clear meanings and intentions, tend to remain on the surface of the experiences they address: the operation of sexism in the case of Kruger and the business of racism in the case of Weems. In other words, they identify the processes of objectification, but not the lived effects of that process described by Fanon ([1952] 2008). In the work of many postmodern political artists, there is little or no sense of the traumatic effects of being on the receiving end of forms of oppression. What distinguishes Ah Kee's 'unwritten' series is that the images go below the skin; they are a visceral representation of the effects of racism. To interpret this series in a more psychological vein, the perspective demonstrated by Ah Kee is akin to an identification with the aggressor – a key response to trauma (Ferenczi [1932] 1949). This type of identification is how trauma undoes subjectivity; it renders the subject in the soul-destroying terms of the coloniser.

In the psychoanalytic trauma literature, this idea of identification with the aggressor is first theorised in the 1930s by both Sándor Ferenczi and Anna Freud in very different ways. It is Ferenczi's description of this state, however, that is particularly pertinent for Ah Kee's work. Ferenczi ([1932] 1949) coins the term 'confusion of the tongues' to capture the way that identity is shattered by traumatic experiences, leaving the victim forever porous to the feelings and projections of others. In notes from 1932, the year Ferenczi delivered the 'Confusion of the Tongues' paper, he describes not just a skinless openness to the feeling and thoughts of others, but a loss of one's own form as an effect of trauma:

'Shock' = annihilation of self-regard – of the ability to put up a resistance, and to act and think in defence of one's own self; perhaps even the *organs* which secure self-preservation give up their function or reduce it to a minimum. (The word *Erschütterung* is derived from *schütten*, i.e. to become 'unfest, unsolid,' to lose one's own form and to adopt easily and without resistance, an imposed form – 'like a sack of flour'). (Ferenczi [1932] 1955: 253–4)

The victim of trauma, in other words, suffers a kind of colonisation of the soul, their bodily fate forever marked by the experience. Ah Kee's 'unwritten' series embodies these processes of losing one's own form, of becoming *unfest* or unsolid. These images speak of that deeply damaging process; they are about the irreparable wrongs suffered – souls destroyed, or annihilation.

Miguel Gutiérrez Peláez (2009) observes that Ferenczi's term *Erschütterung* is usually translated as 'shock' or 'psychic shock' from *schütten*, to become 'unfest, unsolid.' He notes, however, the distinction between the corporeal and psychic consequences of trauma in Freud's usage:

> According to the dictionary of Roudinesco and Plon (1998), in the entry on 'traumatic neuroses,' Freud uses the term *Erschütterung* in *Beyond the Pleasure Principle* (Freud, 1920) to denote the somatic character of trauma and *Schreck* [fright] for its psychic aspect. (Peláez 2009: 1227)

This distinction between shock and fright is a useful one for thinking about another aspect of Ah Kee's unwritten images: they are 'unsolid' forms that also manifest the feeling of fright. Perhaps they could be described as both brutalising and brutalised images. In other words, a curious doubled perspective is enabled in which the heads are the result of an annihilating gaze, victims of it, and yet their ghoul-like etiolated appearance gives them the power to assail. The heads are at once victims and aggressors – a truly startling confusion of the tongues. In other words, Ah Kee's images do not just point to the operation of racism; they lay bare the disturbing psychical effects.

The work of the late Gordon Bennett also addresses trauma in a highly visceral way. While much of his work can be classified as highly cerebral critical postmodernism, there are also works that are deeply affecting. For example, his notepad drawings from 1992 expose some of the atrocities of Australian colonial history with a lacerating directness. Rarely shown during his lifetime, they were recently exhibited in Australia and Canada in an exhibition called 'Gordon Bennett: Be Polite' (2016–18). The subject matter of the drawings includes rape, dispossession, and hangings. Compositionally these works are much simpler than his paintings, but they have a political punch and incisiveness that recalls the powerful work of German artists like George Grosz and Otto Dix in the aftermath of World War I.

Bennett's 'welt' series of paintings, begun in France in December 1991, also have this same deeply affecting visceral quality. He explains that they were constructed by painting over 'a [Jackson] Pollock drip style underpainting with black' (Bennett 1996: 48). One work in the series, *Self Portrait: Interior/Exterior* (1993), stands out for me as emblematic of the scarifying effects of racism. It is a wall-mounted triptych. Reading from left to right, the first component is a stock whip on the end of which are manila-coloured tags with letters of the alphabet. Next to the whip are two rectangular canvases stretched over pine frames to make a shallow box: the first is like the lid, and the second shows the cavity. The two paintings are almost coffin-like in appearance as the dimensions are based on the artist's body: his height, width, depth. The overpainted Pollock drips suggest both veins and forms of scarification that make the paintings seem like skins. The first painting shows a black surface slashed by bloody welts as if the painted skin has been whipped open. These marks draw attention to the whip hung alongside the canvas. The other painting with the recessed interior is inscribed with the masochistic message in raised deep red letters 'cut me'. It is unclear where the damage begins in this triptych. Does it start with the whip, or the desire to be cut? Reading left to right, as we customarily do, one might think of this work as showing the action as coming from outside. That reading is complicated here, however, by the assertion of agency – 'cut me' uses the imperative form, but the command asks for an injury already received. As a self-portrait, it is a confounding and confronting image that profoundly entangles outside and inside, painting and skin, laceration and self-laceration. Like Ah Kee's 'unwritten' series, there is a complicated entwinement of victim and aggressor in this work – the complicated doubling of Ferenczi's 'confusion of the tongues'.

More usually, Bennett keeps such strong feelings at bay by using the familiar vocabulary of political postmodernism, the ideas of deconstruction, along with the techniques of quotation and image–text combination, so well honed by precursor American artists such as Barbara Kruger, amongst many others.[1] This kind of identity politics art, as next generation conceptualism, deliberately appeals to 'the mind of the viewer rather than his eye or emotions' to use conceptual artist Sol LeWitt's infamous phrase ([1967] 1992: 836). Indeed, this is how Bennett talked about his practice: 'There is a conceptual distance involved in the making of my work and my work was largely about ideas rather than emotional content emanating from some stereotype of a "tortured" soul' (quoted in Wright 2007: 97).[2]

That concentration on ideas and the legacy of conceptual art is evident in much of Bennett's work. For example, Bennett's *Double Take* (1989) has the bite and visual acuity of the best political conceptualism. In this small painting, he used the dot-style of painting associated with Aboriginal art of the Western Desert to rework the visual language of the so-called proclamation boards of 1829–30. These infamous boards were conceived by George Frankland, the Surveyor-General of Van Diemen's Land (present-day Tasmania), as a kind of pictographic writing. According to art historian Tim Bonyhady (2018), the proclamation paintings are the most significant paintings of Tasmania's Black War, an intense and bloody frontier conflict, which raged from 1824 to 1831. The painted boards were described in 1829 by George Augustus Robinson, the future Chief Protector of Aborigines of Port Phillip, as 'a means of facilitating a friendly communication with the aborigines of the interior' (Bonyhady 2018: 131). The paintings were supposed to be left in the bush to communicate this unlikely, if not duplicitous, message.

The boards were comprised of four cartoonish scenes, arranged one on top of the other. The top two scenes were intended to convey to Aboriginal people fraternity with the European settlers, while the lower portion shows how European justice ought to operate. Bennett reproduces the lower portion of the image. In the original, an Aboriginal man is shown spearing a settler and then being hanged. Below that image the situation is reversed: a settler shoots an Aboriginal man and then he too is hanged. In Bennett's version, the Aboriginal man is hanged whether he is the victim or the perpetrator. The title *Double Take* operates as a multilayered pun. First, there is the double take of the settlers: they clearly 'take' in both instances. Additionally, the work evokes the usual sense of the term 'double take' to convey a delayed reaction, in this instance shock or disbelief at behaviour completely counter to the ideal of impartiality suggested by the original boards. *Double Take* is a sharp critique of colonial hypocrisy.

Following the approach of queer theorist Eve Kosofsky Sedgwick (2003), I have, in previous work, called this way of making political art a paranoid approach to art making (Best 2016). Sedgwick contrasts what she calls paranoid readings and reparative readings. She advocates reparative interpretations of cultural material in place of the much more common 'paranoid' interpretations. She argues that paranoid interpretations routinely adopt a posture of suspicion and operate as a kind of 'exposure' of traces of oppression or injustice. Crucially, she argues paranoid suspicion is central to critical practice in the humanities and propelled by the desire on the part of theorists and critics to avoid surprise, shame, and humiliation (Sedgwick 2003: 136–8). For Sedgwick, a reparative motive seeks pleasure rather than the avoidance of shame, but it also signals the capacity to assimilate the consequences of destruction and violence. While the feelings to be avoided are clearly identified, the feelings to be embraced are not. They could include joy, surprise, hope, interest, and excitement.

In contemporary art, the paranoid approach is typical of the anti-aesthetic tradition and identity politics art, which also favour critique and the exposure of wrongdoing. The anti-aesthetic tradition is one of the dominant approaches to political art. Typically, it privileges critique over aesthetic engagement and rejects the importance of traditional aesthetic concerns such as originality, beauty, feeling, expression, and judgement. In the 1960s, 1970s, and 1980s, this tradition of art making was associated with conceptual art and conceptualism, institutional critique, feminist and critical postmodern practices. Artists like Barbara Kruger, Allan Sekula, Adrian Piper, Martha Rosler, Victor Burgin, Hans Haacke, Mary Kelly, Guerrilla Girls, and Jenny Holzer are representative of this type of political art.

More recently, the work of Fred Wilson, Coco Fusco, Renée Green, Emily Jacir, Alfredo Jaar, and James Luna, along with many, many others, can also be understood as foregrounding the exposure of wrongdoing. These artists often work in the visually deadpan or unremarkable mode of later conceptualism. I do not want to suggest here that these artists are making bad art because they adopt an emphatically political stance; these artists are extremely well known internationally for precisely that reason. Rather my point is that paranoid art has become almost synonymous with political art. As Sedgwick explains, for cultural criticism, 'it seems to me a great loss when paranoid inquiry comes to seem entirely coextensive with critical theoretical inquiry rather than being viewed as one kind of cognitive/affective practice among other, alternative kinds' (2003: 126). In this spirit, I suggest that alongside the long-standing tradition of making paranoid political art, there are also alternatives – the reparative kind I consider next.

To qualify, I am using the terms 'repair' and the 'reparative' in a very particular way. The conventional usage of the term 'repair' suggests a redemptive or restorative gesture: making amends in human relationships, returning something to a usable state in the case of artefacts and clothing, or to a prior state of functioning in the case of cars and houses. Philosopher Elizabeth Spelman distinguishes three main types of repair of artefacts: returning something to a functional state, restoring something as closely as possible to the original state, and what she calls 'invisible mending' where the repair is undetectable (2010: 15). In other words, she emphasises the quality or extent of the repair measured against a prior condition. In contrast, Sedgwick's reparative reading practice pays little attention to restoration. Here, she borrows from psychoanalyst Melanie Klein, for whom the reparative position signals the capacity to tolerate ambivalence, that is, to hold together both positive and negative feelings about something. This phase in human development contrasts with the period in infancy when these feelings are split apart: something or someone is experienced as alternately wholly bad or wholly good. The maturity of the reparative phase or position is indicated by the ability to tolerate the coexistence of good and bad qualities in the same person or experience. The reparative position is not, then, simply about undoing or reversing damage; ambivalence precludes that wholly positive orientation. This way of thinking about repair should enable the incorporation of intense negative emotions and experiences such as the horror of annihilation, anger, and despair alongside positive feelings like tenderness, pleasure, love, and hope.

Repair

Brisbane-based Indigenous artists Judy Watson and Robert Andrew make work that is reparative in this rich and affectively complex way. Their work also escapes the didactic framework of much political postmodernism, yet it is no less confronting for taking a more indirect approach. While both artists have addressed a range of themes, the works I want to consider here are about the massacres of Aboriginal people in the Frontier Wars of the colonial and modern periods.

Historical research into massacres in the colonial period is still woefully incomplete. To address this lack, historian Lyndall Ryan has been leading a team of researchers who are painstakingly uncovering the history of frontier violence in Australia. In the introduction to their recently published online map – it went live in 2017 – they note the paucity of research and the granular nature of the research to date:

> Colonial frontier massacre is a largely under-researched topic in Australia. Most studies relate to particular incidents, such as Risdon Cove in Tasmania (1804) which remains highly contested even today or at Myall Creek (1838) where all but one of the twelve perpetrators were arrested and brought to trial and seven of them were convicted and hanged. Such incidents are considered as unique and overshadow many others that are simply lost from sight. (Ryan et al. n.d.)

The Myall Creek massacre is the subject of Robert Andrew's work *Reveal* (2018). The work was commissioned for the exhibition 'Myall Creek and Beyond' curated by Aboriginal artist and curator Bianca Beetson for the New England Regional Art Museum in Armidale in 2018. The exhibition commemorated the 180th anniversary of the Myall Creek massacre. That massacre at Henry Dangar's cattle station on the traditional Country of the Wirrayaraay people was premeditated, as were the majority of massacres in Australia (Ryan 2018). The Myall Creek massacre took place when the overseer William Hobbs, his senior stockmen and ten Wirrayaraay warriors were all absent from the property. Consequently, the victims of the massacre were left defenceless; they were the remaining old men, women, and children who were peacefully living on the banks of the Myall Creek. Lyndall Ryan and Jane Lydon estimate that approximately thirty people were killed (2018: 1). Ryan classifies the murder of six or more people as a massacre.

What is unusual about this massacre is the fact that the perpetrators were tried, found guilty, and punished: seven of the eleven involved were hanged. It is one of only two cases in Australia where this happened; the second is the Forrest River massacre in Western Australia in 1926 (Ryan and Lydon 2018: 5). It is no doubt because of this unusual history that the Myall Creek massacre has become a rallying site for the reconciliation movement in Australia. For example, descendants of both perpetrators and victims attended the opening ceremony of the memorial at Myall Creek on 10 June 2000. Key instigators of the memorial, Sue Blacklock (a descendant of the people massacred) and John Brown (Uniting Church minister), explain their aspirations for remembrance:

Figure 1.2 Robert Andrew, *Reveal* 2018, ochres, oxides, aluminium, acrylic, electromechanical elements. Image courtesy of the artist.

We hope that this ongoing focus on the massacre, and the trial that followed, may drag us towards a more honest understanding of our history, and the possibility of more just and open acknowledgment of our tangled journey in Australia over the past two centuries. We further hope that the reflection might open more just and life-affirming opportunities for our future together in the land. (Blacklock and Brown 2018: xiii)

The orientation towards a hopeful future is a very moving response to the remembrance of historical atrocity. The combination of an 'honest understanding of our history' with the hope for 'life-affirming' coexistence follows the kind of reparative complexity Sedgwick outlines. So too does Andrew's work.

Reveal (2018) is typical of Andrew's kinetic works, which he has been making since graduation from the Queensland College of Art Contemporary Australian Indigenous Art (CAIA) programme in 2013.[3] He calls *Reveal* a 'palimpsest machine' (Andrew 2018: 17). The term 'palimpsest' describes the overwriting or writing over performed by this sleek drawing machine. The drawing or printing mechanism shuttles across a large vertical white chalk surface, powered by open source software. The moving parts are modelled on the operation of a desktop printer, except in this instance the shuttle moves both horizontally and vertically over the initially white ground, which remains stationary. Instead of ink, the machine uses water to slowly spell out the text. In the case of *Reveal*, it is a documentary account of the Myall Creek massacre that is inscribed onto and into the chalk surface. Andrew's kinetic drawing machines are programmed to last for the required exhibition time.[4] In this instance, at the very beginning of the exhibition the machine was positioned on an entirely white surface that concealed a large floor-to-ceiling window. As the water jets hit the chalk surface, ochre was revealed and mixed with the chalk. The glass window and the view beyond the window slowly came into view as the water dissolved the surface in the shapes of the letters.

At first sight, it is not clear how the words were appearing, that is, whether the machine was adding or subtracting substance. The action of subtraction seems counter-intuitive, given our understanding of the typical operation of inkjet printing. Even with Andrew's simpler single-word works, the subtraction of the surface of chalk is not immediately clear. For example, *Moving out of Muteness: Nganga (language) denied* (2013) and *Transitional Text – BURU* (2016) spell out single words from Andrew's ancestral language Yawuru: 'buru' (Country) and 'nganga' (language). In both cases, the palimpsest machines were mounted on the wall so that the process of subtraction was harder to perceive – ochre seems to appear rather than chalk disappearing. The appearance of the window in *Reveal* made subtraction more obviously the mechanism at work as the layers of chalk and ochre are shown to dissolve and disappear.

The dissolution of the surface suggested bullet holes, wounds, bleeding, and scarring. The pooling of ochre on the floor below was redolent of a river of blood. Alongside the wounding and witnessing the machine enables, there is also the surprise of the work, its sheer ingeniousness, and its very satisfying and elegant performance of its assigned task. The mechanical parts make a pleasant low-level burring noise as they skate across the surfaces. The machine is minimalist in style, comprised of shiny metal components that contrast with the rich earthy ochre it reveals. In other words, there are many aesthetic pleasures as well as sorrows in this work. In terms of affective tone, it is thus subtle and complicated. Perhaps most astonishingly, it inscribes an account of a terrible atrocity, but it does so with hope. Andrew reports:

> Through the palimpsest process of scraping back and re-inscribing the surface, new images emerge. The changing runs and bleeds of the chalks and ochres provide an opportunity to look and to see beyond the words. This is a way that I address our different ways of constant remembering. I am also drawing attention to changes that bring renewal. The white-wash of colonial histories is eroded and previously suppressed stories and images emerge. The residues of history fall towards the floor making way for new images to remain. (Andrew 2018: 17)

As Andrew's commentary indicates, the palimpsestic process of writing and rewriting operates as a metaphor for the complexity and mutability of memory and remembrance. The work brings together the terrible deeds of the past with this prospect of other voices and visions coming to light. The palimpsest machine thus lays bare the history of the Myall Creek massacre, while simultaneously revealing a new, more optimistic view. In the installation itself, this idea of the removal of whitewash making way for a new vision was presented quite literally. At the conclusion of the exhibition, the garden beyond the gallery was visible through the window. In Andrew's works with Yawuru language, the revival of language is of course also part of cultural renewal and an optimistic worldview.

Judy Watson's work similarly combines difficult truth telling with aesthetic pleasure to address shameful events of the colonial past. In her case, her strategy is to use very beautiful seductive surfaces to soften and contain the searing information about past atrocities. Watson is very explicit about her approach:

> Art as a vehicle for invention and social change can be many things, it can be soft, hard, in-your-face confrontational, or subtle and discreet. I try and choose the latter approach for much of my work, a seductive beautiful exterior with a strong message like a deadly poison dart that insinuates itself into the consciousness of the viewer without them being aware of the package until it implodes and leaks its contents. (Quoted in Martin-Chew 2009: 226)

The combination of beauty, seduction, and strong messages is nowhere more evident than in her work on Aboriginal massacres. She has been making work about Aboriginal massacres for many years now; she reports that she began researching this important topic in the 1970s (Watson 2017: 121). Her investigations have resulted in a number of paintings as well as her film from 2015 *the names of places*, which is the culmination of her research.[5] The film was first shown in an exhibition titled 'When Silence Falls' at the Art Gallery of New South Wales in Sydney, which addressed traumatic events that have not been properly discussed or acknowledged. The film has since been exhibited all around the country and has an accompanying interactive map.[6] The single-channel film shows a shifting map of the Australian continent over which scroll the innumerable place names where massacres have taken place. Watson's map, like that of Lyndall Ryan's research team, was made with the collaboration of historian Jonathan Richards. The film is approximately twenty minutes long and is comprised of a continuous list of place names for virtually the entire duration. This mode of representing frontier violence is deliberately unsensational; nonetheless, the sheer quantity of massacres leaves the beholder in no doubt of the horror written across the continent.

Watson's painting *a picnic with the natives – the gulf* (2015) was exhibited in the exhibition 'When Silence Falls' alongside the film. Exhibited in this context, the link to massacres comes very quickly to the fore. Yet, at first sight, the large-scale painting on unstretched canvas might be viewed as a beautiful evocation of the blending of land and water in the Gulf Country of the two northern provinces of Australia: the Northern Territory and Queensland. The intense colours bring to mind the ancient water from her Waanyi Country in North West Queensland, which is located on the Queensland side of the Gulf of Carpentaria. In an artist's talk about *a picnic with the natives*, Watson refers to the colour and extreme age of artesian water from Lawn Hill Gorge, the 'dinosaur water' which she describes as having a 'subterranean greeny blue look to it' (2016). The painting is filled with this kind of otherworldly colour; swirls of blue and green unsettle the map of the Gulf made by the colonial explorer Matthew Flinders. The swirls of colour seem to lap at the clear contours supposedly separating land and sea, rendering them unstable. That Western map forms one of the layers or realities of the image. More insistent and anchoring is the upper layer of the image, comprised of many white dots with red centres scattered across the land – these points suggest the locations of massacres. This topic has a deeply personal significance for Watson: Watson's great-great-grandmother Rosie narrowly escaped the Lawn Hill massacre. With her friend, Rosie hid behind a windbreak; she was bayonetted through the chest and carried that scar for life.

The title of the work, *a picnic with the natives*, initially might seem innocuous; however, it is a euphemism for a massacre, drawn from colonial documentary sources. Specifically, it is a phrase used by Inspector Paul Foelsche to describe an expedition to murder Aboriginals around the Roper River in the

Northern Territory. According to historian Tony Roberts, Foelsche issued these cryptic, but sinister, instructions: 'I cannot give you orders to shoot all natives you come across, but circumstances may occur for which I cannot provide definite instructions' (2009). Roberts reports that Foelsche used the strange turn of phrase 'a picnic with the natives' in a letter to a friend: 'He boasted in a letter to a friend, John Lewis, that he had sent his second-in-command, Corporal George Montagu, down to the Roper to "have a picnic with the natives"' (2009). The phrase, with its terrible perversion of fraternity and sociability, was also used as the title for Gordon Reid's book on the Northern Territory: *A Picnic with the Natives*: *Aboriginal–European Relations in the Northern Territory to 1910* (1990). Used in this way, the phrase is clearly presented as characterising relations between Aboriginals and Europeans in the Northern Territory in the colonial period and the early twentieth century.

An earlier work by Watson, *massacre inlet* (1994), also refers to the Gulf Country of North Eastern Queensland. Massacre Inlet is an actual place name in Queensland on the Gulf of Carpentaria. In Australia, there are many such place names that speak of the history of colonial violence: for example, Murdering Creek, Murderer's Flat, Massacre Inlet, Murdering Point, Murdering Gully, Slaughterhouse Creek, and Skull Hole.[7] Louise Martin-Chew reports that Watson is 'intrigued by the names of places and the meaning and history they hold' (2009: 116). In this case, Massacre Inlet is reported to be the site of a massacre in the late nineteenth century. According to the Queensland Places Project compiled by historians Marion Stell and Peter Spearritt: 'Massacre Inlet, north of Hells Gate, marks the place where European settlers from the Westmoreland homestead slaughtered nearly all the Ngyanga Aborigines in 1884 in reprisal for an attack' (2018).

Watson's *massacre inlet* is another large unstretched canvas with luminous colour: a stark white form cracks through the middle of the canvas while swathes of colour pool and flow around it: crimson, red, and pink. Darker tones anchor and earth the washes of colour. Martin-Chew reports that the 'canvas mourns the lives lost in our past, with a central skeletal form and other sections scrubbed back through the layers to represent bare bones in the canvas, which is otherwise stained red' (2009: 116). The scrubbing back of colour has the effect of making the central spine of the work seem as though it has been uncovered below the sea or soil of red pigment. I imagine bones revealed by an archaeological dig, wounded bodies left in the landscape to perish. The spine is also redolent of an inlet with tributaries, as indicated in the title. Other lines in the canvas evoke a contour map: land forms from above. In that evocation the scale shifts from body size – the approximate size of the canvas – to an aerial view. In short, this is a space of extraordinary ambiguity and uncertainty: forms twist and turn, moving between scales and representational possibilities. What is bone, what is contour? Blood and bone, blood and soil, all these associations come to mind as the title interacts with the ambiguous space. Martin-Chew has exquisitely captured the extraordinary spatial ambiguity that is characteristic of Watson's painting. She writes:

> As representations of landscape, more internal and metaphysical than actual, they are fresh in their tackling of the subject from the inside out. Watson has worked in this manner since the late 1980s, after initially training as a printmaker. Multiple layers in each canvas create a drift, locating the viewer above, below, or somewhere within. (Martin-Chew 2009: 14)

This spatial and formal ambiguity in *massacre inlet* evokes a deep connection between body and land, while also suggesting Country stained with blood. For Indigenous Australians, Country includes not just land, but also stories and all living things; thus injuries to people affect place and vice versa.

Blood is also very strongly suggested in *pale slaughter* (2015), the last work of Watson's I want to discuss. Watson makes extensive use of text in this work and yet it does not tip into the constrained and cramped language of political postmodernism. Down the middle of the work is a list of the names of fourteen weapons. In personal correspondence, Watson explained that the names come from a list of weapons imported into Fremantle during colonial times, as well as being the weapons she noted were mentioned in contemporaneous accounts of massacres. The list tells of changing technologies of slaughter: Colonial Muskets (a musket-loaded gun replaced by breech-loading rifles in the mid-nineteenth century), Brown Bess (nickname for a British army musket, produced 1722–1860s), Snider Enfield (British breech-loading rifle), Martini Hendry (British breech-loading rifle used from 1871, replaced Snider Enfield), Dean, Adams and Deane (revolver from 1855), Smith & Wesson (American firearms since 1852), Scabbards, Bayonets, Muskets, Light Cavalry Swords, Revolvers, Elliots Carbines (1760 onwards), Baker Rifles (muzzle-loaded gun in service 1801–37), Minie Rifle (French rifle in use mid-nineteenth century), and Winchester (American repeating rifle designed in 1866). Below the list are outlines of boomerangs, one of the weapons that would have been used in defence against these various mechanical weapons. The boomerangs are numbered down the left-hand side of the canvas. In her communication with me, Watson reported that she based this layer of the image on a line drawing of boomerangs made by a private collector that she came across during her fellowship at the British Museum in 2013. On the right-hand side of the canvas are the names of two places: Gallipoli and Coniston. Everyone in Australia would know the name of Gallipoli; the World War I battle on the Turkish peninsula of that name is commemorated each year on Anzac Day.[8] It is not the celebration of a military victory as one might suppose, but the site of a huge sacrifice of life, since over 8,000 Australian soldiers died, thirteen of whom

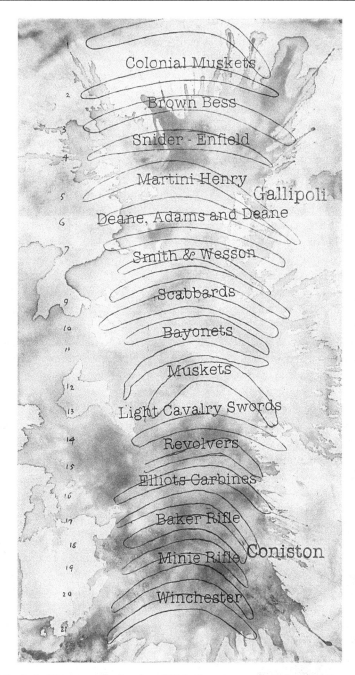

Figure 1.3   Judy Watson, *pale slaughter* 2015, pigment, acrylic paint, pastel, watercolour pencil on canvas, 179 x 96 cm. Collection: National Gallery of Australia. Image courtesy the artist and Milani Gallery, Brisbane.

were Aboriginal. At least seventy Aboriginal men were involved in the Gallipoli campaign, despite the fact that it was illegal for them to enlist, as they did not have Australian citizenship (Bell 2017). That event was in 1915; thirteen years later in 1928, the Coniston massacre occurred in the Northern Territory. It is referred to as the last state-sanctioned massacre in Australia and the last event of the Frontier Wars. It should be as well known as Gallipoli. It is not. The massacre, in which over sixty Aboriginal people were killed, was an unjust and violent reprisal for the murder of a white dingo trapper, Fred Brooks. One of the main perpetrators, Constable William Murray, was a Gallipoli survivor.[9]

Watson's subtle juxtaposition of different wars and different weapons leaves all of this unspoken, but the names provoke thought and investigation. What happened at these two places, what were these many and varied weapons used for? The loss of life is framed by beautiful washes of colour that evoke coral seas, blood, bruises, reefs, landforms, and islands. The seductive exterior Watson consistently crafts to carry the terrible truth of frontier violence is very much in evidence. These three examples of her work, all large-scale paintings on unstretched canvas, show how Watson has developed a language of lush, complex, and layered images that also point to the terrible histories of massacre sites in Australia. In this way, she eschews the typical mode of making critical political art, characterised by paranoid or didactic thinking. Her work is reparative in the complicated sense Sedgwick gives to that term. The ambivalence Sedgwick emphasises as the hallmark of the reparative position is evident here in the combination of aesthetic pleasure with clear references to historical atrocities. Beautiful images of massacres might seem ethically troubling or even morally wrong to those concerned about unwanted traffic between aesthetics and politics, but as Brett Ashley Kaplan argues in relation to Holocaust art, beautiful representations enhance remembrance (2007: 2). Remembrance is key to the repair these works make possible.

CONCLUSION

For me, as a long-time advocate of the affective dimension of art, the very moving artworks I have been discussing demonstrate a powerful and productive alternative to the typical ways of making paranoid political art. Such strong and complex artworks allow the atrocities of colonialism to be registered, and perhaps even internalised and felt. In the unflinching vision of Vernon Ah Kee and Gordon Bennett, the damage of trauma, and the permanent scars it causes, are represented with unprecedented directness and force. The depiction of scarring and scarification makes the damage in these works both literal and visceral. Mutilation is emphasised. These works thereby very forcefully show damage that cannot be undone. It is not possible to return to a state prior to the advent of colonisation. In the work of Watson and Andrew, acts of colonial violence are presented more allusively, but no less effectively. While both embrace aesthetic pleasure, their approaches to the depiction of violence differ markedly. For Andrew, facing our violent past enables renewal. In *Reveal*, the story of the Myall Creek massacre emerges on the window taking away substance to let the light in. With the shades removed, a horizon emerges beyond the gallery and new ways of seeing and being seem possible. In Watson's paintings, beauty is like an outer skin with the historical subject matter as a kind of interior that is slowly released. As the subject matter comes into focus, the beauty does not dissipate; rather it acts like a holding environment for the volatile content – allowing it be felt, to be remembered. All four artists engage the eye and the emotions, not 'just the mind'. In this way, the irreparable and repair are presented in equally powerful and affecting ways.

NOTES

1. In an interview with Bill Wright, Bennett states, 'I learnt about deconstruction and semiotics, which I applied to my practice' (Wright 2007: 102).
2. In an interview in 1993, Bennett describes a shift in his practice as aiming for an impersonal mechanical mode: 'Part of the reason I'm using projectors too is to remove myself to the point at which I become like a printing press. I'm not painting what I feel, I'm tracing it on the surface of the thing' (quoted in Gellatly 2007: 120 n.17).
3. On the success of CAIA, see Buttrose (2015).
4. See the discussion of time sequences in Whittle (2015).
5. The film was made with Greg Hooper and Jarrard Lee. Watson always uses lower case for her titles. In correspondence with me, she explains: 'I like the look of lower case in text . . . It might be like my unstretched canvases that float out beyond the parameters of your vision rather than being defined by strict borders.'
6. Watson's interactive map (made with collaborators Greg and Angus Hooper) can be accessed at <http://thenamesofplaces.com/tnop/> (last accessed 18 October 2019).
7. See the list of place names suggestive of murder and massacre at <https://www.creativespirits.info/aboriginalculture/history/massacres-the-frontier-violence-thats-hard-to-accept> (last accessed 18 October 2019).
8. Anzac is an acronym for Australian and New Zealand Army Corps. The soldiers from these two nations were grouped together in Egypt before the landing in Gallipoli in April 1915.
9. Watson, in personal correspondence, indicated that the main organiser of the massacre was a Gallipoli veteran. She pointed me to Midlam's (2010) article, which indicates some of the ways the Gallipoli experience fed into the massacre.

REFERENCES

Andrew, Robert. 2018. 'Artist's Statement.' In *Myall Creek and Beyond*, 17. Armidale: New England Regional Art Museum.

Bell, Michael. 2017 'Aboriginal Presence on Gallipoli Grows.' *Australian War Memorial* blog, 25 April. <https://www.awm.gov.au/articles/blog/aboriginal-presence-on-gallipoli-grows> (last accessed 20 October 2019).

Bennett, Gordon. 1996. 'The Manifest Toe.' In *The Art of Gordon Bennett*, edited by Gordon Bennett and Ian MacLean, 9–62. Sydney: Craftsman House.

Best, Susan. 2016. *Reparative Aesthetics: Witnessing in Contemporary Art Photography*. London: Bloomsbury.

Blacklock, Sue, and John Brown. 2018. 'Foreword.' In *Remembering the Myall Creek Massacre*, edited by Jane Lydon and Lyndall Ryan, xi–xiii. Sydney: NewSouth Publishing.

Bonyhady, Tim. 2018. 'A Means of Facilitating a Friendly Communication with Aborigines in the Interior.' In *The National Picture: The Art of Tasmania's Black War*, edited by Tim Bonyhady and Greg Lehman, 130–1. Canberra: National Gallery of Australia.

Buttrose, Ellie. 2015. 'To the Fore: The Growing Legacy of QCA's Bachelor of Contemporary Australian Indigenous Art.' *Art Monthly* 279: 52–5.

Fanon, Frantz. [1952] 2008. *Black Skin, White Masks*, translated by Richard Philcox. New York: Grove Press.

Ferenczi, Sándor. [1932] 1949. 'Confusion of the Tongues between the Adults and the Child – (The Language of Tenderness and of Passion).' *The International Journal of Psychoanalysis* 30: 225–30. Originally delivered at the Twelfth International Psycho-Analytic Congress, Wiesbaden, September 1932.

Ferenczi, Sándor. [1932] 1955. 'On Shock.' In *Final Contributions to the Problems and Methods of Psycho-analysis*, edited by Michael Balint, 253–4. London: Hogarth.

Gellatly, Kelly. 2007. 'Citizen in the Making: The Art of Gordon Bennett.' In *Gordon Bennett*, edited by Kelly Gellatly, 8–24, 120–3. Melbourne: National Gallery of Victoria.

Kaplan, Brett Ashley. 2007. *Unwanted Beauty: Aesthetic Pleasure in Holocaust Representation*. Urbana: University of Illinois Press.

Leonard, Robert. 2009. 'Your Call.' In Vernon Ah Kee, *Vernon Ah Kee: Born in this Skin*, 5–13. Brisbane: Institute of Modern Art.

LeWitt, Sol. [1967] 1992. 'Paragraphs on Conceptual Art.' In *Art in Theory, 1900–1990*, edited by Charles Harrison and Paul Wood, 834–7. Oxford: Blackwell.

Martin-Chew, Louise. 2009. *Judy Watson: Blood Language*. Melbourne: Miegunyah Press.

Midlam, Amanda. 2010. 'Lest We Forget: The Coniston Massacre.' *Online Opinion*. <https://www.onlineopinion.com.au/view.asp?article=11211> (last accessed 26 October 2019).

Peláez, Miguel Gutiérrez. 2009. 'Trauma Theory in Sándor Ferenczi's Writings of 1931 and 1932.' *International Journal of Psychoanalysis* 90: 1217–33.

Reid, Gordon. 1990. *A Picnic with the Natives: Aboriginal–European Relations in the Northern Territory to 1910*. Carlton: Melbourne University Press.

Roberts, Tony. 2009. 'The Brutal Truth: What Happened in the Gulf Country.' *The Monthly*, 1 November. <https://www.themonthly.com.au/issue/2009/november/1330478364/tony-roberts/brutal-truth> (last accessed 18 October 2019).

Ryan, Lyndall. 2018. 'The Myall Creek Massacre: Was it Typical of the Time?' Paper presented at the Myall Creek and Beyond symposium, Oorala Aboriginal Centre, University of New England, Australia.

Ryan, Lyndall, and Jane Lydon. 2018. 'Introduction: Remembering Myall Creek.' In *Remembering the Myall Creek Massacre*, edited by Jane Lydon and Lyndall Ryan, 1–14. Sydney: NewSouth Publishing.

Ryan, Lyndall, William Pascoe, Jennifer Debenham, Stephanie Gilbert, Jonathan Richards, Robyn Smith, Chris Owen, Robert J. Anders, Mark Brown, Daniel Price, Jack Price, and Kaine Usher. n.d. *Colonial Frontier Massacres in Australia, 1788–1930*. <http://c21ch.newcastle.edu.au/colonialmassacres/introduction.php> (last accessed 15 October 2019).

Sedgwick, Eve Kosofsky. 2003. *Touching Feeling: Affect, Pedagogy, Performativity*. Durham, NC: Duke University Press.

Spelman, Elizabeth V. 2010. 'Restoration: Philosophical and Political Contexts.' In *Restorative Redevelopment of Devastated Ecocultural Landscapes*, edited by Robert L. France, 15–20. Boca Raton, FL: CRC Press.

Stell, Marion, and Peter Spearritt (eds). 2018. 'Burke Shire.' *Queensland Places* database. Centre for the Government of Queensland, The University of Queensland. <https://www.queenslandplaces.com.au/burke-shire> (last accessed 18 October 2019).

Watson, Judy. 2016. 'On *When Silence Falls*.' Art Gallery of NSW, 24 February. <https://soundcloud.com/artgalleryofnsw/sets/when-silence-falls> (last accessed 16 October 2019).

Watson, Judy. 2017. 'Artist's Statement.' In *Defying Empire: Third National Indigenous Art Triennale*, 121. Canberra: National Gallery of Australia.

Weems, Carrie Mae. 2000. Audio interview for 'MoMA 2000: Open Ends'. <https://www.moma.org/multimedia/audio/207/2012> (last accessed 10 January 2020).

Whittle, Dianne. 2015. 'Moving Out of Muteness – A Conversation with the Artist.' *National Gallery of Victoria* blog, 30 May. <https://www.ngv.vic.gov.au/moving-out-of-muteness-a-conversation-with-the-artist/> (last accessed 16 October 2019).

Wright, Bill. 2007. 'Conversation: Bill Wright Talks to Gordon Bennett.' In *Gordon Bennett*, edited by Kelly Gallatly, 96–105. Melbourne: National Gallery of Victoria.

2. CIRCULATING BODIES: RETELLING THE TRAUMA OF THE ALGERIAN WAR THROUGH PHOTOGRAPHY AND ART

Amy L. Hubbell

TRAUMATIC IMAGES OF THE ALGERIAN WAR

From 1954 to 1962, Algeria fought for its independence from France after almost 130 years of colonial rule. The long and bloody war resulted in hundreds of thousands of deaths, the annihilation of thousands of villages, and the mass exile of Algerians and French alike, with nearly two million Algerians moved to relocation camps (Cohen 2002: 221), and almost a million Europeans repatriated to France who are commonly called Pieds-Noirs. After the signing of the Evian Accord on 19 March 1962, which officially ended the war, the violence intensified. The agreement, however, granted general amnesty for crimes committed during the war, providing an official silence that allowed the French to delay acknowledging the war as one until 1999. Until that time, the published memories of Algeria were primarily nostalgic representations of a peaceful and beautiful homeland to the Pieds-Noirs. As historian William B. Cohen explains, 'This has not been a chapter in their history of which the French are proud, and they have appeared to many to have preferred amnesia to facing their dismal record in Algeria' (2000: 489).

During the wilful silence in France over the war, a predominantly nostalgic image of Algeria was circulated among its former French inhabitants. Living in exile in France, this generation wanted to focus on the idyllic childhood they had before the war began. Most often, they painted their homeland as a Lost Paradise in their written and photographic works. A series of photodocumentary books popped up between 1980 and the late 1990s in which iconic buildings, sweeping landscapes, European architecture and monuments, and even Roman ruins in Algeria appeared. The goal of these photographic works was often to create a recognisable image of the past, one that would evoke positive memory in an effort to keep the image of Algeria fresh in their minds (Hubbell 2011: 169). The oft-repeated landscapes served a secondary effect of crowding out the unpleasant images of the more recent past (Hubbell 2015: 209–10). The visual memory of the war itself remained largely undocumented until the Algerian Civil War broke out in the 1990s, which prevented the Pieds-Noirs from making return voyages and caused many to examine the more disturbing images they had stored in their minds but largely, at least publicly, suppressed. Once the war was officially named by a law passed in the French National Assembly on 10 June 1999, the memory of specific wartime traumas began to be explored intensively in academic and autobiographical texts and depicted graphically in visual works.[1]

By 2005, when France's so-called Memory Wars over how the Algerian War should be written into history were at their height (Guendouzi 2017: 236), and the younger generation of Pieds-Noirs were grappling with their chaotic childhood memories of violence, graphically violent images of the past began to be circulated online, in films, and in art.[2] Once again, the European returnees took the lead in addressing the history, memory, and visual representation of the past in Algeria. Their autobiography began to acknowledge the most troubling memories of growing up amid regular shootings, bombings, and massacres, and the visual representation of the past became increasingly bleak. Historians and filmmakers went to the archives which progressively became available in search of evidence that might explain the shocking images that remained in their minds. Historian Benjamin Stora is one of the many who used his research to understand the troubling images that he retained from his childhood in Algeria (2015: 5).

Some of the most violent images of the Algerian War circulated on Pied-Noir websites and listservs.[3] Dead bodies from the war seemed to proliferate as images became digitally accessible and shared more freely. The photographs were primarily of mutilated corpses, often of faces only, and many were photos of Algerians allegedly killed by the Algerian Front de Libération Nationale (FLN) for having committed acts against their religion such as smoking (punished by removal of the nose) or more serious crimes such as failing to support the independence movement, and especially for having supported the French military. Algerian soldiers who fought for the French are known as Harkis, and the Pieds-Noirs have taken up the task of commemorating the Harkis' experience alongside their own since the end of the war. The images of emasculated and decapitated Algerians are some of the most commonly reproduced, yet the story behind the images has been repeatedly rewritten. While the photographed victims are labelled as Harkis and personally named on the

Association Harkis Dordogne website, which dates the deaths between July and August 1962, the same images also appear on Simone Gautier's website dedicated to the 26 March 1962 Rue d'Isly massacre (Gautier 2014).[4] On her site, Gautier attributes these deaths to the FLN and notes below the image: 'ils n'ont pas voulu suivre le Ramadan' ('they didn't want to observe Ramadan'). The photo is dated 27 May 1956.[5]

The reclaiming of the same image from site to site, with different names and affiliations given to the pictured victims, is indicative of the ways in which the traumas of the war have been represented. Despite intending to bring acknowledgement for past traumas, the reuse and reappropriation of horrific images contributes to the confusion that remains in the memory of the Algerian War. The recirculation of the same images in completely opposing contexts undermines the validity of the horror represented (that is, are these men victims of the FLN *or* are they victims of the French military?). In *The Image and the Witness*, Frances Guerin and Roger Hallas explore how traumatic photos lose their meaning by examining examples from the US war in Iraq:

> On the one hand, all of these images are disseminated in abundance, and they carry political conviction way beyond their status as representation. On the other, like many public images of trauma, they also continue to be denigrated, dismissed, questioned and cast in doubt. (Guerin and Hallas 2007: 3)

While the intention of disseminating these images is often related to claims of or demands for truth, the atrocities depicted defy belief. The images often evoke denial and contestation rather than recognition and acknowledgement. Photography has the ability to function as concrete evidence, and yet, the image is portable, moveable, reusable, and unstable; its meaning is dependent on its context. Susan Sontag explains in *Regarding the Pain of Others*, 'And photographs of the victims of war are themselves a species of rhetoric. They reiterate. They simplify. They agitate. They create the illusion of consensus' (2003: 8). Photographs of victims, both living and dead, can be resituated in political and personal ways. They are used to make sense of one's own suffering and to make statements about collective forms of trauma.

Given the ability to resituate photography in ways that change the meaning of the suffering contained within it, what then can we understand from art, created by a victim of the trauma, that reproduces and reinterprets horrific scenes? This chapter explores the effects of recirculating photographic images of dead, living, and surviving bodies in art by Nicole Guiraud, who survived a famous bombing in the Algerian War. Response to the reused and repeated images ranges from denial and shock to recognition. Relying on theoretical works on photography of traumatic events and the work of memory, this chapter examines how images of traumatised bodies are circulated and integrated into Guiraud's art with the aim of understanding how individual suffering can be integrated into collective memory and whether repeating images intensifies or mitigates trauma for the artist and her spectators.

Nicole Guiraud

Pied-Noir artist Nicole Guiraud, who now lives in France, is one of the many civilian victims injured during the Algerian War. When she was ten years old, on 30 September 1956, she survived a bomb placed in the Milk Bar in Algiers – a scene made famous by Gillo Pontecorvo's film *The Battle of Algiers* (1966).[6] Three people were killed, fifty wounded – including Guiraud's father – and twelve civilians were maimed. Nicole's left arm was amputated, but this did not stop her from pursuing a career in art and, like her father, becoming an advocate for victims of terrorism. Her artwork consists primarily of painting and installation art that has been shown in France and Germany. Her work demonstrates the psychological process of working through personal and collective war traumas. It contains a mixture of peaceful scenery and massacred bodies, some reproduced from photographs and some created from her imagination.

Guiraud is personally committed to and heavily involved in her community's memory work. She has been an advocate for the recognition of several silenced massacres that occurred during the Algerian War.[7] She has also fought her own public battle against the France 3 television channel, suing it for emotional damages for financing and broadcasting the film *Les Porteuses de feu* (*Fire Carriers*) (2008, dir. Faouzia Fékiri), which celebrates the Algerian women who carried bombs. Although she was unsuccessful in her cause, Guiraud's case was widely shared on social media, making known the point that the women who left the bombs in civilian locations became heroes in Algeria while Guiraud and others like her who survived have permanent physical and emotional consequences to bear for those acts. In 2013, Guiraud published her diary from the war, *Algérie 1962: Journal de l'Apocalypse* (*Algeria 1962: Diary of the Apocalypse*) which recounts the final days of the war and includes photographs of the original journal, personal photographs with her father and other victims, and several pieces of her artwork (Guiraud 2013, 2015).

Immediately after the war, Guiraud found living in France burdensome and she emigrated to Germany as a young adult, but in 2016 she decided to move permanently to Montpellier, France. She routinely participates in Pied-Noir cultural, academic, and commemorative events. Guiraud willingly lets her body stand in as a symbol of the loss of Algeria, and she has given testimony in documentary films and in sociological studies of the Pied-Noir community. Along with depicting her own body on her canvases, Guiraud inscribes other living and dead war victims. She also depicts French soldiers and Algerian liberation fighters in several of her paintings. Although some of the images she reworks are derived from photographs that are well known among the Pieds-Noirs and mainland French of Guiraud's generation, Guiraud frequently situates herself among the dead and suffering.

As a child during the Algerian War, Guiraud is part of the last and young-est generation of Pieds-Noirs who, unlike their parents and grandparents, are not invested in protecting a pacific memory of Algeria. This generation is, for the most part, absent of guilt for colonisation and the war, but they witnessed and survived extreme violence during the war and endured difficult integration and sometimes discrimination in France due to the public discontent over the seven-year war attempting to keep the colony. This generation uses art and literature to make sense of their fragmented memories, and to understand their parents and the larger historic and political context of the war. They examine both personal suffering and communal trauma, and a large part of their knowl-edge of Algeria is entwined with what Marianne Hirsch calls 'post-memory', or memory of their homeland that has been safeguarded and passed down from their parents (1992: 8).[8] As Hirsch indicates, 'Photography is precisely the medium connecting memory and post-memory', and this can in part explain why Guiraud and others turn to photography to work through their own mem-ory of wartime violence (1992: 9). The photo stands in the gaps, providing a sense of historical fact, visual memory, and personal experience for the artist.

Guiraud's artwork includes photographed and painted reproductions of photographed bodies in various states: living, dead, and surviving. The living bodies are those of perpetrators of violence, bodies before violence occurs (her own and others), and bodies before separation from exile or war, and occasion-ally bodies of emergency workers or witnesses of the devastation. These living bodies are often surrounded by dead and traumatised bodies. The dead bodies are commonly those destroyed by the war through torture, terrorist acts, and isolated murders. The dead bodies include children, adults, Europeans, and North Africans. Surviving bodies are alive but visibly scarred, pierced, maimed, or psychologically traumatised. Survivors are represented as having 'out-lived' their 'intended destruction', as Hirsch puts it (1992: 5). In the following sec-tions, I will analyse how these painted representations of bodies function in Guiraud's art.

LIVING BODIES

In 'Family Pictures: Maus, Mourning and Post-Memory', Hirsch studies the jux-taposition of living bodies photographed and the horrific photos of death and how the two relate to each other. Reflecting on Susan Sontag's *On Photography*, Hirsch underscores the 'simultaneous presence of death and life in the photo-graph' (1992: 5). The living cannot be separated from the dead; they are two points in the same narrative. Although Hirsch is investigating the single survivor in the photograph and how she has outlived her intended destruction, I will examine how the living are represented next to the dead in the same image. The dead bring meaning to those who are alive and vice versa, particularly when the narrative is one of war. In the following examples from Guiraud's artwork, the living are perpetrators, rescuers, and those facing imminent destruction. Their stories are entirely caught up with each other. These reproduced images are not candid shots but made with an intended narrative and with the hindsight of personal experience, memory, and historical research. Those about to be wounded sometimes look forward with dread and sometimes look away from approaching disaster.

One of the most famous images that is now emblematic of the Pieds-Noirs is a photograph called *L'Exode* (*The Exodus*) published in the popular French magazine *Paris Match* in 1962 (Unknown 1962). In the black and white photograph, soon to be exiles, both young and old, wait to leave Algiers, sitting on the street, grief stricken, accompanied by their baggage. French soldiers stand behind the families. Holding machine guns, they look on with the ambiguous appearance of either protecting the exiles or forcing them to leave. The photograph, which covers a two-page spread in the popular magazine, has been repeatedly circulated across the Pied-Noir community since its original publication. It appeared, for example, in the 2006 documentary film *Les Pieds-Noirs: histoires d'une blessure* (*Pieds-Noirs: Stories of Pain*) (2007, dir. Gilles Perez) and in *Je me souviens . . . L'Exode des Pieds-Noirs (1962–2012)* (*I Remember . . . The Exodus of the Pieds-Noirs*), a book of collected testimony published in 2012 (Cardinali 2012). Guiraud uses the photo in her installation from the 1990s 'La Valise à la mer' ('The Suitcase in the Sea'), as depicted in a short film of the same title (1991, dir. Dieter Reifarth and Bert Schmidt), in her catalogue for the 'Survivre' ('Survival') exhibit in 2012, and she recreated the magazine pages in a painting for the 'Survivre' show (Guiraud 2012: 33, 36, 41). The image also appears in her published diary (Guiraud 2013: 103). In the installation piece, the iconic image lies across the top of her open suitcase, which is filled with plastic bags of catalogued memorabilia, surrounded by debris on the floor and encircled by a compass which delineates the space of the exploded suitcase.[9] In her painting of the iconic departure scene for the 'Survivre' exhibit commissioned by the city of Perpignan in 2012, Guiraud overlays the words 'Cessez le feu – c'est fini' 'Cease fire – it's over' on the painting and inscribes a verse by poet Edmond Jabès (2012: 29; 2013: 99). Guiraud at once relates her personal departure to an immediately recognisable image of the departure which will resonate with the community of returnees, 'allowing the autobiographical to be overshadowed by the community's memory' (Hubbell 2015: 222).

In another painting entitled *Milk Bar*, Guiraud recreates the scene of the bombing that wounded her and her father in 1956, based on a photograph taken in the aftermath. The iconic event was depicted in Pontecorvo's *The Battle*

Figure 2.1   Nicole Guiraud, *Attentat*.

of Algiers, although the film erroneously attributed the bombing to Djamila Bouhired, as many others have done. The woman who actually left the bomb, Zohra Drif, survived and became a lawyer and famous politician, married to former Algerian president Rabah Bitat. Guiraud uses a photograph of a fully intact woman, Drif, on the day of her arrest. In this way, she resituates the person who wounded her in the place of trauma, positioning her as present at and culpable of the bombing. Drif, whole and unscathed, stands in contrast to the image of Nicole and other dismembered children.[10]

DEAD BODIES

The dead bodies that appear throughout Guiraud's artwork are generally based on photographs that are easily sourced through reverse image searches on the internet. The bodies she has chosen to paint are often ones that have proliferated across various websites, and for this reason, they have also invariably been used to different ends. The images of these bodies range from faint outlines to gruesomely bloodied and tortured bodies. The dead are often spatially positioned to relate to those who survive, as will be explored in the next section of this chapter. The depicted victims are upsetting to look at, yet Guiraud as an artist and survivor has gone beyond mere looking to painstakingly recreate them, to retrace their wounds, to think through how the bodies must have suffered at the time of their death, sometimes emphasising blood and sites of trauma on the body.

In her painted collage piece, a triptych called *Survivre* (*Survival*), the aforementioned decapitated and emasculated Muslim victims (whether they have been murdered by the French, if they are Harkis, or men who refused to follow religious law and slain by the FLN) are reproduced. As an example, the photograph is reproduced on the Wikipedia page on 'torture in the Algerian War', and in a reverse image search, the image was found as part of a political message from an Algerian asking France to apologise for its crimes.[11] Like the stories that have been reformulated over time, the images themselves have been repainted and reassembled by Guiraud. The disembodied faces appear to be photographed and then the photos are displayed in jars in the painting. This is a reference to (and a painted reproduction of) Guiraud's earlier installation series 'Le Monde en bocal' ('The World in a Preserving Jar'), in which memorial fragments are enshrined in sealed glass jars and stored on shelves (Guiraud 1998). In that installation series the photographed men's faces are clearly displayed with a partly legible inscription in German 'und Tod' ('and death') (Guiraud 2013: 95). Guiraud reproduces different versions of this photo across her artworks. For example, she repaints the work with French words 'est la terreur' ('is terror') and includes a reproduction of the painting in her published diary (2013: 104; 2012: 54–5).

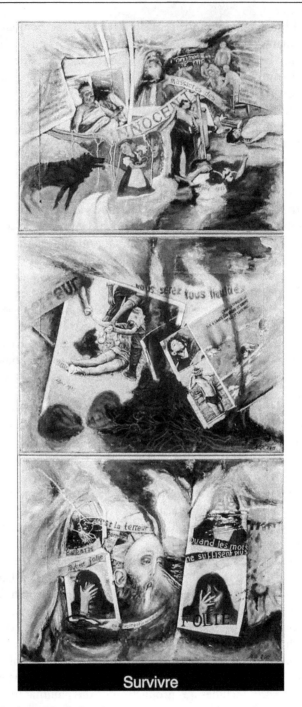

Figure 2.2   Nicole Guiraud, *Survivre*.

Guiraud includes at least four different photo booth-style images of herself, showing physical signs of emotional trauma, to accompany the men's severed heads in *Survivre*. She reworks the different copies of her own face showing her mouth scratched out, her eyes closed, her eyes open and traced as though permanently forced to see, and her eyes hidden in her hands (2012: 54–5; 2013: 104). What does it mean to interject her own contemporary photo amongst these massacred bodies, victims like her but Algerians who did not survive? What does it mean to mutilate her own photographed mouth and eyes in ways that evoke the torture inscribed on the decapitated men? Her depicted psychological suffering relates a reaction to and reproduction of the horrific nature of torture. By mutilating an image of her own face and placing it in a jar alongside the murdered men, Guiraud demonstrates the unspeakable nature of trauma, as described in the text 'when words are no longer enough'. She allows her body to relate to the body of other victims to fill in the narrative. She enmeshes the edges of the photos in the painting in a way that makes the puzzle pieces fit, although they are jammed together.[12] Guiraud clearly relates to the pain and suffering these men endured before dying, and she depicts her own suffering alongside theirs.

In two other similar works, *Massacre des innocents* (the top third of the triptych in Figure 2.2) and *Milk Bar* (Figure 2.3), Guiraud depicts four more dead and bloodied bodies. These particular bodies are painted in a photographic style in *Massacre des innocents* and in a more painterly and vividly coloured way in *Milk Bar*. The original photo of the bodies is not easily found in a reverse image search. Although the source photograph of two men and one woman is published in Guiraud's diary, another seemingly photographed body has been inserted into the central part of the paintings. The man of unknown origins is lying shirtless on his back, fully extended with his face turned away from the spectator.[13] Guiraud has reworked these same bodies over two different paintings, but she has changed the date from Algeria 1955 to 1956 (Hubbell 2018). In the source photo of the three dead bodies printed in Guiraud's diary, she labels the image 'les bains de sang' ('blood baths') (2013: 96). In the painting *Massacre des innocents*, Guiraud represents herself as a fictionalised body – a Little Red Riding Hood not knowing what terror lurks ahead, looking back over her shoulder at the wolf who follows her without seeing the horrific dead bodies that lie ahead. Guiraud the adult emerges next to the child as a torn photograph, placing the artist at the crossroads, an adult survivor between the fantasised child and the dead bodies.

In a third untitled reproduction of the dead bodies, Guiraud paints the corpses on the street with blood flowing across the footpath (2013: 99). A soldier walks along the path unknowingly about to be faced with the bodies which are situated around the corner. The soldier looks down at one body

Figure 2.3   Nicole Guiraud, *Milk Bar*.

covered by newspapers. This painting resonates with a passage in Guiraud's personal diaries where she writes about a traumatic experience in Algiers:

> 27 avril 1962
>
> Je descends en ville avec Mado. Dans la rue Michelet, il y a des cadavres sur les trottoirs, c'est affreux. On les enjambe pour éviter les flaques de sang. Quelqu'un a jeté une couverture ou un journal sur le visage. Mado dit qu'il ne faut pas regarder leurs yeux. On fait comme tout le monde, on regarde ailleurs. Mais on a peur quand même et nous nous dépêchons de rentrer. (Guiraud 2013: 32)

> 27 April 1962
>
> I go into town with Mado. On Rue Michelet, there are bodies on the footpath, it's horrible. We step over them to avoid the pools of blood. Someone has thrown a blanket or a newspaper over their faces. Mado says you mustn't look at their eyes. We do the same thing as everyone else, we look away. But we're still scared and we hurry to get home. (Guiraud 2015)

This painting can be read as another attempt to work through horrific visions of the past through research and reproduction of the terrifying aspects of what she survived. The fact that the cadavers reappear over three separate paintings shows the extent to which the dead bodies affected her.

Recreating massacred bodies from both known and unknown events and inserting her own experience within those iconic traumas, Guiraud shows how these deaths could have been her own, and how her body is a part of the larger traumas of the war. In some cases, as with her reproduction of a known photo of the bodies from the Rue d'Isly massacre being put into an ambulance and inscribing this into the Milk Bar bombing which maimed her, Guiraud reconfigures the attacks to relate her own experience to others.[14] She also inscribes Zohra Drif, the person who left the bomb, into the painting in a way that lets her stand in for all FLN fighters. As Guiraud transposes a historical trauma at the end of the war into her own which occurred at the beginning, she creates a personal and communal narrative of the war through her art.

SURVIVING BODIES

As demonstrated by Nicole Guiraud's 2012 art exhibit entitled 'Survivre' ('Survival'), the surviving bodies like her own are the ones that are sometimes the hardest to depict but also the ones that need the most care. The surviving bodies in Guiraud's work are bodies that show physical signs of trauma but are also representations that indicate the psychological anguish of surviving the war. Without discussing the exact traumas entailed with survival, Hirsch analyses a multiplied copy of an image of a relative named Frieda who survived the Holocaust. Hirsch explains:

> She is the survivor who announces that she has literally sur-vived, lived too long, outlived her intended destruction, the survivor who has a story to tell, but who has neither the space nor the audience to do so in the instantaneous flash of the photograph. (Hirsch 1992: 5)

In a similar way, through her art, Guiraud announces her own and others' survival of the intended destruction. Through art, she has the time to reconsider and recast the story of that survival for her audience.

In her 1991 film and art project titled *Der Koffer. La Valise à la mer* (*The Suitcase in the Sea*) (dir. Dieter Reifarth and Bert Schmidt), Guiraud sits within her installation art and testifies to the moment that her arm was blown off. She shares the intensely personal and traumatic moments of her past, but she remains inscribed within the community of Pieds-Noirs by framing her experience within the exodus symbolised by her suitcase and various objects and images related to the war. Her own physical amputation has come to represent

Figure 2.4   Film still from *Der Koffer. La Valise à la mer.*

the community's metaphorical amputation from Algeria. The most commonly repeated surviving body across Guiraud's artwork is her own. She uses a photo of herself and other child bombing victims taken in the Hôpital Mustapha and published in *L'Algérie médicale* (Lombard 1957: 67). These images, like many others examined here, have often circulated with political motivations and they were more recently republished in Guiraud's diary (2013: 97). Although another survivor of the Milk Bar bombing, Danielle Michel-Chich (2012), rejects the use of her photograph as a means of seeking restitution for the community's losses, Guiraud nonetheless recirculates her own body freely. In many cases, the photo of the child amputees seems to legitimise her art and confirm her capacity to speak about the Algerian War. Her surviving body stands defiant against the ones who tried to kill her.

In many of her pieces, Guiraud inscribes the outline of these amputated children's bodies. She and the other children hover ghostlike above the scenes of destruction. In the upper left quadrant of the *Milk Bar* painting, Guiraud's body, along with three other survivors and one dead child, are embossed onto the canvas. In correspondence with Guiraud, she explained that the dead child is an imagined child symbolic of the other innocent victims of the war. As her own childhood body hovers above the scene of attack, Guiraud is separate from but a witness to the moment of devastation.

Repetition and Making Meaning of Suffering

By representing three different phases of the body – living, dead, and surviving – and by using photographs of real bodies intertwined with those that are symbolic or imagined, Guiraud addresses her own and others' trauma in the war. Through repetition and reframing, however, she also undermines the truth of the stories the victims themselves might share. She easily manipulates, recasts, and reforms the narratives. This is a way for her to work out her own trauma in the war, but it can be seen as exploitative of the others she depicts. Her personal trauma is so great that she does not question her right to reconsider the horrific scenes she survived and witnessed. However, there is no consideration for the wishes of the others depicted or any pain that her works may stir up in the spectator. As an example, in her 'La Valise à la mer' exhibit, Guiraud uses a well-known photograph that appeared in *Paris Match* in 1962. The photo is a close-up of a child's bloodied face. As she sits and holds this photograph in the film, the viewer might think that is Guiraud's bloodied face after the Milk Bar bombing. Through research, however, the photo is identifiable as Delphine Renard, a four-year-old girl who was blinded by a bomb placed outside her window by the Organisation de l'Armée Secrète (OAS) that was intended to kill French Minister of Cultural Affairs André Malraux. Renard contests the journalists who photographed her in her autobiography *Tu choisiras la vie* (2013) because she says by photographing her, they delayed her treatment.[15] Despite Guiraud's frequent use of text within her art, in this case she does not provide an explanation. Instead, the images themselves create a narrative that directly relates her experience of survival to Renard's despite their divergent histories.[16]

Repetition is a common strategy in Pied-Noir remembrance and it is one that Guiraud also employs. Reparative nostalgia which is often highly visual (see Boym 2001) functions to temporarily reattach the exile to their homeland and allow them to feel connected to a time prior to the rupture of exile. Repeating beautiful images of home provides respite from a present characterised by absence and pain and allows the exile to feel temporarily restored. In photographic collections, the repetition of the same locations is one way to solidify communal remembrance. As I wrote in 'Accumulating Algeria: Recurrent Images in Pied-Noir Visual Works', 'The sheer volume of repeated images takes up space, crowding out the individual versions in favour of the familiar and resonating one. Personal memories, both good and bad, are pressed out in favour of the more popular' (Hubbell 2015: 218). Here, the repeated corpses in many ways become the only ones that exist. As Hirsch proposed in 'Surviving Images: Holocaust Photographs and the Work of Postmemory', photos have potential to be used to promote forgetting even when the images themselves are hard to forget:

> If these images, in their obsessive repetition, delimit our available archive of trauma, can they enable a responsible and ethical discourse in its aftermath? How can we read them? Do they act like clichés, empty signifiers that distance and protect us from the event? Or, on the contrary, does their repetition in itself retraumatise, making distant viewers into surrogate victims who, having seen the images so often, have adopted them into their own narratives and memories, and have thus become all the more vulnerable to their effects? If they cut and wound, do they enable memory, mourning, and working through? Or is their repetition an effect of melancholic replay, appropriative identification? (Hirsch 2001: 8)

In Guiraud's case, the repeated images from the archive of trauma have a blunting effect. Sontag, in *On Photography*, points out:

> Photographs shock insofar as they show something novel. Unfortunately, the ante keeps getting raised – partly through the very proliferation of such images of horror. One's first encounter with the photographic inventory of ultimate horror is a kind of revelation, the prototypically modern revelation: a negative epiphany. (Sontag [1977] 2005: 14)

Effectively, then, the more an image is repeated because of its veracity and uncontainable message, the less impact it has on its viewer. If shock is the desired emotional response, we are always in need of something stronger, newer, or previously unseen. However, when it comes to digesting and understanding the trauma depicted, if the spectator is to understand and acknowledge the horror in the image, the viewer's response to the image is hardened. This may, in fact, be a desired outcome for the trauma victim who reproduces the sites and sights related to their own metaphorical demise. Survival, for him or her, requires scarring, and scars provide protection from future wounds.

The activity of circulating images of trauma to elicit response, then, is counterproductive. The image can shock only if it is not fully seen, not acknowledged, and not recognised or not accepted by the viewer. The moment we move beyond the superficial horror and begin to recognise the victims, its power to shock fades. We begin to interact with the pain depicted, to imagine the lives of those who suffered and sometimes died, and while acknowledging that trauma, we may also be hardened to the destruction that humans are able to wreak and endure.

When Guiraud recirculates her own story inside of and alongside broader traumas experienced in her community such as the Rue d'Isly shooting or the exodus in 1962, the message of the image is inevitably changed, reappropriated, and re-narrated with specific intent. Guiraud's own image becomes a symbol of survival – not only her own, but also that of the Pieds-Noirs. Guiraud simultaneously tells her survival story and copes as a traumatised witness. Her body works as a bridge, as depicted in *Massacre des innocents* in which she positions herself between threat of devastation and actual violence. In the history of the Algerian War, Guiraud was both an actor and a witness; there is repetition because she survived. As one that outlived her intended death, she grapples with the devastation she witnessed and experienced. When she rehearses and revisits past trauma, she invites others to witness the devastation that marked her.

Repetition affords the viewer more opportunities to examine the traumatic image, allowing an eventual engagement with and response to what is seen. Proliferation of the same images also distils the available repertoire of images into those select few that have survived. Visual memory becomes whittled down to what has most often been seen. These particular repeated images become the select ones we know and recall. The shock value at the beginning is lessened. As Sontag explains in *On Photography*:

> Once one has seen such images, one has started down the road of seeing more – and more. Images transfix. Images anesthetise. [. . .] An event known through photographs certainly becomes more real than it would have been if one had never seen the photographs [. . .] But after repeated exposure to images it also becomes less real. The vast photographic catalogue of misery and injustice throughout the world has given everyone a

certain familiarity with atrocity, making the horrible seem more ordinary – making it appear familiar, remote ('it's only a photograph'), inevitable. (Sontag [1977] 2005: 15)

Repetition and recognition can reduce the power of the trauma, especially as contexts shift. The assemblage of supposedly real images can also construct narrative in false ways.[17] Hirsch writes in 'Family Pictures': 'The horror of looking is not necessarily *in* the image but in the story we provide to fill in what is left out of the image' (1992: 7). The story created through Guiraud's juxtaposition and recreation of photographic images, by positioning her own body within the narrative of other traumas in Algeria, demonstrates the simultaneous impact of witnessing and surviving the horror of the Algerian War.

CONCLUSION

Just like the nostalgic images of Algeria and the repeated scenes of a beautiful past that crowd out unwanted memories of the past, there is a limited stock of images from the war and a limited selection of that limited stock which is circulated to represent the war. By circulating the same images in different contexts, much like in photodocumentary texts, these circulated bodies begin crowding out other memories of the past, creating recognisable iconography of the war in a sorrowful and painful way. This also creates frames of recognition that can be easier to examine. By placing the living alongside the dead and suffering, Guiraud creates a new narrative of the war using her own artistic language to sort out her personal memory. For example, by placing the living body of Zohra Drif artistically at the site of the Milk Bar in ruins, a scene that Drif herself never witnessed (as recounted in Drif 2013), Guiraud reconstructs the history of the war.[18] She forces the woman who placed the bomb to be placed in the site that was destroyed. Likewise, Guiraud places herself, a survivor, among dead Muslims, to show her own shock and horror as a witness of violence.

As Guiraud works through her own acknowledgement of unspeakable acts inflicted on her and others in the war, she asks us to also acknowledge the atrocities committed. By depicting traumatised, violated, murdered bodies as well as amputated and suffering survivors, Guiraud's art initiates the viewer into the experience of trauma. According to Hirsch, if we recognise the images because we have seen them already,

> we can begin to move beyond the shock of seeing them for the first time, again and again. We can also move out of their obsessive repetition, for they are both familiar and estranged. And thus they reconstitute a viewing relation that cannot be repaired, but that can perhaps be re-envisioned in ways that do not negate the rupture at its source. (Hirsch 2001: 33)

In this way, by re-examining the same images with recognition of the extreme trauma of the Algerian War, the viewer may begin to transform her relationship to the horrific past. In Guiraud's text in the catalogue accompanying the 'Survivre' exhibit, she writes:

> Survivre à une enfance brisée par la guerre et par l'exode . . . Oui, car la vie est plus forte que la peur. Après la mort vient toujours la résurrection. Et lorsqu'on les honore, les Ombres des disparus sortent de l'oubli et du néant et sont de nouveau parmi nous, les Survivants. (Guiraud 2012: 51)

> Surviving a childhood broken by the war and the exodus . . . Yes, because life is stronger than fear. After death resurrection always comes. And when we honour them, the Shadows of the dead come out of oblivion and nothingness and they are again among us, the Survivors.

Through her depictions of the trauma of exile, of the disappeared alongside the living, she shows us the value and strength of survival.

Nicole Guiraud will undoubtedly continue to highlight the ruptures she re-envisions in her work. She launched a new art show, 'Entre Racines et Horizons' ('Between Roots and Horizons') in 2018 in Fréjus, France, which valorised Pied-Noir art – both traumatic and nostalgic. She also illustrated a book of poetry called *Deux enfants dans la guerre 1954–1962* (*Two Children in War 1954–1962*) which was co-produced with Gerard Crespo (Guiraud and Crespo 2018). In an interview about the art show, Guiraud said, 'C'est le miracle de l'art qui permet d'exprimer des choses terribles qu'on sublime. C'est la resilience. On arrive à vivre avec et à donner aux autres aussi' ('That's the miracle of art that allows us to express horrible things that we suppress. It's resilience. We manage to live with it and to give to others as well') (Chabert 2018). While Guiraud will not forget the traumas from her past, whether we choose to look and to recognise, and how we are able to understand the recontextualised and reconfigured images will determine how the larger traumas from the Algerian War will be remembered.

NOTES

1. Prior to 1999, the war was referenced as 'police operations' or 'the events'. The Algerian War for Independence was formally named as one on 10 June 1999 in the French National Assembly. Subsequently Law 99–882 was adopted on 18 October 1999, which legally substituted the words 'Algerian War or battles in Tunisia and Morocco' ('la guerre d'Algérie ou aux combats en Tunisie et au Maroc') for 'police operations undertaken in North Africa' ('opérations effec-tuées en Afrique du Nord') (Loi n° 99–882). All translations are my own unless otherwise indicated.

2. The year 2005 corresponds to the unpopular French law to recognise the positive aspects of colonialism (which was quickly repealed), the dying out of the older generation of French Algerians known as Pieds-Noirs, who often fought to keep Algeria French up to and even beyond independence in 1962, and the handover from the memory guardians to the younger generation. See works by Benjamin Stora (Stora and Jenni 2016) and Eric Savarèse (2008), which engage with this time of remembrance.

3. Images began to be circulated by email through the Association Jeune Pied-Noir (Young Pied-Noir Group) as early as 2008. Some of the first photos of wounded bodies were of Nicole Guiraud and other maimed children convalescing in hospital after attacks in the Battle of Algiers in 1956, circulated on 24 January 2008. On 15 March 2008, images from the Rue d'Isly shooting were circulated by email. New and repeated images of dead bodies became commonplace on the emails after that point (Association Jeune Pied-Noir 2019).

4. On the Association Harkis Dordogne site in the story 'Massacres de Harkis de juillet à août 1962 (Deuxième partie)' ('Massacre of the Harkis from July to August 1962, Part 2'), the authors try to tell the story of the individual Harkis who were killed and they reproduce this frequently circulated image from the war. Simone Gautier set up her website because her husband was killed along with eighty other Europeans at the Rue d'Isly shooting. Two hundred were wounded during a peaceful demonstration when the French military opened fire on the crowd. Gautier has actively sought images of her husband on that day to better understand what happened to him. Her site later expanded to cover other massacres during the war. Guiraud also uses this specific image in her art as explored in this chapter.

5. On Gautier's long timeline of attacks, she includes images of wounded Algerians and Europeans, including Nicole Guiraud, and two graphic slideshows of mutilated corpses.

6. Although Pontecorvo's version of the bombings is the most known and has impacted the cultural memory of the Algerian War, this particular scene is full of historical inaccuracies which the victims themselves had sometimes accepted as fact until new testimony, notably by Zohra Drif (2013), and historical work corrected that vision in the 2000s and 2010s.

7. Massacres were officially obscured by government restriction to archives, and also events were too traumatic for many individuals to recount in the aftermath of the unpopular war. Guiraud has been involved in bringing public attention to the 5 July 1962 massacre in Oran. This particular massacre of Europeans on Algerian Independence Day was silenced by the French and Algerians alike, as explored in Jean-Pierre Lledo's film *Algérie, histoires à ne pas dire* (*Algeria, Untold Stories*, 2007). According to testimony, the French military were locked in their barracks and unable to intervene because civil order had been handed over to the Algerian police force. The number of dead has been widely disputed and ranges from 30 to 5,000. See Hubbell (2020) for more details.

8. Although Hirsch calls post-memory 'that of the child of the survivor whose life is dominated by memories of what preceded his/her birth' (1992: 8), I include the children who were born but not old enough to understand or fully remember what they witnessed.

9. See Hubbell (2015: 223) for more in-depth analysis of this work.
10. In addition to the images of living exiles and living liberation fighters, Guiraud also recreates her own family photos, often in an Algerian garden, before the attack. Guiraud appears whole, but these paintings also contain sketched outlines of dead children who seem to lurk in the shadows, disrupting the nostalgic image she may otherwise portray. The living bodies lead to a path of foreshadowed destruction, taken from real and imagined figures that have long accompanied Guiraud on her path to survive the trauma of the war.
11. The caption on the disputed photo reads, 'Photo extraite de la brochure de propagande *Aspects véritables de la rébellion algérienne* publiée en 1957 par le Gouvernement général de l'Algérie et censée représenter deux musulmans torturés et décapités par les "rebelles" du FLN' ('Photo taken from a propaganda brochure on the Truth about the Algerian Rebellion published in 1957 by the Algerian Government and said to represent two tortured and decapitated Muslims by FLN "rebels"'). The photo is available through Wikimedia Commons, titled 'Severed Heads and Penises of Two Algerian Men – 1956'.
12. In *Survivre*, another dead decapitated body is drawn in the bottom right corner; a girl's head with blood coming from it appears to be peacefully sleeping, with her body possibly somewhere off the canvas.
13. The photograph of this man lying alongside three other dead bodies appears in the short film *Der Koffer. La Valise à la mer* (Dieter Reifarth and Bert Schmidt, 1991) and is presumably a part of Guiraud's installation piece.
14. The photo was used as publicity for a documentary on the Rue d'Isly shooting called *Le Massacre de la rue d'Isly: le grand silence* (*The Rue d'Isly Massacre: Total Silence*) (2008, dir. Christophe Weber).
15. The OAS was a French paramilitary terrorist organisation which fought to keep Algeria French after the independence process had been decided. In her book, Renard writes about this photo of her taken after the OAS bombing in detail: 'Il m'est arrivé de ne plus pouvoir le supporter. D'autant plus que le reporter qui l'avait pris avait ainsi retardé les secours, lesquels attendaient pour m'emporter à l'hôpital Cochin, gaspillant de précieuses minutes' (2013) ('There have been times when I could not stand that photo. Even more so because the reporter who took it delayed the first aid workers who were waiting to take me to Cochin hospital, wasting precious time').
16. Guiraud's 'La Valise à la mer' exhibit predates Renard's autobiography by more than twenty years. It is unclear whether Guiraud knew the story of Delphine Renard and intentionally reappropriated the image, or if she used the photograph as one among others of mutilated and dead bodies to contextualise her own experience.
17. For example, when researching images for this chapter, I came across a photo of Nicole Guiraud as a child standing with the adult Zohra Drif, an image that could only have been artificially constructed.
18. Drif recounts the Milk Bar bombing in detail in her 2013 book. Once she left the bomb and waited long enough to be sure no one would find it, she fled the scene. She did not return after the bomb detonated.

REFERENCES

Algérie, histoires à ne pas dire. Documentary. Directed by Jean-Pierre Lledo. Algeria: Albarès, 2007.

Association Jeune Pied-Noir. 2009. 'Jeune Pied-Noir: le site des Pieds-Noirs, des Harkis et de leurs amis.' <https://jeunepiednoir.pagesperso-orange.fr> (last accessed 4 October 2019).

The Battle of Algiers. Film. Directed by Gillo Pontecorvo. Italy: Igor Film, 1966.

Boym, Svetlana. 2001. *The Future of Nostalgia*. New York: Basic Books.

Cardinali, François (ed.). 2012. *Je me souviens . . . L'Exode des Pieds-Noirs (1962–2012)*. Paris: Michel de Maule.

Chabert, Chrystel. 2018. '"Entre racines et horizon": 9 artistes pieds-noirs racontent leur Algérie.' *Franceinfo: culture*, 10 April. <https://www.francetvinfo.fr/culture/arts-expos/peinture/entre-racines-et-horizon-9-artistes-pieds-noirs-racontent-leur-algerie_3282475.html> (last accessed 17 November 2019).

Cohen, William B. 2000. 'The Algerian War and French Memory.' *Contemporary European History* 9.3: 489–500.

Cohen, William B. 2002. 'The Algerian War, the French State and Official Memory.' *Historical Reflections/Réflexions Historiques* 28.2: 219–39.

Der Koffer. La Valise à la mer. Documentary. Directed by Dieter Reifarth and Bert Schmidt. Frankfurt: Frankfurter Filmschau, 1991.

Drif, Zohra. 2013. *Mémoires d'une combattante de l'ALN: zone autonome d'Alger*. Algiers: Chihab éditions.

Gautier, Simone. 2014. 'Alger 26 mars 1962.' <http://alger26mars1962.fr/index.php?option=com_content&view=article&id=117:5-7-les-attentats&catid=30&Itemid=132&showall=1&limitstartssss (last accessed 17 March 2021).

Guendouzi, Amar. 2017. 'Contemporary Algerian Francophone Fiction, Trauma, and the "War of Memories".' *Journal of Romance Studies* 17.2: 235–53.

Guerin, Frances, and Roger Hallas. 2007. 'Introduction: The Image and the Witness.' In *The Image and the Witness: Trauma, Memory and Visual Culture*, edited by Frances Guerin and Roger Hallas, 1–20. New York: Wallflower Press.

Guiraud, Nicole. 1998. *Le Monde en bocal*. Berlin: Galerie Peter Hermann.

Guiraud, Nicole. 2012. *Survivre*, edited by Mairie de Perpignan and Cercle Algérianiste. Montpellier: Colleccio Font Nova .

Guiraud, Nicole. 2013. *Algérie 1962: Journal de l'Apocalypse*. Friedberg: Éditions Atlantis.

Guiraud, Nicole. 2015. *Algeria 1962: Diary of the Apocalypse*, translated by Amy L. Hubbell and Muhib Nabulsi. Friedberg: Éditions Atlantis. <http://editionatlantis.de/wordpress/wp-content/uploads/publinks/Nicole%20Guiraud%20-%20Diary%20of%20the%20Apocalypse%20.pdf> (last accessed 17 March 2021).

Guiraud, Nicole, and Gérard Cortés Crespo. 2018. *Deux enfants dans la guerre 1954–1962: peinture/poésie* Paris: Éditions de l'Onde.

Hirsch, Marianne. 1992. 'Family Pictures: Maus, Mourning and Post-Memory.' *Discourse* 15.2: 3–29.

Hirsch, Marianne. 2001. 'Surviving Images: Holocaust Photographs and the Work of Postmemory.' *The Yale Journal of Criticism* 14 (Spring): 5–37.

Hubbell, Amy L. 2011. 'Viewing the Past through a "Nostalgeric" Lens: Pied-Noir Photodocumentaries.' In *Textual and Visual Selves: Photography, Film, and Comic Art in*

French Autobiography, edited by Natalie Edwards, Amy L. Hubbell, and Ann Miller, 167–87. Lincoln, NE: University of Nebraska Press.

Hubbell, Amy L. 2015. 'Accumulating Algeria: Recurrent Images in Pied-Noir Visual Works.' In *Framing French Culture*, edited by Natalie Edwards, Benjamin McCann, and Peter Poiana, 209–27. Adelaide: University of Adelaide Press.

Hubbell, Amy L. 2018. 'Layering Over the Wounds of Algeria in Contemporary Pied-Noir Art.' *EuropeNow: Journal for the Council of European Studies* (March). <https://www.europenowjournal.org/2018/02/28/layering-over-the-wounds-of-algeria-in-contemporary-pied-noir-art/> (last accessed 17 March 2021).

Hubbell, Amy L. 2020. 'Remembering the 5 July 1962 Massacre in Oran, Algeria.' In *Places of Traumatic Memory: A Global Context*, edited by Amy L. Hubbell, Natsuko Akagawa, Sol Rojas-Lizana, and Annie Pohlman, 218–40. London: Palgrave Macmillan.

Le Massacre de la rue d'Isly: le grand silence. Documentary. Directed by Christophe Weber. France, 2008. <http://www.programme.tv/le-massacre-de-la-rue-d-isly-le-grand-silence-11011688/> (last accessed 17 March 2021).

Les Pieds-Noirs: histoires d'une blessure. Documentary. Directed by Gilles Perez. France: France Télévisions Distribution, 2007. Original edition, 2006.

Les Porteuses de feu. Film. Directed by Fékiri Faouzia. France: France 3, 2008.

Loi n° 99–882 du 18 octobre 1999 relative à la substitution, à l'expression 'aux opérations effectuées en Afrique du Nord', de l'expression 'à la guerre d'Algérie ou aux combats en Tunisie et au Maroc'. <https://www.legifrance.gouv.fr/affichTexte.do?cidTexte=JORFTEXT000000578132&categorieLien=cid> (last accessed 17 March 2021).

Lombard, P. 1957. 'La Clinique chirurgicale infantile et d'orthopédie de la Faculté de Médecine d'Alger.' *Algérie médicale* numéro spécial: 67ff.

Michel-Chich, Danielle. 2012. *Lettre à Zohra D*. Paris: Flammarion.

Renard, Delphine. 2013. *Tu choisiras la vie*. E-book edition. Paris: Gallimard.

Savarèse, Eric (ed.). 2008. *L'Algérie dépassionnée: au-delà du tumulte de la mémoire*. Paris: Syllepse.

'Severed Heads and Penises of Two Algerian Men – 1956.' Photograph. May 1956. *Wikimedia Commons*. <https://commons.wikimedia.org/wiki/File:Severed_heads_and_penises_of_two_Algerian_men_-_1956.jpg> (last accessed 17 March 2021).

Sontag, Susan. 2003. *Regarding the Pain of Others*. New York: Picador.

Sontag, Susan. [1977] 2005. *On Photography*. New York: Rosetta Books.

Stora, Benjamin. 2015. *Les Clés retrouvées: une enfance juive à Constantine*. Paris: Stock.

Stora, Benjamin, and Alexis Jenni. 2016. *Les Mémoires dangereuses: de l'Algérie coloniale à la France d'aujourd'hui*. Paris: Albin Michel.

Unknown. 1962. *L'Exode*. Photograph. *Paris Match*.

3. AN i FOR AN EYE: THE COLLECTIVE SHAPING OF EXPERIENCE IN THE AGE OF MACHINE-MEDIATED ART

Ellen Marie Saethre-McGuirk

INTRODUCTION

This chapter concerns the way in which the incessant and exponential use of photography in social media, as a means to form and visually communicate experiences, not only permeates our lives, but also shapes our experience of the world.

In my current research, I am particularly interested in Instagram as a visual communication platform where we share such images. Its global audience and userbase reflects the colonising nature of it and similar platforms for visual communication, stretching across national boundaries and cultures. I argue that the digital landscape created by Instagram and similar platforms begets digital social environments. Aesthetic expressions are given form in these environments, and to a certain degree are reciprocally shaped, taking on similar appearances and manifestations, forming what can be called an Instagram aesthetic. Furthermore, visual representations as subjects for further reflection and experience are not impervious to the organising structures that dictate social media platforms. The effects of this social environment on aesthetic expression are not confined to the digital social environment alone. Rather, these organising structures extend beyond the boundaries of the platforms themselves, reorganising the experience of life and the given form of experienced life through the immediate subject matter. By taking into account the importance of the social nature of these digital tools, I attempt to further nuance the understanding of human interaction and communication mediated by machines as dynamic and adaptive to the advantages and restrictions of such technologies. In short, whereas traditional photography can be thought to interrupt the relationship between the individual and the world, contemporary digital photography shared through social media is different. It entails a machine-mediation that fundamentally shapes and reorientates not only the aesthetic eye, but also experience itself. In this sense it is a disruption, which is followed by new aesthetic forms and experiences. Furthermore, as a disruption, it is made all the more socially significant through the global use of visual communication through social media.

I will draw on two main thinkers in developing this argument. One, who from a historical perspective has been a significant voice in forming the discussion concerning photography, namely Susan Sontag. And the other, who offers a more contemporary perspective on art, visual communication, and technology: Alva Noë. After presenting my starting point for this examination and addressing discussions concerning photography and visual communication, I continue with an in-depth reading of Sontag and Noë, addressing art as a tool for organising life. My argument is that machine-mediation offers advantages and imposes restrictions, and that we adapt to these affordances so successfully that we fundamentally disrupt our experience of the world. It shapes collective but also personal experience, and there are aesthetic implications of this disruption on the experience of life. Finally, I will comment on the downstream effects of this process on contemporary life. Acquiring greater insight into why this is so is especially relevant in order to gain an understanding of how visual communication and social media shape the lives of those who typically use them, such as young adults, for entertainment, to engage themselves in issues, and to share information.

A Starting Point

My starting point for this discussion is a visual study I completed in 2018, and which I exhibited as photographic research outputs in the form of the exhibition 'Norwegian Sublime: Landscape Photography in the Age of the iPhone' (Saethre-McGuirk 2018a, 2018b). The exhibition, held at The Frank Moran Memorial Hall Gallery at the Queensland University of Technology in Brisbane, Australia, was a cumulation of my interest in the aesthetics of digital social environments and the ways in which we give visual form to aesthetic experiences, which began in 2015. The exhibition consisted of nineteen photographs, where art photography and other traditions of photography were intertwined with a social media aesthetic. The aim was to investigate through these works this new aesthetic and our relationship to everyday landscape scenery, to uncover how we can both view and unfold our contemporary relationship to nature.

Figure 3.1 *Tomma 20160325 130212*. This was taken as part of a sequence of images with only a few seconds or minutes between each image, emphasising the speed and ease with which images can be produced today. This sequence was central in a piece written for *The Conversation* (12 August 2018) about the art-as-research project 'Norwegian Sublime: Landscape Photography in the Age of the iPhone' and its findings, titled 'Why We Need Some Perspective on Landscape Photography in the Instagram Age'.

Figure 3.2 *Tomma 20160325 130218*. Sequencing photographs is reminiscent of the production of a moving image, allowing the photographer to experience snippets of time and place through the act of photographing and the end photograph. Figures 3.1 and 3.2 are from the exhibition 'Norwegian Sublime: Landscape Photography in the Age of the iPhone', Frank Moran Gallery, Queensland University of Technology, Brisbane, Australia, 20 June–6 July 2018.

Unintentionally coinciding with Instagram's abandonment of the compulsory square posting format, or possibly influenced by it, I found that this change to the practical framing possibilities relieved the composition of a dominating and characteristic creative constriction. The square both offered and demanded a limited range of possible compositions. With the change, users of the photo-sharing social network service had greater freedom to address subject matter and genres which for practical purposes often necessitated other framing options. As one audience and userbase commentator noted, 'Rejoice: The Iron-Fisted Reign of the Square is Dead' (Stinson 2015). But it was also significant in that by removing Instagram's square posting format, the more shrouded ways in which the amalgamation of the app, the camera, the users, and the community created an aesthetic dynamic and overshadowed the image itself were exposed.

Communicating the effects of social media interaction on the visualisation of aesthetic experiences, the exhibition allowed me to visually question not only how art as an activity, and specifically photography as art, but also social media as a technology organises and shapes our experiences of the world. I explored those more unseen ways in which the subjects were framed through the intersection of technologies and digital social environments. In practical terms, this meant looking beyond composition techniques and the practicality of placing the subject matter in the image space, be it square or otherwise. As with all photography, the technology was significant in forming the image: the cameras themselves, which were most usually iPhone or Android phone cameras, and their distinctive technical limitations would affect the depths and layers, highlights and shadows as compositional elements available to the framing of the subject matter. In addition, objective incongruities differentiating how the camera and the human eye measure and are sensitive to light, as well as how they can focus on subject matter and judge perspective, play into the forming of the image. As an extension of the technology permitting the forming of these images, the app was inadvertently also framing the subject matter; some colours and compositions tended to work better for the typical size of the portrayed image and the platform itself. Furthermore, the digital social environment and the community of users would interact with my images, endorsing, validating, and sanctioning my framing of my subject matter and the subject matter itself through social cues and indicators of approval, in short, through *likes*. By presenting my image to that digital social environment, I was not only entering that environment; I was inadvertently learning to frame my subject matter by responding and reacting to the digital, social nods given to me by the community as well. The different layers of affordances offered by the tool, technology, app, platform, and social media landscape lay in-between art and experience, affecting the imagery and, as I suspected, changing the experience as well (see Debord [1967] 2004).

Finding it necessary to further develop this discussion after 'Norwegian Sublime', I began looking at how Instagram in particular had seemingly influenced other areas of aesthetic experience. Mainstream media recurrently claims that Instagram has changed the food we eat (Tandoh 2016; Lee 2017; Reynolds and Helou 2018), often citing how the visual presentation of the food and the plate has taken over in importance in comparison with how the food tastes. From Michelin star restaurants to food truck chefs, the visual aesthetic experiences of food that were shared by the community seemed to have been taken to a new level, overshadowing olfactory and gustatory stimulation. Similarly, fashion industry commentators had noted how these particular visual framing processes were calibrating forces, affecting the ways in which fashion was presented at shows, and what is more, how fashion was designed, claiming that there was an increase in the attention paid to the photogenic qualities of an outfit, such as shapes, volumes, and colours (Schneier 2014), rather than somatic sensations or other aspects of fashion. One such commentator brought the tension between the visual emphasis and the felt emphasis to the fore when noting that 'by definition couture – clothes that take a seamstress hundreds and even thousands of hours to make by hand, which are [. . .] made for a single individual, to her body and her specifications – derives its worth from the experience of intimacy' (Business Times 2017). These tensions are ultimately signs of opposition to different perceptions of value and significance; oppositions which seemingly became increasingly more poignant the closer one came to the highest echelons of the arts.

This widened view embracing other sources of aesthetic experience accentuated a key distinction between the three areas. As opposed to food and fashion, no longer being primarily about eating and wearing, the visual arts still seemingly enjoyed being primarily and straightforwardly concerned with the visual. There seems to be less tension between the value and significance of the visual in relation to what aesthetic experiences art concerns. However, this can be nuanced. The visual arts are inclined to differentiate between the qualities and visual affordances of different ways of presenting visual art. A painting is something different than a photograph of it, and a photograph is something else than a digital image. Scale, space, place, and atmosphere situate visual art in the world in different ways, and such qualities cannot easily be translated into a two-dimensional platform existence. This is made more complicated by some works having crossover qualities, allowing them to exist as true iterations in both the real and the digital spheres. Photographic works seem to appreciate this duality more often than other artworks, even though some photographs might be specifically created to complement the visual attributes and affordances of a digital platform.

It would seem, then, that contemporary machine-mediation need not have a significant effect on experience. But, while this unpacking of the visual is fine

Figure 3.3 *Tomma 20160325 1309*. This is the last in a series of three photographs that plays on the act of framing, the aesthetics of the technical affordances of the iPhone camera, traditions of contemporary landscape photography, and the presentation of landscapes on social media – a favoured subject matter amongst many users of social media platforms such as Instagram.

as far as it goes, it only considers the visual as an experience had or something seen and then reflected back into visual art. It ignores the impact of the layers of affordances in-between art and experience. Taking a comprehensive view of the complexities of the act of framing, however simple that initial act of framing may be, our ways of visually giving form to images seem to have been augmented along with the increasing changes to photography as a machine-mediated genre and activity.

To extend the line of visual inquiry started in 'Norwegian Sublime', and to cross-inform this thesis that machine-mediation fundamentally shapes and reorientates not only the aesthetic eye, but also experience itself, and is in this sense a disruption, it is necessary to look to theoretical inquiry concerning photography. Juxtaposing my inherently practitioner-based insight with theoretical study, my approach is also an attempt to strengthen the non-hierarchical and dialectical relationship between the practical and the ideal (see Keahey 2019).

The Framing of Experience

Susan Sontag's seminal work *On Photography* ([1977] 2008) is positioned within the contemporary field of thought which accompanied the development of photography after the last world war, although it is at the same time undeniably predigital. Because of this, part of *On Photography* can be read as outdated and irrelevant in light of the technologies and practices that permeate contemporary creative practice. An example of this is Sontag's reflection on the increased frequency of photographs taken and the effect these images and photographs have on us. 'Recently,' Sontag commented in 1977, 'photography has become almost as widely practiced an amusement as sex and dancing – which means that, like every mass art form, photography is not practiced by most people as an art' ([1977] 2008: 8). In comparison with an age where the use of iPhones and Android phones is pervasive and visual communication permeates society through social media, Sontag's reflection on the widespread use of photography seems excessively sensitive, if not highly exaggerated. While one could rightfully argue that photography by definition has always been machine-mediated, as also in Sontag's time, the extent to which this machine-mediation characterises contemporary photography in the digital age is truly unprecedented. Our era's prolific picture-taking and sharing has resulted in the creation of an incomprehensible number of images, seemingly perpetually increasing in number and forever remaining unperishable, inhibiting our ability to visually forget anything, while ironically debilitating our capacity to remember anything, too.

What is more, for Sontag photography is closely tied to the physical nature of photographs. Photographs are for her miniatures of reality that anyone can take or take possession of. Yet what one takes possession of is the photograph, not the image as such. Lamenting over the physicality of photographs, Sontag reflected on how images as photographs and as objects also age: 'plagued by the usual ills of paper objects; they disappear; they become valuable and get bought and sold; they are reproduced' ([1977] 2008: 4). Thus, even though the photograph could be produced and reproduced, it was nonetheless reliant on its physical nature. Being physically delicate, the photograph's lifespan was mostly dependent on the owner's affection for the image. Such a stance may not find much resonance with the contemporary reader. When Sontag states that '[m]ovies and television programs light up walls, flicker and go out; but with still photographs the image is also an object, lightweight, cheap to produce, easy to carry about, accumulate, store' ([1977] 2008: 3), she is clearly referring to the printed photograph. In comparison, today's image either already is or is capable of being emancipated from its owner once it is taken. Images do not need to be objects. They are not even lightweight; they are virtually weightless. As long as you have the equipment, you can freely take an almost endless amount. And to carry them, accumulate them, and store them requires little more than the device you took the image on. These differences are significant because the image is no longer tied to any material object. It can be taken, shared, and reproduced without ever having taken on a physical form. Its reach is unrestrained.

Although these contemporary developments might distance us from Sontag's thought, she nonetheless retains her relevance. Her discussions touching on the physicality of the photograph also refer to the significance of context to determine meaning. In reminding us that the meaning of photographs can change according to the context in which they are seen, and because a photographic image can be seen and understood in one context just as easily another, Sontag argues that whatever the context the photograph had at one moment is inevitably 'succeeded by contexts in which such uses are weakened and become progressively less relevant' ([1977] 2008: 106). In comparison with today's images, Sontag's photographs were only to a certain extent removed from the contexts from which they could derive meaning. This effect is nothing if not amplified for the contemporary image shared on social media. On visual social media platforms, images are pared of external contexts, allowing reality to be understood in plural, encouraging the presence of individual interpretations. Viewers of these photographs are as such true tourists of reality, as Sontag also suggests, where the world and every subject in it 'is depreciated into an article of consumption, promoted into an item for aesthetic appreciation' ([1977] 2008: 110).

The idea of context, or even the lack of context, is meaningless without subject matter, and here, too, Sontag retains her relevance. Through her discussions about the first-order experience of the world and the second-order experience of the world through the photograph, she reflects on how we both use and experience the photograph in its own right. These discussions are still pertinent today. The act of practically framing the subject matter in the image space in relation to the camera's distinctive technical limitations, tainting the forming of the image, is more than just catching that specific subject matter as an image. Sontag's reflections deepen our understanding of the most basic forms of framing the subject matter, both as subject matter in an image space and as photographically seeing and experiencing the world as an act of framing an image. Crucially, Sontag's photograph is also offered to others in the photographer's own circle to see; family, friends, and neighbours alike belong to the image's community and as such are privy to the visual grammar of the photograph. And even more, they are initiated into a shared visual ethics of photography.

Going deeper into Sontag's thoughts on this matter, we find that she goes far in affirming that we experience the world through photographing it. She does so in three ways which are significant to our argument at hand. Firstly, Sontag argues that the photograph is both a grammar and an ethics of seeing the world. In this we find that the photograph, as a composition, frames the world for the viewer to see, and in that both articulates the world and endows that frame of the world significance and states that we have the right to observe this view of the world. It is a shared visual ethics, determining the standards of what we can and cannot visually address. Secondly, she reasons that the camera as a tool trains us to see the world in a dissociative way through its use and through seeing these compositions. In part due to the technical incongruities of the camera versus the human eye but also through being a part of a community of viewers, we develop a habit of photographically looking for subject matter to be seen. This dissociative seeing creates distance to the world; indeed, Sontag also claims that we learn to see ourselves photographically, too, not just the world ([1977] 2008: 85). Thirdly and lastly, Sontag claims that taking a photograph becomes a way of experiencing and a way to experience the world. What is more, *seeing* a photograph is a way to have an experience of the world, as well. These photographic experiences are initially second-order experiences, which become direct, first-order experiences of the world through habitually looking and seeing the world through photographs. These three points are significant to Sontag's argument as a whole, but they also bring us closer to understanding how contemporary photography through its presence on social media both permeates our lives and shapes our experience of the world. These three points require further illumination.

In relation to the first point, Sontag claims that in making the decision to photograph a subject, and as such pointing at that subject, the photographer is implying that that subject matter is important ([1977] 2008: 28). The photographer deems it something worth seeing and confers on others the right to observe that subject matter, too. We do not look directly at the subject matter ourselves, but rather look an image of the subject matter that the photographer has taken. Because of this, Sontag claims that photographs 'are a grammar and, even more importantly, an ethics of seeing' ([1977] 2008: 3). As a grammar or even an ethics of seeing, both the photographer and the observer of the photograph are given a licence to see that subject matter in that particular way. This is different from merely looking at the subject matter. To look at a subject is to turn your head towards that specific thing, but to see it is to follow the photographer's pointing and to understand a subject in relation to a context and meaning. Subject matter which otherwise would have been passed by and subject matter of the glories of nature alike are pointed at, conferred value, and seen. That thing, the photograph seems to say, is made beautiful in this way. The photographed world thus becomes the new standard of how to see the world in the most pleasing, beautiful way (Sontag [1977] 2008: 85).

Secondly, by habitually observing reality through the lens of what would look best practically framed in the image space and in relation to the camera's limitations, the photographer becomes estranged from the world. The photographer is looking for things to be seen, and in this the photographer's relationship to the world becomes depersonalised:

> Like a pair of binoculars with no right or wrong end, the camera makes exotic things near, intimate; and familiar things small, abstract, strange, much farther away. It offers, in one easy, habit-forming activity, both participation and alienation in our own lives and those of others – allowing us to participate, while confirming alienation. (Sontag [1977] 2008: 167)

The camera and our use of it is at fault here, Sontag seems to indicate. It trains us to see the world at a distance. This photographic habitual seeing is what Sontag calls dissociative seeing ([1977] 2008: 97). It is 'both intense and cool, solicitous and detached; charmed by the insignificant detail, addicted to incongruity', she claims ([1977] 2008: 99), unremittingly taking on the student's eye when visually taking in the world. However, Sontag's dissociative seeing is nonetheless short-lived and transitory. On the face of it, it is a habit that can eventually dissipate. Dissociative seeing must therefore be constantly renewed by shock of either subject matter or technique to stay fresh (Sontag [1977] 2008: 89) and, it would seem, to keep the habit alive in us so that we are able to see where others merely look at ordinary things. As such, the act of photographing and habitually observing the mundane subject matter of the world through photographic seeing is not enough. Dissociative seeing needs to interrupt and be different from ordinary seeing; indeed, Sontag claims it must interrupt ordinary seeing, violate it even ([1977] 2008: 89, 90–1).

Thirdly and lastly, Sontag reasons that the photograph is not a mere report nor a true representation of the subject matter; its role is beyond such a simple task of depiction. This leads us to the uncomfortable relationship between photographs and experience. To fully understand this point, we can start with the tourist. Tourists then, like now, photographed the world in a near obligatory fashion. The photograph functions as 'indisputable evidence', Sontag remarks, 'that the trip was made, that the program was carried out, that fun was had' for those near and dear who did not participate in the consumption of the experiences as well ([1977] 2008: 9–10). Those travelling and experiencing different events are thus so compelled to fulfil their duty of documenting the experience, that the urge to photograph everything is indiscriminatory, and so photography, as limitless notes on reality, Sontag states, 'transforms reality into a tautology' ([1977] 2008: 111). In their attempt to entrap the world, reality itself is continuously reiterated through the photograph and, in doing so, that which has been photographed becomes a new reality. So effective is the photograph at reiterating reality through photographic habitual seeing that in comparison with it, reality is often experienced as a let-down (Sontag [1977] 2008: 146). What is more, the two are not even retroactively linked, in that the photograph does not even intend to nor is meant to lead the viewer back to some original experience (Sontag [1977] 2008: 116).

For those who do not travel with or as a tourist, these photographs play an important role in making a substitute world (Sontag [1977] 2008: 162). In that most people do not travel the world or experience the same events, everyone who is privy to that photograph is also invited to participate in the photographed experience. It must be noted, though, that this participation is merely the appearance of participation, in that the act of placing the camera between the photographer and the world when taking a photograph is in effect an act of non-intervention (Sontag [1977] 2008: 11). Moreover, that which the viewer is privy to is indeed not the photographed experience per se, but an image as a first-order meeting with that which was pointed to and given photographic form. The experience is that of taking a picture, not having the experience of the thing taken a picture of. Therefore, neither the viewer not the photographer interacts with the world through the photograph.

The effect of this is an ever deepening chasm between reality and our understanding of it, as long at the habitual photographic seeing of the world continues to be in play. Being in the world through photography, we become less capable of distinguishing between an image and what it is an image of when reflecting on our experience of the world (Sontag [1977] 2008: 179). And while we have become dependent on images for interpreting the world, the glories of nature have at the same time been transformed into corny images too much like photographs to merit any deeper thought (Sontag [1977] 2008: 85). Capturing experiences of the world and interpreting the world, however, are at first of different orders; but through photography, the first-order experience becomes captured and interpreted in the photograph and thus the photograph in itself becomes the new first-order experience. The reality of the old first-order of experience is ultimately only known, then, by its traces. The result of this is that that if '[t]o collect photographs is to collect the world' as Sontag asserts ([1977] 2008: 3), then to take a photograph is to create it.

Photography, both as taking and seeing an image, becomes a form of dissociated knowing the world without knowing the world through first-order sensuous experience. It is, as Sontag states, 'a way of outwitting the world, instead of making a frontal attack on it' ([1977] 2008: 116). Yet what we outwit is not just the physical world, it is also our experience of time as a part of the physical world. As a new first-order experience, and relieved of the usual ills of paper objects, the image is also relieved of time itself. Where old photographs gave body to our mental images and constructed memories of the past, the photographs of now transfigure the world into a series of second-order realities ready to be superseded by the first-order experience of the photograph. This gives us 'an instantly retroactive view of experience [. . .] [where] [p]hotographs give mock forms of possession [of time]: of the past, the present, even the future'

(Sontag [1977] 2008: 166). In this way, we can conclude together with Sontag that any photograph by definition is indeed a memento mori (Sontag [1977] 2008: 15), but in addition we can reflect that to create the world in the photograph is to also end our experience of it.

LOOPING BACK, REORGANISING LIFE

Once brought into being through dissociative seeing, and now a first-order experience of the world, one can reflect on what happens once images are created and shared in unfathomable numbers, at unearthly velocities, and at rapid frequencies. Now, even one's most modest image can potentially be had as anyone's first-order experience of the world. The photograph and image have become objects of consumption, where whole communities of users, not only one's near and dear, get to participate in the consumption of the image and what it has to offer. Sontag falls short at offering an understanding of the new level of framing that takes place in this digital, social environment. Today, we find that there is more to the place of the image and the way in which we collectively interact with the world through images and art.

Whereas I have discussed experience as it is given form in photographs and as images, which as Sontag claims is not practised as art, I propose to look to art to get closer to what machine-mediation does in relation to our visual experience of the world. This will help further nuance machine-mediation and our use of it as dynamic and adaptive. Perhaps we do adapt to the affordances of machines, and we do it so effectively that we surrender our experience of the world with it. Therefore, to open up the idea of the reflexivity of framing and experience, I look to Alva Noë and his *Strange Tools: Art and Human Nature* (2015). Here, Noë goes far in offering a definition of art through his discussions about what art is and what it does. This can help differentiate between that which is and that which is not art; a differentiation which is interesting when trying to make a distinction between that which is an experience given form as a creative output and offered to others to see and that which is a mere visual communiqué released on social media platforms. It can also reveal why the image as art on platforms such as Instagram can potentially play such a significant role in the lives of those who habitually use those platforms.

Starting with Noë's primary position, we find that art brings to light our own organisation of our lives and simultaneously loops back and reorganises us (Noë 2015: 3216). Central to this idea is that we, as human beings, are in the business of first-order organising ourselves. First-order activities, Noë holds, organise our being and action in the world and are a phenomenon of human life. Such activities are, for example, 'walking, talking, singing, thinking, making and deploying pictures for this task or that' (Noë 2015: 516). However, as human beings, we can be more deeply engaged in life than merely through

actions forever moving us forward in time. Indeed, we are easily at once organised by a first-order activity at hand while we at the same time carry on with
our action in the world by using different methods and cues to guide our attention (Noë 2015: 146–7). 'It is our nature to acquire [such] second natures', Noë
states (2015: 147), showing how we do not differentiate between natural and
learned activities as patterns of organisation.

Taking its cue from this point, art (and, as it were, philosophy) as an organisational and reorganisational practice displays to us ourselves as walkers, talk-
ers, singers, thinkers, makers, picture deployers, and more. To clarify what this
means, Noë shows what choreography as a form of art offers us. Choreography,
Noë states, 'shows us dancing; choreography exhibits the place dancing has,
or can have, in our lives. Choreography puts the fact that we are organized by
dancing on display' (2015: 252). Furthermore, Noë broadens this understanding to state that '[A]ll the arts [. . .] seek to bring out and exhibit, to disclose
and to illuminate, aspects of the way we find ourselves organised' (2015: 286).
The key to this, though, is that where art brings to light our own organisation
of our lives, it simultaneously loops back and reorganises us. By illuminating
how we organise ourselves and giving form to the act and practice of organisation, we are imagining into being new ways of organising ourselves and thus
enabling ourselves to do so. Drawing on the work of philosopher of science
Ian Hacking (1999) and his idea of looping, Noë's use of the term 'looping'
implies that art essentially gives us resources and is a practice for illuminating
the ways we find ourselves organised, as well as new resources to *rethink* how
we organise or are disposed to organise ourselves (2015: 3788). Importantly,
we cannot otherwise freely choose to step back and see things differently nor to
release ourselves from the structures and activities that organise us (Noë 2015:
4014, 4135), and therefore we cannot by choice loop back and reorganise our
ways of organising ourselves, either. For this reason, art is not merely an activity. Rather it is a genuine and important practice for gaining a meta-perspective
on our being in the world, for stepping back, finding ourselves, making sense
of the ways we are organised, and, following this, to reflect on this organisation
and to rethink the ways in which we organise ourselves. Art arrests us in our
forever, moving forward through actions in time, creates a thinking space along
with the resources to think with, and then releases us.

Thinking of art as such a reorganising practice which exposes 'the concealed ways we are organised by the things we do' (Noë 2015: 322) presents a
framework for a definition of what art is, based on what art does or potentially
can do for us as human beings. As such a framework, there are two implications to this defining idea of art which are relevant to the argument at hand.
Firstly, following Noë, it means that art is a mode of investigation, a method of
research on our human nature that we are dependent on (see Noë 2015: 322,
2104, 3395). It is human nature to organise and reorganise ourselves and for

this, we think through using tools such as art and writing. By gaining a meta-reflection on the organisation of life, we are fulfilling our human potential to be in the world. Secondly, just because it is human nature, it does not mean that this practice is automatic in full. To see our organisation of the world, to allow oneself to loop back, and have the resources to reorganise the world, demands action. The two points are to a certain degree interconnected, but the position and the implications of the latter are significant in their own right. Nonetheless, these two points require further consideration.

In relation to the first point, art is essentially how we 'grapple with what we already know (or think we know). It is the domain in which we try to get clear about the ways we think and respond and assign value' (Noë 2015: 3347). Because of this, art is not experience preserved in the form of art. Art is not, simply put, canned experience and so, as Noë states, 'not everything that consoles, entertains, or moves us is art' (2015: 1306). In that art does not exist as a response trigger or stimulus, it is not defined by its ability to merely stimulate aesthetic or other experiences in the brain. The virtues of all art, it follows, are the subjective and non-physical features that do not correspond to any particular stimulus depicted in the work. A work of art is as such not an experience or the equivalent to an experience, but rather something that affords the opportunity to reflect and reorganise the possibility of that experience. Therefore, while art has value to us both as individuals and as human beings, it does not produce knowledge about the world or our being in the world in the same way that science does. In fact, as Noë claims, '[a]rt imparts no knowledge' (2015: 3162). As such, art teaches nothing, but rather invites you to inspect it and interrogate it; to see what it is offering for you to look at (Noë 2015: 2752). Art is in this sense a tool, a strange tool, something which we as humans think through, to solve problems, and to enable us to frame new problems. Art, like writing, is for thinking (Noë 2015: 770) and to make sense of ourselves as active human beings in the world (see Noë 2015: 723).

Secondly, and in contrast to this understanding of art, images as mere illustrations simply show us this or that depiction (Noë 2015: 2764). They cannot visually remove our tools for the organisation of our action in the world from their context nor make them strange, and so they cannot bring out the organisational embedding that we have otherwise taken for granted (Noë 2015: 505). Illustrations as such are one of the many other types of images that are not art, including visual communiqués, which are visual statements of something seen or something experienced and which can be released onto platforms such as Instagram. Where art brings something from being in the world into view, illustrations simply show something to look at. And where art asks for the unseen in the world to be looked at by pointing at it and requesting us to see the unseen, illustrations make no such demands on us. When something that is unseen in the world is seen in this way, 'that function, that rhetoric, that invisibly familiar practice, is disrupted' (Noë 2015: 2740), and art can find form.

With this in mind, visual communiqués on the one hand and art on the other hand are two different types of business, with two different missions to fulfil. But while this is an easy distinction to make in theory, differentiating between the two in practice is at times not as simple as, say, discriminating between an image of a man and an image of a person (see Noë 2015: 2717). Taking Noë's example, an image of a man such as Martin Luther can portray the role of 'father, priest, theologian, [or] founder of a new religion' (2015: 2717). But any other image of Martin Luther can also visually describe the inner man, Martin Luther, the person. As an extension of this idea, an image from experience or even the depiction of a scene can portray roles, too. For example, an image can depict a sunrise, a mountain range, or a lake. Similarly, those images as art can individually also display something other than the scene itself; a beginning, an obstacle, or a moment in time, without regressing to the level of symbols or signs. These can be different levels of understanding an image, too, in addition to a comment on the different types of images.

Noë does not go into further detail about how we can differentiate between the two beyond his framework. And to a certain degree, that is not important, either. Nonetheless, it can be noted that art for Noë seems to have physical qualities that are significant. This leads him to necessarily differentiate between how one would react to pictures of artworks as opposed to the artworks themselves (see Noë 2015: 2175). Any response to art would also have to factor in the qualities that visually situate visual art, such as scale and installation. But even seen without these qualities, art's defining character as practice does not change. For this to take place, we must look past the depiction and the role of the image, past the most basic understanding of the subject matter based on a pseudo-formal analysis and its factual and expressional artistic motif (see Panofsky [1939] 1972: 14). We must instead see it bringing to light our own organisation of life and it must be capable of showing that to us, too.

The visual differences between the art and depiction can be subtle. They can easily be mixed up in the eyes of the beholder. Noë does not offer an easy answer to this, but rather squarely places the responsibility to see the inner things of the image in the hands of the beholder. When he advocates that one must activate art by activating yourself, Noë is confirming that art only affords you something, it does not do it for you (2015: 3383). At the same time, Noë indicates that the image will do you no favours, claiming that picture makers make pictures that both show you something and also 'invite you to wonder what you could possibly see in or with or thanks to a picture' (2015: 792).

What Noë seems to be doing, then, is not differentiating between that which is art and that which is not, but rather saying that some art gives form and offers the form of these inner things more easily than others. Indeed, one could conclude, Noë seems to be saying, that even bad art is still art, and it is up to the viewer's ability or interest to activate it, that is, to understand the image at that level. So, while seeing the organisation of life, looping back, and having the resources to reorganise the world is a practice that might be genuine and important, it is not completely automatic; it can be made stronger or weaker, easier or harder, facilitated or encumbered, accelerated or impeded. What is more, it can be changed or altered.

MACHINE-MEDIATION AND THE LOOPING OF EXPERIENCE

As an effect of this practice, Noë can claim that art 'corrupts us [. . .] and it does so in a way that conceals this very fact from us' (2015: 3162). Yet this is by no means a negative comment. There is an underlying assumption that looping back is good; the possibility in and of art fulfils us as human beings in the world. This brings us to a final point of reflection.

Accepting that images often enjoy the ability to exist as equal iterations in both the digital and real and that bad art is still art, art practice as an image on visual social media platforms such as Instagram can exist amongst a ceaseless stream of visual communiqués and pulses over an endless digital landscape. And, in the same way that art conceals its corruptive nature from us, social media platforms conceal that they allow reorganisation practices to be tampered with and counterfeited, too: we see and give form to art and images, but that sight and tools for giving form may reciprocally shape the practice as a whole.

The digital landscape is a social landscape and a community where we become socialised into seeing all images alike, pared down of any particular cultural, political, or expressive connotation, and where we become schooled to primarily view the image as something to quickly consume. Framing, as a compositional tool and as what follows the use of technological tools, is expanded by the existence of this social landscape. From sharing an image privately from within the confines of a photo album or on a wall, to the public space of an exhibition, the technology that allows for universal sharing of the image changes how an image can be activated or consumed to the extent that it is in fact a catalyst. The community itself becomes a framing structure, socialising us into an understanding of how to see the world and experience it through a particular taste for photographic seeing. Sontag states that

> by the nature of photography, [. . .] preferences [. . .] are, for the most part, merely reactive. Taste in photography tends to be, is perhaps necessarily, global, eclectic, permissive, which means that in the end it must deny the difference between good taste and bad taste. (Sontag [1977] 2008: 143)

When the image says that the thing is made beautiful in this way, the community can confirm this standard of how to see the world, and in doing so the community influences the shaping and reorientation of the aesthetic eye and our experience of the world itself. In this view, it is of no consequence that image as art is stripped bare of the qualities that visually situate the work. As Noë seems to indicate, while these images may or may not be easily defined as art, through them we still create the image of the world in which we reside (see Noë 2015: 3299). We can take this further: through these images, the community creates the image of the world in which we reside.

For Sontag, the make-believe iteration of the world in images becomes a new first-order experience, so that by being in the world through photography, we become less capable of distinguishing between an image and what it is an image of, when reflecting on our experience of the world ([1977] 2008: 179). So, whereas it seems that Sontag argues that the dialectic of seeing has been interrupted by the discontinuous habit of dissociative seeing, one can now argue that the dialectic of seeing has instead become disrupted in full.

The camera, Sontag held, trained us in dissociative seeing. But there is more to it now: while the camera still trains us in dissociative seeing, the digital community rewards us for it. A seemingly endless stream of similar images is like receiving accolades. The habit thus becomes an addiction. Constantly seeing the world through photographic seeing and uninterruptedly consuming first-order experiences through the image, there is nearly no time or opportunity to see the world in anything but a dissociative way. Whereas we once were sporadically habitually taken over by dissociative seeing, looking for a make-believe iteration of the world to see, one can argue that it has become our primary way of meeting the world. Everything seen is experienced in terms of potentially being framed as an image. These images, then, bring to light not the organisation of our lives, but an opaque interpretation of the organisation of our lives; it is a dissociative understanding of the organisation of ourselves.

The looping practice has been disrupted not at the point where looping and reorganisation occurs, but at the point where we interpret the organisation of ourselves to begin with. Like a stream of mock-ups of the organisation of life, or like a dress rehearsal, these alternative, false looping practices trick us into neglecting the fact that, in the end, we have not fulfilled the potential of art or the image, nor, in light of Noë, of our human nature. It feels real, and so it is. Here, I am brought back to 'Norwegian Sublime'. Exploring those more unseen ways in which the subjects were framed through the intersection of technologies and digital social environments and partaking in those communities did not just alter my style of photography, my eye, so to speak; it altered my experience of being in the world. I was no longer photographing nature. Rather I was experiencing the framing nature for presenting it as an idea of an experience.

ALL THINGS CONSIDERED

Habitual being in the real world, looking, and experiencing the world, is necessary for us not to be reduced to seeing the world through the opacity of the photograph as image. It is necessary for us to be picture makers, to truly study the organisation of life, and to allow these works to afford us the tools to reorganise ourselves. Picture making as an act invites dissociative seeing, and it is feasible that all picture making, with any practical tool, invites some level of dissociative seeing. Perhaps it is that the camera amplifies this by being a physical filter that tampers with seeing and framing of the world in placing the image in the image space, in the discrepancies between the lens and the eye, and in relation to images on the app, the visual preferences that the app technically encourages.

Nonetheless, the digital, social landscape and our addiction to it does more than merely amplify dissociative seeing. It makes dissociative seeing a new normal. First-order experiences then, can only be had through such a filter. And hence picture making, the study of our organisation of ourselves, is through this filter, too. The implications of this addiction on our aesthetic eye, visual grammar, and ethics of seeing is that we *must* put the camera between us and the world, because that is how we have trained ourselves to experience the world. We take pictures of events and the world because that is now how we are in the world. In its raw form, certain events and reality are left unfamiliar and abnormal. We cannot freely step back from this organisation of ourselves, be it counterfeit or otherwise. Ironically, for that we must call on engagement with the world, through picture making in the real. Indeed, we must leave the image behind.

REFERENCES

Business Times. 2017. 'Fashion in the Instagram Age.' *The Business Times*, 10 July. <https://www.businesstimes.com.sg/life-culture/fashion-in-the-instagram-age (last accessed 29 March 2021).

Debord, Guy. [1967] 2004. *Society of the Spectacle*, translated by Ken Knabb. London: Rebel Press.

Hacking, Ian. 1999. *The Social Construction of What?* Cambridge, MA: Harvard University Press.

Keahey, Jennifer. 2019. 'Knowledge in Action: Negotiating Power in Development.' *Action Research* (March). <https://doi.org/10.1177/1476750319837328> (last accessed 18 March 2021).

Lee, Sarah. 2017. 'Picture Perfect? How Instagram Changed the Food We Eat.' *BBC News*, 29 December. <https://www.bbc.com/news/uk-england-london-42012732> (last accessed 10 October 2019).

Noë, Alva. 2015. *Strange Tools: Art and Human Nature*. Kindle edition. New York: Hill and Wang.

Panofsky, Erwin. [1939] 1972. *Studies in Iconology: Humanistic Themes in the Art of the Renaissance*. Oxford: Westview Press.

Reynolds, George, and Anissa Helou. 2018. 'How Instagram Changed Food.' Radio programme. BBC Radio 4, 5 November. <https://www.bbc.co.uk/programmes/m00010pv> (last accessed 10 October 2019).

Saethre-McGuirk, Ellen. 2018a. 'Norwegian Sublime: Landscape Photography in the Age of the iPhone.' Exhibition. <https://eprints.qut.edu.au/119875/> (last accessed 16 March 2021).

Saethre-McGuirk, Ellen. 2018b. 'Why We Need Some Perspective on Landscape Photography in the Instagram Age.' *The Conversation*, 12 August. <https://theconversation.com/why-we-need-some-perspective-on-landscape-photography-in-the-instagram-age-100093> (last accessed 10 October 2019).

Schneier, Matthew. 2014. 'Fashion in the Age of Instagram.' *The New York Times*, 9 April. <https://www.nytimes.com/2014/04/10/fashion/fashion-in-the-age-of-instagram.html> (last accessed 29 March 2021).

Sontag, Susan. [1977] 2008. *On Photography*. London: Penguin Books.

Stinson, Liz. 2015. 'Instagram Ends the Tyranny of the Square.' *Wired*, 27 August. <https://www.wired.com/2015/08/instagram-says-goodbye-square-photos/> (last accessed 7 October 2019).

Tandoh, Ruby. 2016. 'Click Plate: How Instagram is Changing the Way We Eat.' *The Guardian*, 2 November. <https://www.theguardian.com/lifeandstyle/2016/nov/02/click-plate-how-instagram-changing-way-we-eat-food> (last accessed 10 October 2019).

PART TWO

ETHICS

4. THE ETHICS OF FILMMAKING: HOW THE GENETIC HISTORY OF WORKS AFFECTS THEIR VALUE

Mette Hjort

Organised by Ted Nannicelli and Marguerite La Caze at the University of Queensland in 2018, the (New) Visuality: Ethics and Aesthetics symposium invited reflection on the dynamic, even causal, relations between ethical and aesthetic value: 'Under what conditions does ethical value in a media "text" yield aesthetic value – and how does the platform in which the "text" appears affect this?' 'Text', in this chapter, refers to audiovisual works associated with the milieux of motion picture production, for example, to short films or full-length feature films. Whereas 'platform' is often used to refer to a given (technological) means of distribution, I interpret the term's referent more broadly. 'Platform', I contend, also refers to contexts of production, to the intentionally devised and systematically sustained structures that underpin the very making of a given audiovisual work.

Responding to the above question, the aim is to make a case for seeing the ethical features of a given process of production as having clear implications for the artistic value of the relevant audiovisual work. Berys Gaut's ethicist position offers a good starting point for this approach, but falls short nonetheless (Nannicelli 2017: 405), due to the philosopher's emphasis on text-immanent properties and neglect of the conditions underpinning the actual interaction between agents – for example, between actors, producers, and the director – during the making of the work. I begin with a reconstruction and critique of Gaut's ethicist position, so as to argue for an expanded ethicism that gives weight to concepts of harm and vulnerability as they relate to the way in which works are made. Focusing on the 'genetic' (Nannicelli 2014: 179)[1] histories of specific audiovisual works, I subsequently develop a spectrum of artistically relevant ethical merits and demerits and provide an indication of how the position of a given work on this spectrum should be determined. Erik Poppe's *Utøya: July 22* (2018) and iconic Danish youth films from the 1970s by the directors Lasse Nielsen and Ernst Johansen define the two ends of the relevant spectrum. Having considered the implications of especially the ethically deficient production processes for the works' artistic value, I offer thoughts about how those committed to an expanded ethicist position can effect change resulting in ethically robust production practices. Such change, I argue, is of considerable importance, inasmuch as it creates the conditions for ethically valuable filmmaking practices, and through this, for works of greater artistic value.

Developing his ethicist argument with reference to the general idea of 'ethical values being "associated" with aesthetic values' (Gaut 2007: 58), Gaut distinguishes between the claims of the autonomist, the contextualist, and the ethicist. The focus throughout is on ethical and aesthetic values as features of works, with the ethical (or unethical) characteristics of the intentions and actions of the agents producing the works receiving no explicit discussion. Following Gaut, the autonomist holds that 'artworks are never aesthetically improved or worsened by the presence of ethical qualities in the works',[2] whereas the contextualist contends that artworks may be 'aesthetically improved by the presence of ethical merits' but may also be 'improved by the presence of ethical flaws'. Embracing ethicism, as the best alternative to autonomism and contextualism, Gaut contends that the ethicist rightly claims that 'artworks are always made aesthetically better by the presence of ethical qualities in the work' and, by extension, made aesthetically worse by the presence of ethical flaws (2007: 58).

But what, we might ask, is the precise nature of the ethical qualities and flaws that Gaut has in mind? Referring to ethical flaws, Gaut points out that the ones that are decisive for the aesthetic value of works are 'intrinsic' to those same works. Gaut points out that he is not concerned with the 'ethically bad effects that works may have on actual audiences' (2007: 229), partly because he sees them as contingent or extrinsic. The ways in which works may inspire and prompt immoral behaviour in the immediate future, or may even become an actual source of enduring action schemes in the longer run, are thus regarded as falling outside the necessary scope of analysis. For Gaut, the *implicit attitudes* of works, which are presumably the attitudes of an implicit authorial persona, provide the key to understanding what counts as an intrinsic ethical flaw. 'Intrinsic ethical flaws are', as he puts it 'ethical flaws in the *attitudes* that works manifest toward their subjects' (2007: 229; emphasis added).

Elucidating his understanding of implicit attitudes as these are manifested in works, Gaut evokes a contrast between two paintings from 1654, the one by Willem Drost, the other by Rembrandt van Rijn. Both are depictions of the same subject matter, namely Bathsheba, wife of Uriah the Hittite, as she holds a recently received letter from King David, one that is in effect a royal summons to concupiscence and infidelity, leaving no room for choice. According to Gaut, Drost's work manifests an implicit attitude that amounts to an ethical flaw, whereas Rembrandt's painting is deemed to express an appropriate ethical stance that brings ethical value, and through this, aesthetic value to the work:

> it is the quality of moral attention, its awareness of the tragedy of Bathsheba's situation, its invitation to feel sympathy for her and its acute sensitivity to the existence of a fully-rounded person with an interior life that go a large way to explaining why Rembrandt's is such a great picture. Conversely, it is the moral nescience, the sense that Bathsheba is narrowly the construct of male concupiscence, the object of a sexual interest that is oblivious to any sense of the interior life of its object and indifferent to the evil that is about to be enacted, that explains in large part why Drost's painting falls short of the artistic greatness that Rembrandt's picture so effortlessly commands. (Gaut 2007: 24)

Like all works, the paintings by Rembrandt and Drost manifest attitudes and these, in turn, encourage responses on the part of the viewer. Whereas the attitude expressed in Rembrandt's painting is one of kindness and sympathy for a victim of lust, the attitude manifested in Drost's representation is entirely complicit with the erotic imagination of the predatory abuser of power.

For Gaut, the concept of a 'merited response' (2007: 233) provides a means of explaining, not only why some works have greater aesthetic value than others, but also why ethical deficiencies/merits detract from/contribute to aesthetic value, as the case may be. Referring once again to the contrasted paintings, we may note that both depict a woman who, faced with a royal abuse of power in response to her beauty, has little choice or agency, a woman, in short, who is a victim. The response that is appropriate to the situation – the merited response – is one that aligns the viewer with the victim through a sympathetic engagement with her plight and vulnerability. Rembrandt's painting is seen as superior to that of Drost, in the sense of having greater aesthetic value, because its manifestation of a pervasive attitude of sympathy encourages the viewer to respond in ways that are merited by the depicted woman's plight. Drost's painting, however, fails to invite the viewer to see Bathsheba as the victim that she is, fuelling instead a lustful imagination. It encourages, in short, a response that cannot be said to be merited by the woman's situation. Whereas some merited responses encompass ethical norms and considerations, others do not. However,

> if the prescribed responses are unmerited, because unethical, that is a failure in the work. What responses the work prescribes is of aesthetic relevance. So, if the prescribed responses are unmerited because unethical, that is an *aesthetic* failure of the work – that is to say, is an aesthetic defect in it. (Gaut 2007: 233)

PRODUCTION ETHICS: ON THE ACTUAL ATTITUDES BEHIND THE IMPLICIT ATTITUDES OF WORKS

Encompassing research by Ted Nannicelli (forthcoming; 2020), Jane Stadler (2008), Robert Sinnerbrink (2016), Carl Plantinga (2018), Jinhee Choi and Mattias Frey (2013), and Hjort (2011, 2012a, 2012b, 2013b, 2018a, 2018b), among others, the field of film production ethics is a rapidly expanding one, bringing significant new dimensions to the already flourishing general field of production studies (Nannicelli forthcoming). As a field, film production ethics takes seriously the task of identifying, clarifying, and strengthening the force of ethical norms as they relate to film production. What is at stake here is how living beings – women, children, animals, and specific professional groups (actresses, stunt persons) – but also, for example, the natural environment, are treated during the making of motion pictures.[3] While the empirical data with which production ethicists work typically stems from concrete cases of abuse, the field's collective aims extend well beyond any mere documentation of unethical behaviour. Attention given to norm-breaking has implications for regulatory frameworks – for example, as these relate to the protections afforded to children while on set – for it is increasingly clear that these have failed to capture the full scope of the norms that must be regarded as indubitably relevant and sound. Production ethics thus prepares the ground for, or actually involves, activist undertakings. The aim, that is, may be to articulate and defend norms for the purposes of effective mobilisation and, ultimately, the introduction of regulatory changes. In some cases, the goal may be the less stringent one of simply developing fairer practices based on common understandings.

Especially relevant for present purposes is the place of conceptual clarification and analysis within the scope of film production ethics. Robust arguments regarding how we should value motion pictures, about the circumstances in which it is legitimate to attribute ethical and artistic value to cinematic works, can only be essential. Such arguments offer a context for assessing behaviour, on the part of filmmakers and film viewers alike, and, if mobilised beyond the narrow confines of academic debate, a means of effecting change.

Prominent examples of the sorts of cases that are of interest to production ethicists are those driving the global movements known as #MeToo and Time's Up. A combination of factors – for example, celebrity activism (Watson 2014), the viral dissemination of testimonies of abuse (Hayek 2017), and the use of big data analytics to track the inequities of women's screen and speaking time (Geena Davis Institute on Gender in Media n.d.) – has helped to sustain #MeToo (originating with sexual harassment survivor Tarana Burke in 2006) and Time's Up (founded by Hollywood celebrities in 2018, in response to revelations about the extent and severity of Miramax producer Harvey Weinstein's abuse). Focusing on the three core goals of safety, equity, and power for women (Time's Up n.d.) and supported by effective fundraising, the Time's Up initiative is likely to have a significant longer-term impact on how women are treated in the context of motion picture production.

There is reason to hope that the #MeToo movement will have the effect of changing how we see the legitimate bases for attributing value to audiovisual works. With implications for the viewability of motion pictures, for the pleasure that viewers are warranted in deriving from films originating in certain production contexts, such changes will inevitably affect the returns of investors and producers. As is well known, economic considerations remain an especially significant factor when determining which projects are to be realised. As a result, a widespread convergence on arguments foregrounding the link between the ethics of a given film's production processes, on the one hand, and an assessment of this same film as either having or lacking certain kinds of value, on the other hand, can be expected to change the dynamics and practices of the industry.

Prompted by revelations of sexual abuse, #MeToo and Time's Up have created a context of relevance for reconsidering, further examining, and carefully probing the ramifications of a wide variety of norm-breaking abuses relating to gender in the history of motion picture production. Such abuses include the systematic neglect and institutionalised effacement from memory of the earliest known female film director Alice Guy-Blaché,[4] but also specific types of violence that were perpetrated against women for the fully intended purpose of producing scenes with specific audiovisual features. It is this latter violation of norms, one upstream of identifiable audiovisual properties manifested during a film's viewing, that concerns us here. The basis for our attributions of ethical and artistic value to a given film, audiovisual properties have both an immediately manifest and an initially opaque dimension. While the former dimension is a matter of perception and cognition during the act of viewing, the latter is a matter of contextual information pertaining, among other things, to the genetic history of the audiovisual properties in question. The claim here is that any unethical behaviour leading directly to a film's having specific audiovisual properties must be taken into consideration when determining how the work is to be valued. If this is the case, then Gaut's ethicist position requires modification, inasmuch as it involves the attribution of ethical and artistic value to a work based purely on its implicit attitudes – all of them assumed to be immediately manifest through perceptual and cognitive processes during the act of viewing. Even if one were to accept that the implied author approach is valid, the problem remains, as Nannicelli (2020) points out: that is, manifest attitudes, except in cases of narrative simplicity, are typically ambiguous.

The call for a modification of Gaut's in many ways appealing position imme-diately raises a host of questions. For example, can ethical and artistic value only be attributed to a film following an extensive research process focusing on the work's genetic history? A requirement to the effect that all film viewers are responsible for informing themselves about a film's production context before engaging in any acts of evaluation is a very tall order indeed, one that is likely to be ignored in practice. In response to cogent observations along these lines we might choose to ask a different question, this one suggesting an answer that expands the scope of the ethicist position, but in ways that are realistic about the behaviours that can be expected of viewers: if viewers become aware of a causal link between ethical violations in a film's genetic history and its mani-fested audiovisual properties, should this awareness affect how they evaluate the work? For example, if viewers initially attributed a high degree of artistic value to a canonised film classic but then discovered that crucial scenes were abusively produced, should the newly acquired knowledge, as a matter of obli-gation and principle, lead to a reassessment of the initial evaluation? My claim is that, yes, indeed, it should. Given the internal connections among a given film's genetic history, its audiovisual properties, and well-founded attributions of ethical and artistic value to this work, it is legitimate to expect viewers to take an interest in contextual matters. Competent viewers who take film watch-ing seriously will, as a matter of course, seek additional information about the circumstances of a film's production, including decision-making leading to distinctive audiovisual features.

The extent to which artistic value based on appreciation of a film's audiovisual properties should be seen as compromised by ethical flaws in the genetic history of the work depends on a number of factors: (1) the extent to which vulnerable agents operating within a command structure where power is unequally distrib-uted are exposed to a variety of risks, for example physical, reputational, or psy-chological risks (Hjort 2012a); (2) the severity of the harm that was inflicted on a victim in order to achieve the properties in question; (3) the vulnerability of the victim, for example by virtue of age, lack of experience, gender, and the absence of institutionalised and properly enforced protections; (4) whether the harm was inflicted for artistic reasons; and (5) how central the harmful strategy was to the making of the entire work. Such distinctions support the idea that films fall on an artistically relevant ethical spectrum, the two limit positions being occupied by strikingly different categories of works. At the one end we find films that merit attributions of artistic value by virtue of their manifested properties, but also attributions of ethical value based on their genetic histories. Additionally, the intentions, decisions, and actions supporting attributions of ethical value are internally linked to the manifested audiovisual qualities in a clear causal history. At the other end, we have a category of works that are fundamentally and pervasively shaped by the intention egregiously to exploit vulnerable victims, the films being a mere means to a perverse and significantly harmful end. In what follows, the aim is to chart the extremes on the spectrum, but also some of the other possible positions, the point being to clarify when, to what degree, and why artistic value is compromised by ethical flaws.

An Artistically Relevant Spectrum of Ethical Merits and Demerits

There are countless examples of production-related testimonies offering support for an expanded ethicist position. The experiences of Salma Hayek, Tippi Hedren, Shelley Duvall, and Maria Schneider during the making, respectively, of *Frida* (2002, dir. Julie Taymor), *The Birds* (1963, dir. Alfred Hitchcock), *Last Tango in Paris* (1972, dir. Bernardo Bertolucci), and *The Shining* (1980, dir. Stanley Kubrick) suggest that ethical flaws are indeed prevalent in the genetic histories of many films, including some of the most celebrated ones. Following a discussion of these cases, I consider *Let's Do It* (*Måske ku' vi*, 1976, dir. Lasse Nielsen) and *Leave Us Alone* (*La' os være*, 1975, dir. Lasse Nielsen and Ernst Johansen), in order to capture an extreme degree of harm and vulnerability and, finally, *Utøya: July 22* (2018, dir. Erik Poppe), which serves to exemplify high ethical standards and exceptional ethical merit. The artistically relevant ethical spectrum ranges from *Utøya*, on the artistically and ethically sound end, through *The Shining*, *Last Tango in Paris*, *The Birds*, to, finally, *Let's Do It* and *Leave Us Alone* on the artistically and ethically unsound end.

In 2017, Salma Hayek published a painfully personal piece testifying to the abuse she had suffered at the hands of Miramax producer Harvey Weinstein during the shooting of *Frida*, a biopic about the celebrated Mexican artist Frida Kahlo. Entitled 'Harvey Weinstein is My Monster Too', Hayek's article was one of many articles devoted to the sexually abusive behaviour of the film mogul and published by *The New York Times* in 2017. Hayek's testimony details the consequences for her, as the producer of *Frida* and as the lead actress playing the role of the Mexican artist, of refusing executive producer Weinstein's desire for sex. Drawing on a robust network, including the director Julie Taymor and actors Antonio Banderas, Edward Norton, and Ashley Judd, Hayek was able to prevent Weinstein from shelving the film that she herself had brought to the Miramax mogul. Hayek found herself unable, however, to reject Weinstein's demand that she participate, as Kahlo, in 'a sex scene with another woman',

one featuring 'full-frontal nudity'. Hayek describes the impact of her subjuga-
tion to Weinstein's predatory will during the shooting of the sex scene between
Kahlo and Tina Modotti (played by Ashley Judd) as follows:

> I arrived on the set the day we were to shoot the scene that I believed
> would save the movie. And for the first and last time in my career, I
> had a nervous breakdown: My body began to shake uncontrollably, my
> breath was short and I began to cry and cry, unable to stop, as if I were
> throwing up tears.
>
> Since those around me had no knowledge of my history of Harvey,
> they were very surprised by my struggle that morning. *It was not because
> I would be naked with another woman. It was because I would be naked
> with her for Harvey Weinstein.* But I could not tell them then.
>
> My mind understood that I had to do it, but my body wouldn't stop
> crying and convulsing. At that point, I started throwing up while a set
> frozen still waited to shoot. I had to take a tranquilizer, which eventually
> stopped the crying but made the vomiting worse. As you can imagine,
> this was not sexy, but it was the only way I could get through the scene.
>
> By the time the filming of the movie was over, I was so emotion-
> ally distraught that I had to distance myself during the postproduction.
> (Hayek 2017; emphasis added)

Knowledge of the conditions under which the sex scene featuring Kahlo and
Modotti was shot necessarily identifies abusive unethical behaviour as the
cause, not only of the very existence of the sequence, but of its having some
of the features that it does. That is, the quality of Hayek's performance in the
scene is directly related to the ethical transgressions reducing her to a mere
means of satisfying a powerful man's illegitimate desires.

Whereas an overall assessment of *Frida* would focus on the extent to which
Hayek and her team were successful, against all odds, in making a film to which
a variety of types of value can be attributed to some degree,[5] assessment of the
particular scene discussed above must focus on how harm, vulnerability, and
unethical intentions combine to produce significant ethical flaws. Arising from
the genetic history of the film, these flaws detract from the work's artistic value.

An ethical assessment of *Frida*:

- *Harm*: Psychological harm caused by executive producer's insistence on
  the Hayek–Judd sex scene. Psychological harm inflicted throughout the
  making of the film, due to executive producer's abusive advances and
  aggressive acts of retribution when rejected. Various harms overcome
  through powerful alliances/friendships, the success of the film, and,
  more recently the collective support of the #MeToo movement.

- *Vulnerability*: Great, on account of gender and outsider status (Mexican, new to Hollywood); mitigated by powerful alliances/friendships.
- *Intentions*: Producer's intentions with the Hayek–Judd sex scene: artistically inappropriate and deliberately unethical (aiming to satisfy personal lust, to humiliate, to intimidate, and to assert power).

Tippi Hedren's experiences during the making of *The Birds* offers another example of thwarted male desire resulting in abusive behaviour during the filmmaking process.[6] The ethical flaws in the genetic history of *The Birds* are somewhat different from those evident in the case of *Frida*, providing support for the idea that varying degrees of harm and vulnerability, and different types of intentions, combine to produce artistically relevant flaws of varying magnitudes. Harvey Weinstein did not engage in abusive behaviour towards Hayek in order to achieve a stronger performance from the Mexican actress; the ultimate goal was not to make the best film possible. *The Birds*, by contrast, appears to belong to a category of mixed intentions combining ego-driven desires – for example, to humiliate a non-compliant woman – with ones aimed at producing the best possible film.

Richard Allen has argued that Hitchcock's long-lasting obsession with Hedren involved what French theorist René Girard ([1961] 1965) calls mimetic desire. Hitchcock's desire, that is, is understood by Allen to have been mediated by his relation to European directors, and, through them, to European actresses in whose image the director sought to fashion Hedren (2013: 185–8). For present purposes, it is relevant to note that Hitchcock seems to have rationalised some of the abuse to which he subjected his leading actress, and to have done so along artistic lines. In the complexity of his self-deceived, but also artistically ambitious mind, his use of the actress as a mere instrument to be manipulated at will was warranted by his artistic goals.[7] In Hedren's case, a wounded male ego combined with artistic ambition to produce a situation requiring the actress to take unwarranted risks for which she was unprepared.[8] More specifically, without prior warning Hedren found herself facing real birds capable of inflicting bodily harm:

> everybody had lied to me, and on the Monday morning, as we were going to start the scene, the assistant director came in and looked at the floor and the walls and the ceiling, then blurted out: The mechanical birds don't work, so we have to use real ones, and then he ran out. When I got to the set I found out there had never been any intention to use mechanical birds because a cage had been built around the door where I was supposed to come in, and there were boxes of ravens, gulls and pigeons that bird trainers wearing gauntlets up to their shoulders hurled at me, one after the other, for a week. (Hiscock 2012, quoted in Palau 2018: 83)

Compared with *Frida*, the artistically relevant ethical flaws of *The Birds* are arguably less severe due to the mixed nature of the authorial intentions.

An ethical assessment of *The Birds*:

- *Harm*: Physical and psychological harm caused by director's decision to have Hedren subjected to scratching birds; psychological harm caused by director's persistent sexual aggressions.
- *Vulnerability*: Great, due to gender.
- *Intentions*: Director's intentions with the scene in which the actress is attached to birds: mixed, to produce authentic acting and through this artistic value; to humiliate and seek revenge for the rebuffing of sexual advances.

Films having ethical flaws due to the *single-minded* pursuit of artistic goals/ value by ethically dubious means occupy yet another position on the spectrum. A notorious instance of this is Bertolucci's collusion with Marlon Brando to use butter as a lubricant in the rape scene in *Last Tango in Paris* (Nannicelli forthcoming). The two older men kept their last-minute decision a secret from the much younger Maria Schneider, the aim having been to achieve genuine 'onscreen humiliation and rage' (North 2018). As Bertolucci put it in a video clip in 2013: 'I wanted Maria to feel, not to act' (North 2018). Reflecting on the adopted strategy as he sought the artistically most valuable film, Bertolucci admitted to feeling guilt about his abusive treatment of Schneider, but no regrets. Indeed, he steadfastly defended the view that 'As a filmmaker [. . .] "you have to be completely free"' (North 2018). Schneider, who died of cancer in 2011, following a troubled history of drug abuse and attempted suicide, never had any doubts about the abusive nature of the scene, or about its long-lasting psychological effects. She referred to her legal rights, which, being unaware of them at the time, she failed to evoke or defend: 'I should have called my agent or had my lawyer come to the set because you can't force someone to do something that isn't in the script, but at the time, I didn't know that' (North 2018). As is well known, Bertolucci's film went on to garner countless awards and to achieve the status of one of film history's most canonised works. This success, due in large part to the abusive scene with Schneider, did little to compensate for the actress's humiliation. Rather, as far as Schneider was concerned, it merely caused further harm:

> People thought I was like the girl in the movie, but that wasn't me [. . .] I felt very sad because I was treated like a sex symbol – I wanted to be recognized as an actress and the whole scandal and aftermath of the film turned me a little crazy and I had a breakdown. (North 2018)

In this case, the parties involved all agreed that the film's genetic history includes abuse, the abuse being viewed as artistically justified by the director and as profoundly harmful and unethical by the victim.

An ethical assessment of *Last Tango in Paris*:

- *Harm*: Lasting psychological harm caused by the director and male lead deliberately withholding information about how the rape scene would be filmed; lasting psychological harm arising from how the film's notorious rape scene affected Schneider's public identity.
- *Vulnerability*: Great, due to gender, age (as compared with much older director and male lead).
- *Intentions*: Director's intentions with the rape scene: artistically informed (to produce great art) and ethically unsound.

Kubrick's *The Shining* offers another example of how artistic goals can be pursued by unethical means, thereby generating ethical flaws that ultimately detract from the work's artistic value. In this case, however, unlike that of *The Last Tango in Paris*, the abuser's strategy has the support of the victim. Referring to Kubrick's abusive treatment of her, Shelley Duvall says: 'From May until October, I was really in and out of ill health because the stress of the role was so great. Stanley pushed me and prodded me further than I've ever been pushed before. It's the most difficult role I've ever had to play' (Hughes 2000, quoted in Palau 2018: 37). Isolating Duvall, ignoring her, withholding praise, and subjecting her to the stress of countless takes – all with the collaboration of the production team – Kubrick used manipulation, bullying, and psychological terror to achieve authentic terror before the camera and thus, as intended, in the finished work. Suggesting elements of self-deception and other psychological complexities, Duvall acknowledges the abusive nature of Kubrick's approach, yet justifies it in artistic terms:

> You always dislike whatever the cause is of pain. You always resent it. So I resented Stanley at times, because he pushed me. And it hurt. And I resented him for it. Why do you want to do this to me? How can you do this to me? You agonise over it. And it is just the necessary turmoil to get out of it what you want out of it. I mean, we had the same end in mind. It was just that sometimes we differed in our means. And by the end, the means met. (Shelley Duvall in *Making 'The Shining'*, 1980, dir. Vivian Kubrick)

Duvall's statement points to a lack of mutual understanding between her and the director, but also characterises the conflict as insignificant by virtue of an eventually, or even persistently, shared, overarching intention. The artistic value of the manifest audiovisual properties thus offers a kind of post hoc justification for the abusive means. What is overlooked by Duvall, but intuitively grasped by Schneider, is that the transgression of ethical principles during the making of a film has consequences for its artistic value inasmuch as ethical demerits necessarily diminish artistic value. In this case, assessing the *extent* of the consequences of the ethical demerits for artistic value requires consideration of the following factors, especially the victim's acceptance of the approach.

An ethical assessment of *The Shining*:

- *Harm*: Psychological harm caused by director's decision to terrorise Duvall throughout the making of the film, and to deprive her of a network of support. Victim later accepts the harm as legitimate, given the artistic goals.
- *Vulnerability*: Significant, due to gender and complicity of the cast and crew.
- *Intentions*: Artistically informed (to produce great art) and ethically unsound.

EXTREME ETHICAL FLAWS AND THE IMPOSSIBILITY OF ARTISTIC VALUE: *LET'S DO IT* AND *LEAVE US ALONE*

Released in the 1970s, at a time of sexual liberation and rebellion, *Let's Do It* (dir. Lasse Nielsen) and *Leave Us Alone* (dir. Lasse Nielsen and Ernst Johansen) were widely applauded in Denmark, by young and older audiences alike, for adopting a youth-centred, anti-authoritarian approach that brought young people's agency and desires to the screen. The films have been canonised on account of their central contributions to the wave of youth films that emerged in the latter half of the 70s. Indeed, stills from the films can be found in countless volumes detailing the achievements of Danish cinema, especially in the category of films for and about children and young people. *Let's Do It* features Karl Wagner as the fifteen-year-old Kim Christensen who is taken hostage by bank robbers along with a young girl, Marianne (Marianne Berg), with whom he becomes romantically, and, indeed, sexually involved; *Leave Us Alone* focuses on the increasingly dysfunctional interactions between teenagers who find themselves stranded on an island. It is fair to say that for decades these modern classics of the Danish cinema were regarded as having considerable cultural and artistic value. In 2018, however, revelations about the making of the films brought to light egregious sexual abuse (Ryom and Christensen 2018).

Prompted by the realisation that his sexual abuser, Lasse Nielsen, was making films with children and adolescents in Thailand, Karl Wagner contacted the daily *Politiken* in order to tell the troubling story about how the director had selected him for the role of Kim Christensen with sexual gratification in mind.

Wagner's decision to come forward became the start of a lengthy process of investigation by journalists and filmmakers from TV 2 and *Politiken*, leading to more testimony from the many adolescents with whom the two directors had worked. The result was a two-part documentary entitled *The Abused Film Children* (*De misbrugte filmbørn*, 2018, Impact TV), detailing the degree and extent of the two paedophiles' abuse during several film productions (including *Let's Do It* and *Leave Us Alone*). Produced with public funds from the coffers of the Danish Film Institute (DFI), the films had served as a front for abuse, but also as a means of facilitating it. Asked about the accusations of rape and molestation levelled against his friend and fellow filmmaker, Johansen, Nielsen, compromising himself too, says:

> I noticed that all the girls he had chosen were very young. And I was surprised to see that two or three of them had very large breasts. At one point they get up and say: 'The sun is shining, let's get rid of the T-shirts.' And that wasn't in the script. It was something Ernst had thought up. But since I was insisting on the boys being naked, I couldn't really say anything about his getting the girls to take off their T-shirts. [. . .] I noticed that he touched the girls a lot. In all sorts of strange places. (Christensen and Bruun 2019)

In 2018, Tine Fischer, founding director of the CPH:DOX festival, declared during her opening speech, which referenced #MeToo, that for the first time in its history, the festival would open with a Danish film. Her eloquent and fiery speech introduced *The Abused Film Children*, the first part of which premiered at CPH:DOX, but it also insisted on a heightened sense of collective responsibility on the part of the audience. Stating that she would not allow the audience to leave the theatre thinking that the abuse holds merely historical interest, she indicated that the screening would be followed by a performance piece. She had, she declared, invited a number of actors to take the stage after the screening, for the purpose of reading anonymised testimonies of abuse shared by Danish actors active in the film industry today. *The Abused Film Children*, she claimed, should be a call for action. The call to action was warranted, for what the two-part documentary revealed, in addition to egregious abuse, was failings on multiple fronts. While there appears to have been a general awareness of transgressive behaviour on the part of the two directors in the film industry at the time, nobody spoke up and many simply looked the other way, or found ways to rationalise dubious situations, for example by evoking the freewheeling mores of the times. Also, when the monies from the DFI eventually stopped flowing in the direction of the abusers, the decision to cease funding the two directors who had produced such celebrated youth films was not recorded or explained in a paper trail. Implicit in Fischer's challenge to the audience was the idea that the elements needed to protect children, adolescents, and adults in the film industry from unethical abuse – regulatory frameworks and protocols or simply mutual beliefs – are lacking or insufficiently robust.

Praised at the time of their release for their carefree attitude towards adolescents' sexuality, the films' many images of naked or half-naked bodies take on a very different meaning in the wake of *The Abused Film Children*. Serious abuse with lifelong consequences is part of the genetic history of the relevant scenes. In determining the severity of the ethical flaws in the production processes, the following factors must be taken into consideration.

An ethical assessment of *Let's Do It* and *Leave Us Alone*:

- *Harm*: Life-long trauma.
- *Vulnerability*: Extreme, due to age (adolescents).
- *Intentions*: Criminal and unethical (sexual abuse, including rape).

The attribution of artistic value to the scenes of naked or half-naked bodies of minors can no longer be defended. Given the extent to which these scenes define the visual style of the works, and given how pervasive the sexual abuse was throughout the making of the films, the only appropriate response, from 2018 onwards, is to focus on the ethical flaws. The ethical flaws in the films' genetic histories are so great as to make unethical any attributions of artistic value to the works. Any such attribution would, in effect, further compound the harm caused by the filmmakers, by re-victimising the adults who bravely stepped forward to share the abuse that has haunted them for four decades.

SETTING AN ETHICAL STANDARD: ERIK POPPE'S *UTØYA: JULY 22*

Anne Gjelsvik, a Norwegian film and media scholar at the Norwegian University of Science and Technology (NTNU) in Trondheim, has written extensively on Erik Poppe's *Utøya: July 22* (2018). In an early commentary on the film she affirms the film as follows:

> Several things are necessary if one is to succeed with a film project like this, and three things stand out in my mind as absolutely essential: thorough preparation, clear aesthetic choices, and decency. My first thought after seeing the film for the first time was precisely that it is decent. (Gjelsvik 2018)

In the present context the term 'decency' signals a synergy of ethical and artistic value, the ethical value in the film's genetic history not only serving to amplify the work's artistic value, but being actually constitutive of it. That is, ethical production strategies and intentions throughout the making of the film led to the film's having precisely the audiovisual qualities that it has. Discernible in the film independently of contextual knowledge, these audiovisual qualities remain unchallenged as we learn about the work's genetic history. In brief, the most fundamental element in Poppe's overarching artistic strategy was his commitment to ensuring that vulnerable parties were not harmed by his film. This commitment was remarkably comprehensive for it extended beyond the pre-production and production phases that produced the work's salient features to encompass the dynamics of its distribution too. *Utøya* is thus especially deserving of inclusion in the category of films on the most virtuous end of the artistically relevant ethical spectrum.

Described in the film's credits as a reality-based fiction, Poppe's film is an attempt to imagine what the young victims attending the Workers' Youth League's summer camp on the island of Utøya experienced when right-wing extremist Anders Behring Breivik hunted them down with a rifle for seventy-two minutes on 22 July 2011. Consisting mostly of a single take, the film follows the eighteen-year-old Kaja (Andrea Berntzen) as she searches the island for her younger sister, Emilie (Elle Rhiannon Müller Osbourne) once the massacre starts. Poppe avoids having the killer fill the frame at any point in the film, the viewer being offered but a mere glimpse of the shooter in an extreme long shot and from the perspective of Kaja. While Poppe shows us the wounded and dying, he steers clear of graphic displays of violence. Lasting exactly the amount of time that the killer went unapprehended on Utøya, Poppe's film is

Figure 4.1   Looking straight at the camera, Kaja's remark about 'never understanding' in *Utøya: July 22* has the effect of challenging viewers to make a significant effort.

93

designed to foster the most thoroughgoing sympathy for the victims. Poppe's intentions are clearly signalled in the opening moments of the film, which feature Kaja speaking to a family member on her mobile phone. As she utters the words 'You will never understand. Listen to me', her eyes look straight into the camera, effectively demanding that we see the film as a way of accessing what it felt like to be hunted, and, in the case of seventy-seven young people, killed by Behring Breivik on 22 July 2011.

Poppe's intention to make a film about the Utøya massacre was not met with enthusiasm when it was announced seven years after the national tragedy. Mindful of the many risks associated with a project dealing with personal and collective trauma from which survivors, their families, and, indeed, the nation were still seeking to recover, critics claimed that the tragedy was still too close, the experiences too raw, and the danger of sensationalising the massacre through moving images simply too great (Gjelsvik 2019). Gjelsvik (2019) is right to claim that Poppe has proved his many concerned critics wrong, having made a film that is thoroughly attuned to, and effectively avoids, the many risks of (re-)victimisation. *Utøya*, far from sensationalising violence or drawing attention to the killer, greatly contributes to the crucial work of respectful national mourning and remembrance, meeting a transgenerational need to understand what Breivik's victims experienced.

Gjelsvik (2019) identifies a number of significant measures that were adopted by Poppe and his team to minimise the impact on vulnerable young actors, as well as on the actual victims and their families, all of whom would be amongst the film's potential viewers. Poppe prioritised the protection of the young actors from the effects of entering into an imagined space designed to bring us as close as possible to the full phenomenological experience of Breivik's victims. The actors were to show us what it felt like to be hunted by Breivik, in a situation of complete uncertainty about the nature of the attack and without any support from the outside world. At the same time the actors were to be protected from the effects of potentially identifying with their roles and becoming consumed by the tragedy. Thus, for example, in an effort to avoid an already sensationalised and re-traumatising production environment, Poppe shrouded the pre-production process – the writing of the script, the financing of the film, and the casting of the actors – in secrecy. Actors who came to the auditions were given no advance information about the particular roles. Especially telling is Poppe's decision to consult the National Support Group for the Victims of 22nd of July, the result of this being, among other things, that a 'balance was sought between telling a true story and avoiding the reconstruction of the experiences of particular individuals' (Gjelsvik 2019). According to Gjelsvik (2019), Poppe included three of the victims (Ingrid Marie Vaag Endrerud, Ole Martin Slyngstadli, and Kristoffer Klunk Nyborg) in the making of the film, as consultants and assistant directors. Indeed, these three survivors were present during the shooting of the film on Frognøya, offering, through their presence, support for the young actors, but also a constant reminder of the need for decency, for clear ethical principles. Finally, Poppe worked with the National Support Group to arrange a number of 'closed screenings in about 40 places in Norway', thereby allowing survivors and their families to see the film in circumstances that recognised their special needs. Thus, for example, any element of suspense relating to the characters' chances of survival was eliminated by furnishing viewers with a full summary of the story prior to the screening (Gjelsvik 2019). Poppe and his team also collaborated with the Norwegian Centre for Violence and Traumatic Stress Studies to offer viewers information about how survivors and their relatives could be expected to respond to the film. Especially vulnerable viewers were given advice about how best to process the relevant reactions and emotions (Gjelsvik 2019). Efforts were also made to ensure that the marketing of the film was limited, thereby restricting the number of occasions on which survivors would find themselves face to face with a poster reminding them of the traumatic events, or in a cinema watching a trailer for the film about their traumatic experiences. To this day, there is no Norwegian trailer for the film.

The artistic value of Poppe's film derives, in part, from the clear and cogent way in which its manifest audiovisual properties give viewers a means of accessing, with the fullest sympathy possible, the experiences of Breivik's victims. Featuring consistent ethical principles designed to avoid harm, the genetic history of *Utøya* has ethical merits that contribute directly to the film's pervasive invitation to sympathy. The film's ethical merits are reflected in the director's attitudes towards harm and vulnerability and in his articulation of ethically appropriate artistic intentions.

An ethical assessment of *Utøya*:

- *Harm*: None inflicted on the participants in the film; the film helps to alleviate the impact of a national trauma.
- *Vulnerability*: Significant (young actors, survivors, and the families of deceased and surviving victims), but mitigated through a range of expert protections.
- *Intentions*: Artistically and ethically appropriate.

The ethical value of the film's genetic history proves to be consistent with and, indeed, constitutive of the artistic value of the work's audiovisual features. The relation between ethical value and artistic value is in this case ideal, the ethical value of the production process serving further to strengthen the film's artistic value, as based on the manifest properties.

Avoiding Ethical Flaws in the Genetic Histories of Future Cinematic Works

In adopting an expanded ethicist position when assessing the value of cinematic works, we are committing ourselves to seeing films created in harmful ways not just as less ethically valuable, but as less artistically valuable than those meeting the higher standard met by Poppe when making *Utøya*. Yet, the expanded position should not merely be about attributions of greater or lesser ethical and artistic value to works during a process of film appreciation. A more thoroughgoing ethicism brings scope for action relating to desirable change in those very milieux that must provide the favourable conditions for genetic cinematic histories devoid of egregious ethical flaws. There are many possible sites for interventions aimed at effecting behavioural change and facilitating the emergence of new conventions, understood as mutual understandings. A few selected examples suffice to make the point that ethicism, in its expanded form, brings with it commitments of a more institutional nature.[9]

First, the ethicist must take an interest in the institutionalised processes that help filmmakers become filmmakers. Film schools, film labs, film workshops, in short, the entire landscape of practice-based training provisions, play a crucial role in creating the conditions for ethical film production. The variety of approaches on offer, ranging from the curricula of well-established conservatoire-style film schools to short workshops run at film labs, is quite significant (Hjort 2013c, 2013d). These approaches help aspiring filmmakers to develop their technical skills sets, but they also shape their attitudes, expectations, and values. The most fundamental purpose of producing motion pictures varies dramatically from one site of practice-based film education to another. At Film-Lab Palestine, for example, in Ramallah, the most important goal of all is to facilitate what Rod Stoneman (2019) calls 'direct speech', the telling of Palestinian stories by Palestinian filmmakers. The same is true, in an African register, of Mira Nair's Maisha Film Lab, in Kampala, Uganda. At the National Film School of Denmark, an especially successful example of a conservatoire-style film school, the purpose of making films was, until recently, defined in terms of a deeply personal and distinctly artistic vision, by the value of art.[10] According to Toby Miller (2013), the purpose of filmmaking is construed rather differently in the established film schools in the United States, where students are taught to have their eyes on the glamour and commercial ambitions of Hollywood, at times even in contexts of collaboration with the US military.

Filmmakers' values are further moulded by the norms that are embedded in various curricular structures, in the ways in which practical exercises are structured or, to use the term preferred by film trainers, scaffolded. At the South African School of Motion Picture Medium and Live Performance (AFDA), there is a 'strong emphasis on collaborative learning [. . .] inspired by the ubuntu philosophy expressed in many African languages, for instance the Sesotho "muntu umuntu babantu" – I am a person through other persons' (Basson et al. 2013: 27). Seeking to instil openness and curiosity, self-reliance, and a strong desire for friendships across national borders, the National Film School of Denmark's Middle East Programme sent student filmmakers to Egypt, Jordan, and Lebanon, where they were to create the conditions for their assigned one wo(man) band filmmaking project by forging friendships with local painters and musicians (Hjort 2013a). By contrast, Miller remembers, while at NYU's Tisch School of the Arts, serving on a 'committee charged with stopping male directors from cutting female actors' bodies in the name of attaining authentic performances from them' (2013: 156). As Miller sees it, the actions requiring investigation were a clear outgrowth of an institutional culture of pervasive sexism. It seems clear that some milieux of practice-based training are more likely to produce film practitioners with a robust moral compass than others. The expanded ethicist position supports those that instil values consistent with the idea that inflicting harm during the making of a film detracts from its value as an artwork.

Second, ethicists can be expected to take a keen interest in the institutional culture of specific production environments. Institutional culture encompasses, among other things, the ways in which a given production company manages access to the milieu in question, as well as the taken for granted modes of interacting with others within that milieu. The significance of access is reflected in observations by Meta Louise Foldager Sørensen, previously a producer of Lars von Trier's films under the aegis of Zentropa and now the CEO of her own company, Meta Film. Following revelations in 2016 about the remarkably poor performance of the Danish film industry with regard to the inclusion of women (Danish Film Institute 2016), Foldager Sørensen made a public promise, during a well-attended forum at the Danish Film Institute, to track gender in all aspects of Meta Film's operations. The aim in doing so, she claimed, would be to foster a heightened awareness of gender imbalances and, through this, eventually to effect change.

Institutional culture also concerns the accepted ways of treating persons within a given hierarchical structure or the existence of robust preferences for more equal relationships. #MeToo has brought to light countless examples of how work environments can be deeply damaging, indeed toxic, for particular groups. The harm in question extends well beyond harassment and humiliation, for some of the institutionally pervasive practices substantially increase the life-threatening physical risks that certain groups must take in order to practise their craft. Focusing on stunt work in Hollywood and Hong Kong, Sylvia Martin (2012), for example, describes how women stunt workers in Hollywood are deprived of the protective padding afforded their male counterparts, due to preferences for scantily clad women on screen.

In assessing the merits or flaws of production milieux it is relevant, now more than ever, to consider attitudes towards the natural environment (Hjort 2016; Nannicelli 2018). Such attitudes pertain to how the natural environment is treated while shooting a film. Actions falling short of a reasonable ethical standard include the refashioning of a pristine beach in the national park on Phi Phi Lae island in Thailand (Cohen 2005), against the advice of environmental experts and activists, when making *The Beach* (2000, dir. Danny Boyle), or Fox Studios' refusal to take seriously its chemical contamination of the Popotla's waters and beaches in Baja California when shooting *The Titanic* (1997, dir. James Cameron) (Miller and Maxwell 2012). We are beginning to see the emergence of production houses that define their identity in terms of sustainability, eco-friendly production methods, and the aspiration to bring about new norms. A good example is Jordnær Film, which was established by Josefine Madsen in 2017, when she was still a student of film and media at the University of Copenhagen. Jordnær Film became Jordnær Creative in 2019, when Madsen was joined by a fellow alumna, Anne Ahn Lund. Jordnær Creative develops tools 'that support the industry in sustainable decision-making'. The production house is part of the global green media network led by Pietari Kääpä and Hunter Vaughan, the aim being to establish 'common sustainable standards' by 'creating strong partnerships' (Jordnær Film n.d.). Led by the next generation of motion picture producers, Jordnær Creative seeks a standard of environmental respect that, if met, guarantees the absence of certain kinds of harms/ethical flaws in the genetic history of future films.

As the field of production ethics develops, awareness of the ways in which ethical demerits negatively affect artistic value will surely be enhanced. It will be important to ensure that the gains are not merely theoretical or conceptual in nature. Rather, the practical implications of acknowledging a link between ethical demerits and diminished artistic value must be vigorously pursued, for this is how the perpetration of further harm will be avoided. Moving forward, collaborative efforts involving scholars, critics, policy makers, educators/trainers, and members of professional guilds and associations will be crucial.

ACKNOWLEDGEMENT

I am grateful to Ted Nannicelli and Marguerite La Caze for their thoughtful comments and generous suggestions.

NOTES

1. In Nannicelli (2020), the preferred terms are 'generative context', 'generative history', 'production context', and 'production history'.

2. In his debate with Felicia Ackerman (1991) over the ethics of basing fiction on real lives, Brandon Cooke highlights one of the consequences of adopting an ethicist position, before ruling in favour of the arguments of the autonomists: 'Either ethical considerations are always overriding, and *much of our creative and appreciative practices are morally corrupt*, or ethical and aesthetic values are incommensurable' (2015: 449; emphasis added). An expanded ethicist position rejects the idea that ethical and aesthetic values are incommensurable and accepts the implications for how creative and appreciative practices are to be assessed.

3. See Miller and Maxwell (2012) for an account of the environmental footprint of the motion picture industry.

4. Guy-Blaché's story is told in director Pamela B. Green's 2018 documentary, *Be Natural: The Untold Story of Alice Guy-Blaché*, which is narrated by Jodie Foster. Guy-Blaché's ten-minute silent comedy *A Fool and His Money* (1912) is noteworthy. In addition to being the work of the world's first known female director, *A Fool and His Money* is also the first known film to feature an African American cast. *Pioneers: First Women Filmmakers*, a DVD released by KinoLorber in 2018, in collaboration with the Library of Congress, features the film.

5. Historical value was an important part of Hayek's motivation for making the film (Hayek 2017). See Hjort and Nannicelli's *Companion to Motion Pictures and Public Value* (forthcoming) for accounts of the variety of types of value that films can have. Issues of co-authorship as they relate to the value of works are also relevant. See Gaut (1997) and Livingston (1997).

6. See Spoto (1999) for an account of what he calls the 'dark side' of Hitchcock's genius.

7. We will recall that Pudovkin (1954) famously identified such behaviour as a pervasive tendency in the production milieux of the then still emerging seventh art.

8. On taking and running risks in connection with film, see Livingston (2012).

9. Nannicelli rightly makes the point that policy matters have 'been deliberately avoided by most philosophers working in' the area of philosophical aesthetics (2020: 25), although such matters are at the very heart of public debates about art and ethics.

10. In 2019, prompted by the dismissal of the revered film educator Arne Bro, students at the film school, widely supported by alumni and such luminaries as former producer Vibeke Windeløv and director Lone Scherfig, called for the resignation of the school's president, Vinca Wiedemann. Wiedemann and her provost, Søren Friis Møller (previously at the Copenhagen Business School), are charged with dismantling the school's most fundamental commitment to art in favour of more academic values, and those driving the league tables.

References

The Abused Film Children (De misbrugte filmbørn). Documentary. Copenhagen: TV 2, Politiken, Impact TV, 2018.

Ackerman, Felicia. 1991. 'Imaginary Gardens and Real Toads: On the Ethics of Basing Fiction on Actual People.' *Midwest Studies in Philosophy* 16: 142–51.

Allen, Richard. 2013. 'Hitchcock and the Wandering Woman: The Influence of Italian Art Cinema on *The Birds*.' *Hitchcock Annual* 18: 149–94.

Basson, Anton, Keyan Tomaselli, and Gerda Dullaart. 2013. 'Audience Response in *Film Education.*' In *The Education of the Filmmaker in Africa, the Middle East, and the Americas*, edited by Mette Hjort, 25–38. New York: Palgrave Macmillan.

Be Natural: The Untold Story of Alice Guy-Blaché. Documentary. Directed by Pamela B. Green. Los Angeles: Be Natural Productions, 2018.

The Beach. Film. Directed by Danny Boyle. Los Angeles: Fox Studios, 2000.

The Birds. Film. Directed by Alfred Hitchcock. Los Angeles: Alfred J. Hitchcock Productions, 1963.

Choi, Jinhee, and Mattias Frey (eds). 2013. *Cine-Ethics: Ethical Dimensions of Film Theory, Practice, and Spectatorship.* New York: Routledge.

Christensen, Claus, and Nicki Bruun. 2018. 'TV 2 kalder mig pædofil-instruktøren.' *Ekko*, 26 February. <https://www.ekkofilm.dk/artikler/tv-2-kalder-mig-paedofil-instruktoren/> (last accessed 18 March 2021).

Cohen, Erik. 2005. 'The Beach of "The Beach" – The Politics of Environmental Damage in Thailand.' *Tourism Recreation Research* 30.1: 1–17.

Cooke, Brandon. 2015. 'Drawing from Life.' *British Journal of Aesthetics* 55.4: 449–64.

Danish Film Institute. 2016. 'Undersøgelse af kønsfordeling i dansk film.' 1 June. <http://www.dfi.dk/nyheder/filmupdate/pressemeddelelser/2016/ny-undersoegelse-om-koensfordeling-i-dansk-film.aspx> (last accessed 18 March 2021).

A Fool and His Money. Film. Directed by Alice Guy-Blaché. Fort Lee, NJ: Solax, 1912.

Frida. Film. Directed by Julie Taymor. Los Angeles: Handprint Entertainment, Lions Gate Films, Miramax, Ventanarosa Productions, 2002.

Gaut, Berys. 1997. 'Film Authorship and Collaboration.' In *Film Theory and Philosophy*, edited by Richard Allen and Murray Smith, 149–72. Oxford: Oxford University Press.

Gaut, Berys. 2007. *Art, Emotion and Ethics.* Oxford: Oxford University Press.

Geena Davis Institute on Gender in Media. n.d. 'The Reel Truth: Women Aren't Seen or Heard: An Automated Analysis of Gender Representation in Popular Films.' <https://seejane.org/researchinformsempowers/data/> (last accessed 18 March 2021).

Girard, René. [1961] 1965. *Deceit, Desire, and the Novel: Self and Other in Literary Structure*, translated by Yvonne Freccero. Baltimore, MD: Johns Hopkins University Press.

Gjelsvik, Anne. 2018. 'Utøya 22. Juli (2018).' *Montages* 13 (March). <https://montages.no/2018/03/analysen-utoya-22-juli-2018/> (last accessed November 2019).

Gjelsvik, Anne. 2019. 'Ingen vanlig kinoopplevelse.' *Norsk medietidsskrift* 26.2. <https://www.idunn.no/nmt/2019/02/_ingen_vanlig_kinoopplevelse?fbclid=IwAR3WGXkMmOuuyuQtWoHcYDc_L1Jcb268U5mTa1AG7mz9ntIlLIr8bfB_9fo> (last accessed 18 March 2021).

Hayek, Salma. 2017. 'Harvey Weinstein Is My Monster Too.' *The New York Times*, 12 December. <https://www.nytimes.com/interactive/2017/12/13/opinion/contributors/salma-hayek-harvey-weinstein.html> (last accessed 18 March 2021).

Hiscock, John. 2012. 'Tippi Hedren Interview: 'Hitchcock Put Me in a Mental Prison.' *The Telegraph*, 24 December. <https://www.telegraph.co.uk/culture/film/starsandstories/9753977/Tippi-Hedren-interview-Hitchcock-put-me-in-a-mental-prison.html> (last accessed 18 March 2021).

Hjort, Mette. 2011. 'The Problem with Provocation: On Lars von Trier, Enfant Terrible of Danish Art Film.' *KINEMA: A Journal for Film and Audiovisual Media* (Fall). <https://doi.org/10.15353/kinema.vi.1236> (last accessed 18 March 2021).

Hjort, Mette (ed.). 2012a. *Film and Risk*. Detroit: Wayne State University Press.

Hjort, Mette. 2012b. 'Flamboyant Risk-Taking: Why Some Filmmakers Embrace Avoidable and Excessive Risks.' In *Film and Risk*, edited by Mette Hjort, 31–54. Detroit: Wayne State University Press.

Hjort, Mette. 2013a. 'Art and Networks: The National Film School of Denmark's "Middle East Project".' In *The Education of the Filmmaker in Africa, the Middle East, and the Americas*, edited by Mette Hjort, 125–52. New York: Palgrave Macmillan.

Hjort, Mette. 2013b. 'Community Engagement and Film: Toward the Pursuit of Ethical Goals through Applied Research on Moving Images.' In *Cine-Ethics: Ethical Dimensions of Film Theory, Practice, and Spectatorship*, edited by Mattias Frey and Jinhee Choi, 195–214. London: Routledge.

Hjort, Mette (ed.). 2013c. *The Education of the Filmmaker in Africa, the Middle East, and the Americas*. New York: Palgrave Macmillan.

Hjort, Mette (ed.). 2013d. *The Education of the Filmmaker in Europe, Australia, and Asia*. New York: Palgrave Macmillan.

Hjort, Mette. 2016. 'What Does it Mean to Be an Ecological Filmmaker? Knut Erik Jensen's Work as Eco-Auteur.' *Projections: The Journal for Movies and Mind* 10.2: 104–24.

Hjort, Mette. 2018a. 'Gender Equity in Screen Culture: On Susanne Bier, the Celluloid Ceiling, and the Growing Appeal of TV Production.' In *Refocus: The Films of Susanne Bier*, edited by Missy Molloy, Mimi Nielsen, and Meryl Shriver-Rice, 130–44. Edinburgh: Edinburgh University Press.

Hjort, Mette. 2018b. 'Guilt-Based Filmmaking: Moral Failings, Muddled Activism, and the Documentary *Get a Life*.' *Journal of Aesthetics and Culture*, special issue, edited by Elisabeth Oxfeldt, 10.1: 6–13.

Hjort, Mette, and Ted Nannicelli (eds). Forthcoming. *Companion to Motion Pictures and Public Value*. Malden, MA: Wiley-Blackwell.

Hughes, David. 2000. *The Complete Kubrick*. London: Virgin Books.

Jordnær Film. n.d. 'CBS Entrepreneurial Day – Explore the Future of Student Entrepreneurship!' <https://cse.cbs.dk/entrepreneurial-day/jordnaer-film/> (last accessed June 2020).

Last Tango in Paris. Film. Directed by Bernardo Bertolucci. Paris: Les Productions Artistes Associés, Produzioni Europee Associati, 1972.

Leave Us Alone (La' os være). Film. Directed by Lasse Nielsen and Ernst Johansen. Copenhagen: Gemini Film, Telefilm, 1975.

Let's Do It (Måske ku' vi). Film. Directed by Lasse Nielsen. Copenhagen: Steen Herdel Film, 1976.

Livingston, Paisley. 1997. 'Cinematic Authorship.' In *Film Theory and Philosophy*, edited by Richard Allen and Murray Smith, 132–48. New York: Oxford University Press.

Livingston, Paisley. 2012. 'Spectatorship and Risk.' In *Film and Risk*, edited by Mette Hjort, 73–95. Detroit: Wayne State University Press.

Making 'The Shining'. Documentary. Directed by Kubrick, Vivian. UK: BBC, 1980.

Martin, Sylvia J. 2012. 'Stunt Workers and Spectacle. Ethnography of Physical Risk in Hollywood and Hong Kong.' In *Film and Risk*, edited by Mette Hjort, 97–114. Detroit: Wayne State University Press.

Miller, Toby. 2013. 'Goodbye to Film School: Please Close the Door on Your Way Out.' In *The Education of the Filmmaker in Africa, the Middle East, and the Americas*, edited by Mette Hjort, 153–68. New York: Palgrave Macmillan.

Miller, Toby, and Richard Maxwell. 2012. 'Risk Off-Screen.' In *Film and Risk*, edited by Mette Hjort, 271–90. Detroit: Wayne State University Press.

Nannicelli, Ted. 2014. 'Moderate Comic Immoralism and the Genetic Approach to the Ethical Criticism of Art.' *The Journal of Aesthetics and Art Criticism* 72.2: 169–79.

Nannicelli, Ted. 2017. 'Ethical Criticism and the Interpretation of Art.' *The Journal of Aesthetics and Art Criticism* 75.4: 401–13.

Nannicelli, Ted. 2018. 'Animals, Ethics and the Art World.' *October* 164: 113–32.

Nannicelli, Ted. 2020. *Artistic Creation and Ethical Criticism*. Oxford: Oxford University Press.

Nannicelli, Ted. Forthcoming. 'Film Production and Ethical Criticism.'

North, Anna. 2018. 'The Disturbing Story behind the Rape Scene in Bernardo Bertolucci's *Last Tango in Paris*, Explained.' *Vox*, 26 November. <https://www.vox.com/2018/11/26/18112531/bernardo-bertolucci-maria-schneider-last-tango-in-paris> (last accessed 18 March 2021).

Palau, Joseph Valentino. 2018. 'I Never Asked for Butter! Ethical Assessment of Film Direction Methods and the Role of Consent in Relation to Aesthetic Value.' MA Thesis, Film & Media, University of Copenhagen.

Plantinga, Carl. 2018. *Screen Stories: Emotion and the Ethics of Engagement*. Oxford: Oxford University Press.

Pudovkin, V. I. 1954. 'Discontinuity in the Actor's Work in the Cinema.' In *Film Technique and Film Acting: The Writings of V. I. Pudovkin*, translated by Ivor Montagu, with an introduction by Lewis Jacobs, 30–41. London: Vision Press. <https://archive.org/details/filmtechniqueact00pudo> (last accessed 18 March 2021).

Ryom, Lasse, and Claus Christensen. 2018. 'Overgreb i danske ungdomsfilm.' *Ekko*, 8 February. <https://www.ekkofilm.dk/artikler/dengang-i-70erne/> (last accessed 18 March 2021).

The Shining. Film. Directed by Stanley Kubrick. Los Angeles: Warner Bros, Hawk Films, Peregrine, The Producer Circle Company, 1980.

Sinnerbrink, Robert. 2016. *Cinematic Ethics: Exploring Ethical Experience through Film*. London: Routledge.

Spoto, Donald. 1999. *The Dark Side of Genius: The Life of Alfred Hitchcock*. New York: Da Capo Press.

Stadler, Jane. 2008. *Pulling Focus: Intersubjective Experience, Narrative Film, and Ethics*. New York: Continuum.

Stoneman, Rod. 2019. 'African Cinema: Perspective Correction.' In *African Cinema and Human Rights*, edited by Mette Hjort and Eva Jørholt, 38–59. Bloomington, IN: Indiana University Press.

Time's Up. n.d. <https://timesupnow.org/about/>.

The Titanic. Film. Directed by James Cameron. Los Angeles: Lightstorm Entertainment, 1997.

Utøya: July 22. Film. Directed by Erik Poppe. Oslo: SF Studios, Paradox Film, 2018.

Watson, Emma. 2014. 'Gender Equality Is Your Issue Too.' *UN Women*, 20 September. <http://www.unwomen.org/en/news/stories/2014/9/emma-watson-gender-equality-is-your-issue-too> (last accessed 18 March 2021).

5. *THE LOOK OF SILENCE* AND THE ETHICS OF ATONEMENT

Marguerite La Caze

Joshua Oppenheimer's (1974–) extraordinary *The Act of Killing* (2012) documented perpetrators of the genocide of hundreds of thousands of communists or 'suspected' communists in Indonesia in 1965–6, encouraging them to re-enact their crimes in the film genre of their choice. These men are largely unrepentant, although one of them, Anwar Congo, appears to show signs of remorse at one point. The film itself can be understood as an attempt at atonement in spite of the attitudes of the perpetrators, and may even lead to real steps to atone, since millions of Indonesians have seen the film and responded with concern to the killings. The film raised awareness of the killings, the impunity of the wrongdoers, and the lack of redress after fifty years.

The follow-up documentary, *The Look of Silence* (2014), filmed before the release of *The Act of Killing*, takes this process of atonement further by considering how the survivors might confront the killers and build relationships with the next generation, the children of the killers.[1] It focuses on the attempt of one survivor, Adi Rukun, to discover the truth of what happened to his brother and to confront those responsible. My chapter discusses the film's presentation of his search for atonement in relation to the concept of communal atonement. One puzzle about atonement is how it is possible if the individuals who committed the wrong do not atone, clearly a difficulty in Indonesia. I consider how the process of making the documentary, participating in it, and the screenings in Indonesia and elsewhere contribute to atonement despite the unapologetic response from the killers.

Atonement

Other accounts of *The Look of Silence* have focused on ethical witnessing (Sinnerbrink 2017) or the question of the monstrosity of the killers (Abbott 2017). Here I concentrate on atonement, to show how atonement speaks to the film as an act, and an act that is an ethical one that performs and encourages atonement. Atonement can involve concepts of apology, compensation, healing, moral transformation, and sometimes punishment or sacrifice as forms of making up for wrongs that have been committed. Although several religious rituals and traditions involve atonement, for example the Jewish celebration of Yom Kippur, or Day of Atonement, my concern here is with secular atonement, both individual and collective, which is beginning to be theorised.[2] Secular atonement does not include a religious commitment and avoids the problems of conflicting religious beliefs and ceremonies. Atonement can often, and often must, be undertaken by someone who is not guilty of the original crime, but may be a bystander, beneficiary, or descendent.[3]

The process of atonement is sometimes called 'making amends' in scholarly discussions. In her book *Moral Repair: Reconstructing Moral Relations after Wrongdoing*, Margaret Urban Walker characterises amends as 'intentionally reparative actions by parties who acknowledge responsibility for wrong, and whose reparative actions are intended to redress that wrong' that make up for the debt to victims (2006: 191). One of the strange features of making amends is that if the wrong is minor, making amends and the recognition of that by victims is relatively easily done and readily accepted as a responsibility. What is strange is not that it is done easily but that atonement is needed less in the case of trivial harms than in more serious cases. However, Walker observes that 'it is often in the most egregious cases of harm that significant reparative actions are resisted and seem shallow, meagre, and incomplete where attempted' (2006: 198). The reasons for this lack of atonement in extreme cases is that acknowledging guilt can be psychologically, politically, and materially painful, and that it is difficult if not impossible for atonement to really make up for the harms of the wrong. Atonement is demanding when many of the victims are dead, and so cannot be directly made amends to, survivors are sceptical about atonement, and the wrongs cannot be righted. It is even more improbable when the offenders do not desire to atone or are even triumphant, as is common in the case of the Indonesian genocide, as Oppenheimer's films make clear.

Philosopher Linda Radzik considers this idea of 'collective atonement' in her book *Making Amends: Atonement in Morality, Law, and Politics* (2009: 175–97). For her, atonement is generally 'an action the wrongdoer carries out' (2009: 7), whereas in the case of institutional and group wrongs, non-perpetrating members of the group share the obligation to atone through their joining the group, sharing an identity with the group, and because in some cases, there is no one else who can do that (2009: 195–6).[4] Furthermore, Kara Barnette considers atonement as 'communal, ongoing, and cross-generational' in relation to memory and atrocities from the past (2017: 61). She characterises atonement this way to distinguish it from atonement as an act or set of acts that can make up for past wrongs once and for all.

Individual atonement may occur in the confessions or truth telling in truth and reconciliation commissions, expressions of remorse, apologies, material compensation, assistance, or community service, and punishment can also be thought of as a form of atonement. Further, community atonement can be carried out through compensation, collective apologies, memorials, monuments, museums, and commemorations. Even if atonement is difficult or close to impossible, we must try to carry it out. Here I ask what kind of atonement can be portrayed, enacted, and encouraged by a documentary. What is that atonement in *The Look of Silence*, which presents a series of unrepentant offenders?

This last problem of institutions, groups, or individuals not feeling remorse for their actions can mean that wrong is not atoned for and also that the victims are still in a precarious or dangerous position. In that situation, communities and those who are not directly responsible for the original crimes can, and arguably should, take on the responsibility to try to atone and to change thinking about the past, and that could lead to the original offenders recognising what they have done. Film, both documentary and fictionalised works, has played an important role in raising awareness and understanding of genocide and other atrocities. For example, the film *Katyn* (2007, dir. Andrzej Wajda) dramatises the full horror of the massacre of more than 20,000 Polish officers and civilians in World War II in 1940, known as the Katyn massacre.[5] The issue of unrepentant offenders has also been portrayed in a number of films. For instance, Claude Lanzmann's film *Shoah* (1985) demonstrates, using a range of techniques, including secret filming, that many of the perpetrators of the Shoah were indifferent to their deeds.

A notable demonstration of the effects of impunity on perpetrators is depicted in *The Act of Killing*.[6] The victims were taken by the paramilitary, including local gangsters, held in concentration camps, and then murdered. One estimate is that up to a million or more people were murdered (Buckley 2016; Schenkel 2015: 97), and that is the figure used in the films. In an interview, Oppenheimer says the figure is between half a million and three million (Goodman 2015: 3). The murders occurred over a period of six months and included feminists, intellectuals, peasants, and teachers.[7] The torturers and killers of the communists and suspected communists are largely unrepentant and are hailed as heroes in Indonesia. *The Act of Killing* shows Anwar Congo, one of these petty gangsters, having some experience of remorse when he asks, 'Have I sinned?' and says, 'I know I have done wrong', but he immediately adds that he 'had to do it'.

This lack of repentance or remorse makes atonement especially difficult, and as another perpetrator says in that film, 'there is no reconciliation, there can be no reconciliation'. However, the film itself can be understood as an attempt at atonement despite these attitudes (Bjerregaard 2014). Tim Grierson observes that the film was criticised for the 'stylised dramatisations overshadow[ing] any examinations of past barbarous deeds' (2015: 2). It was also criticised for neglecting US complicity in the genocide and not interviewing survivors, criticisms Oppenheimer contends are answered in *The Look of Silence* (Behlil 2015: 30), and the second film takes atonement much further. He had a better chance to raise these concerns about impunity in *The Look of Silence* than Indonesian survivors, in spite of the real danger and threat to his own life of raising them within Indonesia.[8] Another consideration is that Oppenheimer, as a US citizen, feels some responsibility due to US involvement in the genocide. While Adi Rukun, a brother of one of the victims, Ramli (or Romli), interviews the perpetrators in this film, it was with Oppenheimer and his team's support and planning that this was possible.

Before responding to these questions, I must briefly describe the genocide that is the context for the films.

The Genocide

The genocide in Indonesia was set off by the murder of six generals and other high-ranking military on the night of 30 September 1965 by members of Sukarno's (president 1945–67) presidential guard and air force. These murders provided the pretext for the political takeover and genocide that followed. Sukarno was the first president of Indonesia after leading the fight for independence from the Netherlands and was one of the founders of the Non-Aligned Movement in 1961 for countries that did not want to be part of either the Eastern or Western Blocs, including India, Egypt, Ghana, and Yugoslavia.[9] His successor, General Suharto (president 1967–98), blamed the Communist Party of Indonesia (PKI) for the killings, and President Sukarno was overthrown in a military coup to be replaced by Suharto, who was backed by the American government led by Lyndon B. Johnson and other Western nations, including Australia.[10] After Sukarno's ousting, he was put under house arrest in Bogor Palace in West Java and died there in 1970.

The genocide can be thought of as a politicide, or targeting of perceived members of a political group, although in some cases ethnicity played a role in who was targeted.[11] As Oppenheimer notes, Suharto and his New Order regime also presided over the genocide in East Timor, where a third of the population was killed, and during that period continued to receive a great deal of financial aid from the US. One of Oppenheimer's concerns is the US role in the genocide.[12] He portrays how the US government funded and trained the military as an internal force against the population, giving money and weapons to the military for the genocide, and supplied the radios used to coordinate the massacres. Moreover, Oppenheimer claims that US Embassy officials were giving kill lists of thousands of public figures to the military during the genocide, saying 'Kill everybody on these lists and check off the names as you go, and give the lists back to us when you're done' (Goodman 2015: 14). Oppenheimer was told this by Robert Martens, who worked at the Embassy in Jakarta at the time. Western countries such as the United States praised measures against the communist party. He also comments on how Goodyear used people held in the concentration camps as slave labour on the rubber plantations, shown in an NBC report in *The Look of Silence*, and asks if the anti-communist campaign 'was a ruse, a pretext, an excuse, for murderous corporate plunder' (Goodman 2015: 15).[13] These details are presented in the film, but not discussed at any length. One of the most amazing things about the two films is that they were made at all, so I will also briefly describe that process.

MAKING *THE ACT OF KILLING* AND *THE LOOK OF SILENCE*

American filmmaker Joshua Oppenheimer first went to Indonesia to teach plantation workers how to make films about union concerns but was disconcerted by the atmosphere of fear he found there, which led him to discover the reasons behind it. As he says, the films are not about 1965 as such, and the events are not explained in the films; they are about 'the impunity, and fear, and silence, corruption and violence in the present' (Blyth 2016). He was encouraged by the workers to film the perpetrators at first alone and then together. What Oppenheimer noticed is that the killers boasted a great deal individually and even more when together, symptoms, he argues, of a collective monstrosity or insanity (Blyth 2016).[14] Ultimately, he decided to make two films, one to understand the bragging of the killers, and one to understand the experience for the survivors living in that atmosphere.

From the beginning the survivors were threatened not to speak by the army, so filming had to be carefully arranged. Because Oppenheimer had made *The Act of Killing* with some of the most powerful perpetrators, such as the vice president, cabinet ministers, and the chief of the Pancasila Youth, the Indonesian paramilitary group, Adi Rukun and Oppenheimer thought that would provide a kind of protection from the regional leaders (Schenkel 2015: 99; Goodman 2015: 6). Oppenheimer spent seven years working with the killers, five of them making *The Act of Killing*, then the interviews for *The Look of Silence* were conducted in 2012 before *The Act of Killing* was released. The crew and Adi Rukun and his family had to go into hiding elsewhere in Indonesia after that (Blyth 2016). When Adi Rukun was conducting the interviews with the offenders, they had a getaway car ready at all times. It should be noted that it was Adi who asked Oppenheimer if he could interview and film the perpetrators himself (Blyth 2016; Goodman 2015: 5). For Adi's confrontations with the killers, Oppenheimer worked with only the Danish crew so that the Indonesian film crew would not be exposed to risk. Adi's family would be at the airport with packed bags waiting for an okay (Blyth 2016; Goodman 2015: 17). Furthermore, everyone Indonesian involved in the films is credited as 'anonymous' for their own safety. After the end of the filming, Oppenheimer had to move to Denmark, and he still gets death threats (Grierson 2015: 6).

Nevertheless, both films have been widely seen in Indonesia. They are distributed in Indonesia by the National Human Rights Commission and the Jakarta arts council (Blyth 2016). Both *The Act of Killing* and *The Look of Silence* are free online for Indonesians to watch so many thousands have seen it. Now I will turn to the documentary itself to see how it presents the issue of atonement.

INDIVIDUAL ATONEMENT (OR LACK THEREOF) IN *THE LOOK OF SILENCE*

The Act of Killing and *The Look of Silence* both won many awards and both were nominated for an academy award for best documentary. Oppenheimer describes *The Act of Killing* as a 'flamboyant fever dream' (O'Falt 2016: 7), with Anwar Congo as 'the main character' (Goodman 2015: 9).[15] Furthermore, he explains how he 'was interested in the relationship between documentary, collaboration, and performance' (Grierson 2015: 2) and speaks of the importance and power of documentary in giving us 'the shock of the familiar', rather than 'the shock of the new' (O'Falt 2016: 4).[16]

Jake Wilson in the *Sydney Morning Herald* criticises *The Look of Silence* for its fictionalising, and compares it unfavourably with *The Act of Killing*, writing that it is 'more lucid but less interesting' (2016: 2).[17] He further claims that the film is 'rather too polished for its own good. Even as he chronicles the search for truth, Oppenheimer turns his subjects into characters in a kind of fiction: it's unlikely any of the confrontations we witness would have occurred without his sponsorship' (2016: 2). It is hard to see how this is a criticism, however. Oppenheimer was able to create an environment where Adi could confront his brother's killers and survive. Also, these interviews would have been much less 'coached' than the interviews Oppenheimer conducted with the other killers over five years. Moreover, Wilson finds the image of optometry working as 'a heavy-handed metaphor' (2016: 3). He hints that the film is really about something else, larger than the story of Adi and Ramli, and even larger than or different from the genocide in Indonesia – such as the lack of the rule of law there and in the US, issues of race, and the genocide of Native Americans (Goodman 2015: 14). Certainly, this point is not denied by Oppenheimer, rather he reinforces it.

Interestingly, Oppenheimer also rejects the term 'storyteller' because it is a flawed metaphor, claiming that he works to 'create new realities' (O'Falt 2016: 3, 5). He says:

> I try to create these realities that are beyond their (the participants') comfort zone and make something visible about that space that was previously invisible. I want to immerse the viewer in that space, but with a moral point of view, and I think that can be achieved without distancing. (O'Falt 2016: 5)[18]

What he means is that the films create a full experience that draws in the viewer so they can understand that moral viewpoint. How I would put it is that they present a reality, a particular interpretation of that reality aimed at the truth, and have a moral message.

Part of that moral message is conveyed by the focus on Adi Rukun throughout *The Look of Silence*, rather than a didactic voice-over or Oppenheimer as interviewer. The film intercuts scenes of Adi interviewing the men involved in his brother's murder with scenes of his mother, father, children, and partner, and him watching the footage of the men boasting about their crimes. *The Look of Silence* presents the process of atonement and reconciliation as one between individuals and focused only on one person, perpetuating the idea of the hero survivor who will make the killers speak the truth and then forgive them if they decide to. Adi and his family had helped Oppenheimer talk to survivors right from the beginning of his project (Goodman 2015: 3). In the film, Adi is trying to find out more about the murder of his brother Ramli, who was killed during the 'Snake River Massacre', where over 10,000 people were killed (Schenkel 2015: 99).[19] Ramli was 'the village head of a farmer's cooperative', so thought likely to oppose the military dictatorship, and he was murdered by the Kommando Aksi, an Acehan paramilitary group (Goodman 2015: 6). Adi is an optometrist living in Northern Sumatra at the time of the film. His brother Ramli was one of the few killed who had witnesses, so his death could be acknowledged, grieved, and his body could be buried. In the documentary Adi confronts a number of his brother's killers, giving some of them free eye tests and an offer of free glasses if they are needed as he does so, and tries to get them to confess responsibility and acknowledge the wrong.[20] However, the killers do not take responsibility. For example, Amir Siahaan, the commander of the Snake River death squads, says, 'We had commanders above us. And we were protected by the government. So you can't say I'm responsible.' He asks Adi where he lives, and he refuses to answer (Goodman 2015: 11). While a number of the perpetrators menace Adi in this way from a position of power, Benedict Anderson questions the extent to which they were rewarded for what they did during the genocide; rather he sees Ramli's killers as 'actually nobodies', and any benefits gained as being from decades of criminality (2012: 282).[21]

There are a number of reasons for the film's focus on Adi's search for Ramli's killers. As Oppenheimer says, 'So, over the decades, from 1965 until I first arrived in 2003 and started working on this, over the decades Ramli became a kind of synonym for the genocide as a whole' (Goodman 2015: 7). Ramli became such a metonym because his murder was one of the few that people had seen take place, as I mentioned above. Most other people could not talk about the death of their loved ones, although they knew they must have been killed. So it appears that the film draws on the need for a metonym for atonement and reconciliation. Rather than referring to every possible act of atonement or attempt to elicit atoning responses, Oppenheimer centres on one person's search for the killers of his brother and others involved in it. He observes of Adi that 'Many younger Indonesians think he's a kind of national hero', that is, for both the public and the media (Grierson 2015: 6; Blyth 2016). *The Look of Silence* was first shown on National Heroes Day, and the trend on Twitter that day was 'Today we have a new national hero and his name is Adi' (Goodman 2015: 13). That status has protected Adi since the release of the film. In that sense, the film presents us with the idealised lone hero, rather than showing he is part of a large family, or that there is a network of children and other relatives of genocide victims that work together in that area. As Tim Grierson points out in *Rolling Stone* magazine, 'the director has [. . .] given what's hopefully a growing movement towards truth and reconciliation a now-recognizable everyman face' (2015: 5).

It was probably necessary for Oppenheimer to focus only on Adi to protect the identities of other family members. During the genocide, Adi's older sister had her head shaved by the local militia, and all the siblings were 'routinely intimidated, harassed and extorted' (Buckley 2016).[22] Moreover, they were threatened by the army to prevent them from being involved in the film (*The Look of Silence*, DVD notes, 2014). There are also a number of reasons why Adi in particular was so determined to participate. Adi is the youngest in the family, and born after the killings, so could see them differently from those directly involved. He is seen by his mother, Rohani, as a kind of replacement for Ramli, and he grew up hearing his mother endlessly telling him about the murder. Now he wants his children to grow up without fear of their neighbours (Goodman 2015: 9) and not be taught that people like his brother deserved to die.

Some critics and audiences objected to the last sequences with Adi's father, Rukun, crawling through the house, not realising he is at home, and saying that he needs help (Stevens 2015). However, Oppenheimer explains that it is the only scene shot by Adi, and shows that his father has forgotten his son, Ramli, but has not forgotten the fear that he might be beaten up in a stranger's house

(Stevens 2015; Goodman 2015: 9; Blyth 2016). For these reasons, the focus on Adi in the film is justified; nevertheless, it is at odds with the ideal of communal atonement and at odds with Oppenheimer's interpretation of his own work. So, before finally considering how atonement is presented and enacted in the film, I would like to consider Oppenheimer's understanding of what he is doing.

OPPENHEIMER AND THE LEGACY OF VIOLENCE

Interestingly, Joshua Oppenheimer explicitly rejects the idea of presenting a heroic or saintly image of survivors, saying:

> *The Act of Killing* exposed the consequences for all of us when we build our everyday reality on terror and lies. *The Look of Silence* explores what it is like to be a survivor in such a reality. Making any film about survivors of genocide is to walk into a minefield of clichés, most of which serve to create a heroic (if not saintly) protagonist with whom we can identify, thereby offering the false reassurance that, in the moral catastrophe of atrocity, we are nothing like perpetrators. But presenting survivors as saintly in order to reassure ourselves that we are good is to use survivors to deceive ourselves. It is an insult to survivors' experience, and does nothing to help us understand what it means to survive atrocity, what it means to live a life shattered by mass violence, and to be silenced by terror. To navigate this minefield of clichés, we have had to explore silence itself. The result, *The Look of Silence* is, I hope, a poem about a silence borne of terror – a poem about the necessity of breaking that silence, but also about the trauma that comes when silence is broken. Maybe the film is a monument to silence – a reminder that although we want to move on, look away and think of other things, nothing will make whole what has been broken. Nothing will wake the dead. We must stop, acknowledge the lives destroyed, strain to listen to the silence that follows. (Quoted in Davis 2014)[23]

Thus, he suggests that films should not present survivors as heroes, even though Adi is thought of and treated as a hero as an effect of the film. It could be argued that while Adi is treated as a national hero, that does not mean that Oppenheimer's film treated him as a hero (Blyth 2016). However, the singular focus on Adi does mean that as an individual he comes to represent all the survivors. The style and structure of the film presents subtle and complex scenarios, which underscore how difficult atonement is in this context.

The Look of Silence is a more conventional film than the *Act of Killing*, although it is carefully crafted, using imagery to convey particular effects, and shows parts of the previous film on a television screen. These scenes are primarily of the killers bragging about what they have done, with Adi Rukun watching, as that is how he discovered who murdered his brother. For Oppenheimer, the two films form a diptych, complementing and enriching each other. (Grierson 2015: 3, 6) The flamboyance of the first film contrasts with the restful, contemplative mood of the second film. Instead of the killers driving through the streets, or acting out roles in loud costumes, Oppenheimer allows the pace of everyday life, the natural sounds, and the spaces of fields and forest to suggest a gentler rhythm. Bright colours in this film come from nature rather than the elaborate costumes the killers don in *The Act of Killing*. The camera focuses throughout on Adi's face, gazing intently, thinking, and yet usually calm, despite what he is hearing in his interviews and on the television when he watches the earlier footage taken by Oppenheimer. Often we hear cicadas and birds in the background providing the soundtrack of the tropical forest. Shots of a bridge over a river evoke the violence hidden behind its stillness, a connection the audience must infer, like the meanings of the butterfly cocoons.

A scene about one-third of the way through the film of an open square with children playing near a makeshift stage, jaunty shops, traffic passing, and Western music coming from the shops appears to have no purpose. It can be seen as similar to the shots of the river, as a scene of life going on as if nothing happened – perhaps disturbing or possibly life-affirming. It also marks a transition to Adi's more focused interviews, where he questions Inong intently, using his technique of the eye test and the promise of new glasses. Here the shots, like that used for the film poster, are close-ups of Inong's face in the trial lenses and then side shots of Adi questioning him. These interviews are intercut with scenes of Adi's mother and father; sometimes his mother is talking about Ramli, and at others she is just relaxing at home. The film can be seen as having two climaxes, which point in different directions concerning the question of atonement and Adi's search for the killers to take responsibility, a point I will return to. One is the scene where a killer's daughter asks Adi to forgive her father and think of them as family – a moment of atonement, perhaps? The other concerns the family of the author who published an illustrated book including details of Ramli's murder.[24] The mother apologises, adding that 'we feel the same way that you do' but this moment is spoilt, as I will explain further on.

The film also has other themes and goals, implied by the title. Oppenheimer's documentary does help us to listen to silence, yet it also helps to make the silence start to speak again. He is trying to 'create a world that's always there, but invisible' and film a 'poem to all that was lost' (O'Falt 2016: 6–7). The film uses images of butterfly cocoons (or jumping beans) to represent what we normally do not see or notice, but that is having an effect (Stevens 2015; O'Falt 2016: 7). They could also signify new life and hope, as Adi's mother holds them and talks to them, very close to the end of the film. Furthermore, the eye tests function as a metaphor for the wilful blindness of the perpetrators to the horrifying meaning of what they did (Goodman 2015).[25] It is not as heavy-handed in its use of imagery as Wilson claims, since the dialogue between Adi and the perpetrators is more important.

For his part, Oppenheimer argues that the problem is impunity, and wonders whether that is why there are 'sweat shop labour and slave labour conditions around the global South?' (Blyth 2016). His concern is with the legacy of the killings, 'the current regime of fear and thuggery and corruption' (Goodman 2015: 3). He says that the situation in Indonesia was like 'wandering into Germany 40 years after the Holocaust, only to find the Nazis still in power' (Oppenheimer, in Behlil 2015: 27). To some extent, the films have led to challenges of that impunity, as I discuss in the final section. Oppenheimer's aim was to 'show how torn this society is, how urgently truth, reconciliation and justice are needed', whereas he saw Adi as specifically looking for reconciliation (Goodman 2015: 6). What happens in and because of *The Look of Silence* is closer to Oppenheimer's goal, although there are elements of Adi's, as I will discuss.

The film also explores the grey zones involved in such an atrocity, in that sometimes the distinction between perpetrators and victims is not completely clear-cut. This issue can arise in two ways: either where victims are coerced to take part in the crimes, as with the *Sonderkommando* and the ghettoes in the Shoah, for example, or where there is little agreement in communities as to who is victim and who is perpetrator in situations of civil war. Primo Levi articulates the first concept in his account of his experiences in Auschwitz (1989: 36–69), which is examined by Claudia Card in her discussion of evil in *Confronting Evils: Terrorism, Torture, Genocide* (2010: 56).[26] However, a term such as 'co-implicated' would be better for the second kind of case. Card argues that diabolical evil, or the worst kind of evil, should be best understood as morally corrupting others. She defines grey zones as those that 'result from choices that are neither gratuitously nor wilfully evil but that nevertheless implicate choosers who are themselves victims in perpetrating evils against others who are already also victims, paradigmatically victims of the same evils as the choosers' (2002: 232). The idea that there are 'grey zones' means that the issue of responsibility becomes 'problematic' because agents are responsible in certain respects and not in others (2002: 216). Card argues that in addition to themselves being victims of evil, and committing similar acts of evil themselves, those in the grey zones 'act under extraordinary stress' (2002: 224). Each situation will be different, since oppressed people or people in extreme situations can be pressured, coerced, and threatened, although they could choose to become complicit, with different levels of pressure. Furthermore, children may be drawn into or forced into conflicts before they have developed a moral sense.

Moreover, as Johann Brännmark (2008) suggests, moral repair and atonement in the grey zones or co-implicated cases is likely to be different from in more clear-cut cases. For example, the first step of acknowledging the wrongs committed will be fraught with difficulty, and the experience of being both victim and perpetrator will be complex and mutually affecting (Brännmark 2008: 172). To some extent, that is true quite generally for the Indonesian genocide, as the army recruited civilians to take part in the killings. More specifically, *The Look of Silence* portrays how Adi's own family is implicated – his uncle (his mother's brother) worked as a guard in the prison where Ramli was held, which he admits on camera. However, he claims to have been under orders and would have been accused himself if he had not obeyed. He also claims that he did not know that Ramli would be killed, which Adi's mother says is a lie. Ultimately, Ramli's uncle refuses to accept any responsibility or express regret. Nevertheless, there is an emotional moment following their discussion where both Adi and his uncle are teary and silent, a silence that is more telling than the uncle's words. For Adi, he should have at least admitted an indirect responsibility. That would have been one step towards atonement.

A troubling aspect for Ramli's mother, Rohani, is that she gave him up after the first attack, under duress, and became in her own mind a collaborator, although that is far too harsh a judgement on herself. Ramli had been attacked but managed to crawl home, but the death squad returned for him and threatened the whole family if he was not given up. They tried to cover this up by saying they were taking Ramli to the hospital (Goodman 2015: 8). It is her acceptance of that pretence that she blames herself for. The existence of these kinds of grey zones is another reason that atonement needs to be communal rather than only individual. So that is the issue I will turn to.

COMMUNAL ATONEMENT

While *The Look of Silence* focuses on one survivor, I argue that the effect of the documentary itself, in empowering victims, survivors, and their descendants, is exemplary, and exemplary as a form of collective atonement. The making of the documentary, participating in it, and its being shown in Indonesia and around the world supports communal atonement in spite of the killers' lack of repentance and the lack of state compensation or care. Oppenheimer's view is that the killers' re-enactments and discussions of what they did provide a document, as he writes: 'Above all, they transformed rumour into evidentiary account. Rendering the spectral explicit allows it to be critically reframed, and this process opens on to the potentially redemptive and retributive possibilities of this project' (Oppenheimer and Uwemedimo 2012: 307). Here it is hinted that the survivors can use the films in a number of ways, ways that could contribute to atonement. It should be noted that much of the work towards reconciliation in

Indonesia has been carried out by grass-roots local organisations, rather than national bodies (Pohlman 2016; Santoso and Klinken 2017: 595). International attention has been drawn to the genocide, *The Act of Killing* was launched in The Hague in 2013, and an International People's Tribunal (IPT65) was held in The Hague in 2015 after the screening of the films and talks with Oppenheimer (Santoso and Klinken 2017: 595).[27] The Tribunal concluded that Indonesia was guilty of a series of crimes against humanity, that of genocide against a national group according to the 1948 Genocide Convention, including mass killing, imprisonment, enslavement, torture, enforced disappearance, sexual violence, and exile (Santoso and Klinken 2017: 598–603).

In Indonesia, the fact the film has been screened very widely means that many people can come to know the truth about what happened and to reflect on the need for atonement.[28] Furthermore, there have been a number of important steps forward since the film was released. The Indonesian president's office admitted that the events of 1965 were a crime against humanity and that truth and reconciliation is needed (Blyth 2016). A Truth and Reconciliation bill was introduced by the government (Goodman 2015: 13) but has not been implemented. This is the first step in what will be a long process. Moreover, in April 2016 the Indonesian government held a two-day symposium on the genocide, with Islamic groups, military, and survivors (Kwok 2016: 1). There have also been discussions between victims and the military, although no apology. Current President of Indonesia Joko Widodo established a reconciliation committee, but did not apologise in his state address on 16 August 2016 to the PKI (the Communist Party of Indonesia), although it had been rumoured that he would (Buckley 2016). Muhammad Rizieq Shihab, the leader of the Islam Defenders Front (FPI), threatened to impeach him if he apologised, so it is not that surprising. Additionally, media silence has ended with testimony of perpetrators published in *Tempo*, Indonesia's most influential news magazine, as Oppenheimer notes (Blyth 2016; Oppenheimer 2014). Lastly, Indonesian history teachers have set out aims for curriculums that present the reality of the genocide and do not scapegoat the victims. In *The Look of Silence*, schoolteachers are shown teaching Adi's son that the communists deserved to be murdered, and that their grandchildren are under suspicion by association.[29]

In relation to the US's role in the genocide, Tom Udall, US Senator, introduced a resolution asking the US government to declassify further documents concerning the killings (Goodman 2015: 14). Earlier released documents showed that the US helped and encouraged the anti-communist groups, as Oppenheimer relates (Buckley 2016). Indonesia's National Commission on Human Rights asked Barack Obama to release documents as well (Kwok 2016), and almost 30,000 pages of records from the US Embassy in Indonesia 1964–8 were released in 2017 by the National Declassification Center, created by Obama in 2009 (Varagur 2017). Journalist Krithika Varagur contends that

It is hard to overstate the impact of the documentaries *The Act of Killing* and *The Look of Silence*, which are respectively about the perpetrators and victims of the 1965–66 killings, on the renewed conversation over Indonesia's mid-century anti-Communist purge. (Varagur 2017)

By this she means the conversation in both Indonesia and in the US.

In contrast, there has been a backlash against this recognition of the genocide, with screenings shut down, supposedly to prevent violence (Schenkel 2015: 101; Kwok 2016: 2). While there was this attempt at censorship, it was undermined by the film being available free online. An anti-communist symposium was held in June 2016 and symposiasts demanded that the communist party 'apologise to the people and the nation of Indonesia' (Kwok 2016: 3). There also still remains the need for monuments for the victims. The only existing material acknowledgements are rare markers of the mass graves that Indonesia is peppered with (Associated Press 2016). In 2016, the government said it would excavate mass graves, and such graves have been excavated in Bali and Central Java (Santoso and Klinken 2017: 595). There is a small grave for Ramli in the palm plantation where he was killed (Goodman 2015: 9).

Atonement is also linked to forgiveness, as a possible response to atonement, and I will briefly consider this issue. This was clearly what Adi Rukun had in mind from the beginning. For instance, Adi said, 'we can forgive them if they can just admit what they've done was wrong' (Blyth 2016; Goodman 2015: 9). Oppenheimer notes that Adi initially hoped that one or more of the perpetrators would be glad to find forgiveness from one of the victims (Goodman 2015: 6). However, Oppenheimer warned Adi that he would not get an apology from the perpetrators (Blyth 2016). He thought it was much more likely that they would 'get defensive and angry' and threatening, after experiencing shame and guilt (Goodman 2015: 6, 10). Indeed, the local perpetrators seem even less perturbed by talking about their crimes than Anwar Congo. He killed around 1,000 people, and after five years of talking to Oppenheimer, expresses some signs of recognising the horror of what he did in *The Act of Killing*, as I noted at the beginning of the chapter.

In an interview, Adi Rukun said that he feels free and free of fear for the first time in his life, because he is not surrounded by people threatening him, and can speak openly about the past (Buckley 2016).[30] Nevertheless it takes a twenty-five-person team, including five full-time workers, to protect him and his family living in another part of Indonesia (Goodman 2015: 16). Hope is also raised in the film through the relationships he begins to build with the children of the killers. When the daughter of one of the killers asks him to forgive her father, and think of them as family, as I described Adi hugs him and shakes his hand, in one of the more touching moments filmed. But she does not apologise, just asks repeatedly for Adi to forgive her father. Also, the partner of the killer who authored the illustrated book, Amir Hasan Nasution, says, 'Adi, we apologise. We feel the same way you do.' And Adi nods. These developments, albeit small, suggests, as Barnette does (2017: 70), that atonement could only come with a new generation, from those who were not involved in the genocide. But the moment is ruined by the sons' noisy claims that they know nothing and Oppenheimer is making trouble. His sons demand they stop showing footage of the author showing off his book. They deny knowing anything and complain that Adi is opening a wound, that he is seeking revenge, that they should forget the past. The scene ends with shot of Adi's pained face, many of which recur throughout the film. The limited nature of these glimmers of atonement supports the need for a broader acknowledgement that does not focus only on individuals. And the last scene of the film, the lights of a truck at night, does not augur well.

CONCLUSION

The Look of Silence responds to a perceived need to make the story about an individual survivor and an individual victim so that people can grasp it, identify with Adi and his murdered brother Ramli, and react against the impunity of the killers. It is successful in portraying that individual search for them to take responsibility, and although Adi does not really find the remorse or apology he seeks, Oppenheimer does expose the guilt and fear he tries to, and suggests that some of the next generation, the children of the killers, will contribute to atonement. Others will continue to deny the genocide or even claim that a communist threat still exists. The film succeeds on many levels in contributing to communal atonement even if, as a work of art, it does not, in the main, portray communal atonement.

NOTES

1. Other films made about the genocide include Robert Lemelson's documentary *40 Years of Silence: An Indonesian Tragedy* (2009), which explains the history and interviews four families affected by it, Chris Hilton's documentary *Shadow Play* (2003), which examines the West's involvement and the propaganda used to attempt to justify the crimes, and Peter Weir's *The Year of Living Dangerously* (1982), which dramatises events leading up to the failed coup attempt.
2. See, for instance, Radzik (2009).
3. Kara Barnette considers atonement in relation to memory (2017: 68–72).
4. I discuss Radzik's view of atonement in more detail in La Caze (2019: 130–8), where I argue that atonement should be understood as moral transformation and as related to but not constituted by reconciliation, as she contends.
5. The massacre was denied until 1990, when Mikhail Gorbachev acknowledged the crime, although the Soviet government refused to categorise it as a war crime, an

act of genocide, or Stalinist repression, so claimed no further accountability was needed. Putin has commemorated Katyn, and expressed regret and contrition, but has not apologised or offered compensation or full disclosure (Bidder 2010).

6. See Sinnerbrink (2016) and 'Indonesian Roundtable: *The Act of Killing*' (2014) for discussions of this film.

7. Furthermore, Jess Melvin describes how from April 1966 ethnic Chinese in Aceh were targeted as a group (2018: ch. 7), while Melvin and Annie Pohlman note the IPT65's findings that motive against ethnic Chinese played a role in Medan, Makassar, and Lombok (2018: 38) and other reports that Chinese were targeted in Central Java, Sumbawa, and South and West Kalimantan (2018: 39).

8. This film's executive producers are Werner Herzog and Errol Morris. They were also producers for *The Act of Killing*, along with Joram ten Brink and André Singer. See Teh and Berghuis (2015) for a discussion of this film.

9. The movement will have its 18th Summit in Azerbaijan in 2019.

10. See Simpson (2012) for a discussion of international involvement in and responses to the genocide. PKI chairman Aidit was captured and killed, while Omar Dhani, air force commander, spent thirty years in jail (1965–95) and died in 2009.

11. See Scott (2018) for a clear summary of the events and Harff (2003) for a discussion of politicide. Melvin and Pohlman (2018) argue that the killings should be understood as genocide, with ideological, ethnic, and religious elements.

12. Oppenheimer says that the US may have been behind the killings of the military that were used to excuse or justify the genocide (Goodman 2015: 14).

13. Oppenheimer observes that the NBC news report shown in *The Look of Silence* celebrates the genocide. *Time* magazine and *The New York Times* both praised the killings (*The Look of Silence*, DVD notes, 2014; Campbell 2015).

14. Johannes Lang (2018) argues that similarly, many of the perpetrators of the Holocaust, particularly members of the SS, were proud of their actions, and boasted about them.

15. Anwar Congo was the forty-first perpetrator Oppenheimer filmed (Oppenheimer 2014).

16. Julian Stallabrass (2013: 12) observes that the twenty-first century's first decade sees a return to documentary.

17. In contrast, Ian Buruma states that 'Oppenheimer's second film, *The Look of Silence*, is a quieter, less flamboyant work and all the stronger for it' (2015: 61–2).

18. Grierson calls *The Act of Killing* a 'vérité-hybrid classic' (2015).

19. *The Look of Silence* was originally called *Snake River* and that is how it is referred to by Anderson (2012) and Oppenheimer and Uwemedimo (2012).

20. The eye tests were Oppenheimer's idea, as a way to build 'an instant intimacy and rapport, to show the perpetrators that Adi sees them, no matter what, as a human being, as any doctor will with their patients' (Blyth 2016). Adi gives an eye test to Inong Syah and also to his uncle.

21. For instance, he is threatened by M. Y. Basrun, speaker in the regional parliament (Schenkel 2016: 100).

22. Adi's two older brothers and Ramli's wife moved, so there are at least three other siblings. Sinnerbrink suggests that the focus on Adi provides 'a source of narrational authority' (2017: 7).

23. Oppenheimer says his influences include Werner Herzog's *Even Dwarves Started Small* (1970) and *Stroszek* (1977), Tsai Min-Liang's *The Hole* (1998), and Robert Bresson's *Diary of a Country Priest* (1951) (O'Falt 2016).
24. One of the killers, Amir Hasan Nasution, whose partner and two sons Adi talks to, wrote an illustrated book (*Embun Berdarah*, or 'Dew of Blood') about the massacres that uses Ramli's name (Oppenheimer and Uwemedimo 2012: 293).
25. Mathew Abbott notes that Inong and the others have a kind of 'epistemic impunity' or culpable unclarity of vision (2017: 408).
26. Johann Brännmark discusses both types of grey zones in his review (2008: 171–2).
27. However, the Indonesian government did not take part. The fifty-year anniversary in 2015 also drew more international attention to the atrocities.
28. Both films were also shown widely in the Netherlands, where survivors and children of survivors have been led to reflect on and discuss the events (Dragojlovic 2018).
29. Communism and Marxist-Leninism are still banned in Indonesia (Santoso and Klinken 2017: 595). There is also a ban on grandchildren of communists getting government jobs (Goodman 2015).
30. Adi Rukun intends to start an optometry shop, using funds from the True/False film festival (Buckley 2016).

REFERENCES

Abbott, Mathew. 2017. '*The Look of Silence* and the Problem of Monstrosity.' *Film-Philosophy* 21.3: 392–409.

The Act of Killing. Film. Directed by Joshua Oppenheimer. UK, Denmark, Norway: Final Cut for Real, Piraya Film A/S, Novaya Zemlya, Spring Films, 2012. DVD notes.

Anderson, Benedict. 2012. 'Impunity.' In *Killer Images: Documentary Film, Memory and the Performance of Violence*, edited by Joram ten Brink and Joshua Oppenheimer, 268–86. New York: Columbia University Press.

Associated Press. 2016. 'Memorial Monument Shines Light on 1965 Indonesia Massacre.' *The Indian Express*, 5 October. <https://www.indianexpress.com/article/world/world-news/memorial-monument-shines-light-on-1965-indonesian-massacre-3066332/> (last accessed 19 March 2021).

Barnette, Kara. 2017. 'Haunting Guilt, Communities of Memory, and the Process of Atonement.' *The Pluralist* 12.1: 60–73.

Behlil, Melis. 2015. '*The Look of Silence*: An Interview with Joshua Oppenheimer and Adi Rukun.' *Cineaste* 40.3: 26–31.

Bidder, Benjamin. 2010. 'Remembering the Katyn Massacre: Putin Gesture Heralds New Era in Russian–Polish Relations.' *Spiegel Online*, 8 April. <https://www.spiegel.de/international/europe/remembering-the-katyn-massacre-putin-gesture-heralds-new-era-in-russian-polish-relations-a-687819.html> (last accessed 3 March 2020).

Bjerregaard, Mette. 2014. 'What Indonesians Really Think about *The Act of Killing*.' *The Guardian*, 6 March. <https://www.theguardian.com/film/2014/mar/05/act-of-killing-screening-in-indonesia> (last accessed 10 June 2021).

Blyth, Antonia. 2016. 'The Look of Silence's Joshua Oppenheimer: "We had a getaway car and bags packed, ready to evacuate".' Deadline, 4 February. <https://www.deadline.com/2016/02/look-of-silence-joshua-oppenheimer-oscars-interview-1201696228/> (last accessed 19 March 2021).

Brännmark, Johann. 2008. Review of Moral Repair: Reconstructing Moral Relations after Wrongdoing, by Margaret Urban Walker. Theoria 74: 169–72.

Buckley, Cara. 2016. 'Adi Rukun, Neither Silent Nor Intimidated.' The New York Times, 12 February. <https://www.nytimes.com/2016/02/13/movies/adi-rukun-neither-silent-nor-intimidated.html> (last accessed 10 June 2021).

Buruma, Ian. 2015. 'The Violent Mysteries of Indonesia.' The New York Review of Books, 22 October, 60–2.

Campbell, Meagan. 2015. 'A Few Questions for His Brother's Killers.' Maclean's, 27 July.

Card, Claudia. 2002. The Atrocity Paradigm: A Theory of Evil. Oxford: Oxford University Press.

Card, Claudia. 2010. Confronting Evils: Terrorism, Torture, Genocide. New York: Cambridge University Press.

Cribb, Robert. 2014. 'Indonesian Roundtable: The Act of Killing.' Critical Asian Studies 46.1: 147–9.

Davis, Edward. 2014. 'Watch: First Clip from Joshua Oppenheimer's Venice-Premiering Doc "The Look of Silence".' IndieWire, 27 August. <https://indiewire.com/2014/08/watch-first-clip-from-joshua-oppenheimers-venice-premiering-doc-the-look-of-silence-273138/> (last accessed 19 March 2021).

Diary of a Country Priest. Film. Directed by Robert Bresson. France: Union Générale Cinématographique, 1951.

Dragojlovic, Ana. 2018. 'Violent Histories and Embodied Memories: Affectivity of "The Act of Killing" and "The Look of Silence".' In The Indonesian Genocide of 1965: Causes, Dynamic and Legacies, edited by Katharine McGregor, Jess Melvin, and Annie Pohlman, 269–85. London: Palgrave.

Even Dwarves Started Small. Film. Directed by Werner Herzog. West Germany: Werner Herzog Filmproduktion, 1970.

40 Years of Silence: An Indonesian Tragedy. Film. Directed by Robert Lemelson. USA: Elemental Productions, 2009.

Goodman, Amy. 2015. '"The Look of Silence": Will New Film Force U.S. to Acknowledge Role in 1965 Indonesian Genocide?' Democracy Now, 3 August. <https://www.democracynow.org/2015/8/3/the_look_of_silence_will_new> (last accessed 10 June 2021).

Grierson, Tim. 2015. 'The Look of Silence: How a New Doc Revisits Indonesia's Genocide.' Rolling Stone, 17 July. <https://www.rollingstone.com/movies/movie-news/the-look-of-silence-how-a-new-doc-revisits-indonesias-genocide-113990/> (last accessed 10 June 2021).

Harff, Barbara. 2003. 'No Lessons Learned from the Holocaust? Assessing Risks of Genocide and Political Mass Murder since 1955.' American Political Science Review 97.1: 57–73.

The Hole. Film. Directed by Tsai Min-Liang. Taiwan, France: Arc Light Films, Central Motion Pictures, China Television, Haut et Court, La Septe-Arte, 1998.

Katyn. Film. Directed by Andrzej Wajda. Poland: Akson Studio, TVP, Polski Instytut Sztuki Filmowej, Telekomunikacja Polska, 2007.

Kwok, Yenni. 2016. 'The Look of Silence and Indonesia's Quest for Truth and Reconciliation.' *Time*, 27 June. <https://time.com/4383283/the-look-of-silence-indonesia-1965-1966-killings-massacre-pki/> (last accessed 10 June 2021).

La Caze, Marguerite. 2019. *Ethical Restoration after Communal Violence: The Grieving and the Unrepentant*. Lanham, MD: Lexington.

Lang, Johannes. 2018. 'The Proud Executioner: Pride and the Psychology of Genocide.' In *Emotions and Mass Atrocity: Philosophical and Theoretical Explorations*, edited by Thomas Brudholm and Johannes Lang, 64–80. Cambridge: Cambridge University Press.

Levi, Primo. 1989. *The Drowned and the Saved*. Translated by Raymond Rosenthal. New York: Vintage.

The Look of Silence. Film. Directed by Joshua Oppenheimer. Denmark, Indonesia, Finland, Norway, UK, Israel, France, USA, Germany, Netherlands: Anonymous, Britdoc Foundation, Final Cut for Real, Making Movies Oy, Participant Media, Piraya Film A/S, Spring Films, 2014. DVD notes.

Melvin, Jess. 2018. *The Army and the Indonesian Genocide*. London: Routledge.

Melvin, Jess, and Annie Pohlman. 2018. 'A Case for Genocide: Indonesia, 1965–1966.' In *The Indonesian Genocide of 1965: Causes, Dynamics and Legacies*, edited by Katharine McGregor, Jess Melvin, and Annie Pohlman, 27–47. London: Palgrave Macmillan.

O'Falt, Chris. 2016. 'How the Oscar-Nominated *The Look of Silence* Uses Art to Spread Activism.' *Indiewire*, 26 February. <https://www.indiewire.com/2016/02/how-the-oscar-nominated-the-look-of-silence-uses-art-to-spread-activism-63862/> (last accessed 10 June 2021).

Oppenheimer, Joshua. 2014. 'The Act of Killing Has Helped Indonesia Reassess its Past and Present.' *The Guardian*, 26 February. <https://www.theguardian.com/commentisfree/2014/feb/25/the-act-of-killing-indonesia-past-present-1965-genocide> (last accessed 10 June 2021).

Oppenheimer, Joshua, and Michael Uwemedimo. 2012. 'Show of Force: A Cinema-Séance of Power and Violence in Sumatra's Plantation Belt.' In *Killer Images: Documentary Film, Memory and the Performance of Violence*, edited by Joram ten Brink and Joshua Oppenheimer, 287–310. New York: Columbia University Press.

Pohlman, Annie. 2016. 'A Year of Truth and the Possibilities for Reconciliation in Indonesia.' *Genocide Studies and Prevention: An International Journal* 10.1: 60–78.

Radzik, Linda. 2009. *Making Amends: Atonement in Morality, Law, and Politics*. Oxford: Oxford University Press.

Santoso, Aboeprijadi, and Gerry van Klinken. 2017. 'Genocide Finally Enters Public Discourse: The International People's Tribunal 1965.' *Journal of Genocide Research* 19.4: 594–608.

Schenkel, Hannah. 2015. 'Clarifying the Past: Joshua Oppenheimer's *The Look of Silence*.' *Metro Magazine* 186: 96–101.

Scott, Margaret. 2018. 'The Truth about the Killing Fields.' *The New York Review of Books*, 28 June, 33–5.

Shadow Play: Indonesia's Year of Living Dangerously. Film. Directed by Chris Hilton. Australia: Hilton Cordell Productions, 2003.

Shoah. Film. Directed by Claude Lanzmann. France, UK: British Broadcasting Corporation, Historia, Les Films Aleph, Ministère de la Culture de la Republique Française, 1985.

Simpson, Bradley. 2012. 'International Dimensions of the 1965–68 Violence in Indonesia.' In *The Contours of Mass Violence in Indonesia*, edited by Douglas Kammen and Katharine McGregor, 50–74. Singapore: NUS Press.

Sinnerbrink, Robert. 2016. *Cinematic Ethics: Exploring Ethical Experience through Film.* New York: Routledge.

Sinnerbrink, Robert. 2017. 'The Act of Witnessing: Cinematic Ethics in *The Look of Silence*.' *Post Script* 36.2–3: 31–45.

Stallabrass, Julian (ed.). 2013. *Documentary: Documents of Contemporary Art.* Cambridge, MA: MIT Press.

Stevens, Dana. 2015. '*The Look of Silence*: The Follow-Up to Joshua Oppenheimer's *Act of Killing* is Just as Beautiful – and Just as Disturbing.' *Slate*, 17 July. <https:// slate.com/culture/2015/07/the-look-of-silence-by-joshua-oppenheimer-reviewed. html> (last accessed 10 June 2021).

Stroszek. Film. Directed by Werner Herzog. West Germany: Werner Herzog Filmproduktion, Zweites Deutsches Fernsehen, Skellig Edition, 1977.

Teh, David, and Thomas J. Berghuis. 2015. 'The Act of Video: Reflections on Video Vortex #7 and Contemporary Video Practices in Indonesia.' *Theory, Culture and Society* 32.7–8: 215–30.

Varagur, Krithika. 2017. 'How the US Came to Declassify 30,000 Pages of American Embassy in Indonesia Files.' *Voa News*, 18 October <https://www.voanews.com/a/us-declassified-indonesian-embassy-files/4075504.html> (last accessed 19 March 2021).

Walker, Margaret Urban. 2006. *Moral Repair: Reconstructing Moral Relations after Wrongdoing.* Cambridge: Cambridge University Press.

Wilson, Jake. 2015. '*The Look of Silence* Review: Joshua Oppenheimer's *The Act of Killing* Follow-Up Powerful but Too Polished.' *Sydney Morning Herald*, 25 November. <https://www.smh.com.au/entertainment/movies/the-look-of-silence-review-joshua-oppenheimer-the-act-of-killing-followup-powerful-but-too-polished-20151125-gl7gcr. html> (last accessed 10 June 2021).

The Year of Living Dangerously. Film. Directed by Peter Weir. Australia, USA: McElroy & McElroy, Metro-Goldwyn-Mayer, 1982.

6. TRUTH, PERFORMANCE AND THE CLOSE-UP: PARADOXICAL CANDOUR IN ERROL MORRIS'S 'INTERROTRON' INTERVIEWS

Robert Sinnerbrink

The face has been central to cinematic presentation from early cinema to present-day digital media. Indeed, the conjunction of the close-up and its preferred subject – the human face – was quickly identified as one of the distinguishing features and artistic affordances of the new medium. Hugo Münsterberg identified the link between the close-up and the face, describing it as analogous to an attentive act of perception that brings its subjects closer to us in ways that other arts, such as theatre, cannot do: 'The close-up has objectified in our world of perception our mental act of attention and by it has furnished art with a means which far transcends the power of any theatre stage' (2002: 87). Jean Epstein praised the power of the close-up to capture the unique vitality and expressive movement of cinema, the *photogénie* expressing the 'soul of cinema' itself (1977: 9). Béla Balàzs defined the close-up as a 'technical condition of cinema', with its power of capturing and expressing the physiognomy not only of human faces but of landscapes and objects, which thereby become 'facialised' and expressive of an intertwining of subjectivity and objectivity (quoted in Doane 2003: 91). This fascination with the potentiality of the (facial) close-up was not confined to early film theorists but also extended across subsequent generations of film theory. As a mediating figure, Sergei Eisenstein reframed the manner in which the close-up tended to be treated as isolated or decontextualised, and drew attention to its significatory dimensions, arguing that its key feature is the link between focus and scale, the potential for desubjectification through scaling (magnification) (1949: 228–34). Christian Metz, in keeping with his attempts at articulating the significatory 'language' of cinematic images, described the close-up as a rhetorical form of synecdoche (part for whole) relation (1974: 67ff.). Gilles Deleuze, in his philosophical taxonomy of images and signs, referred to the close-up as extracting the depicted object 'from all spatio-temporal co-ordinates', raising the face or 'facialised' objects to the level of an expression of impersonalised affect, the close-up as expressing the 'state of an Entity' with particular affective force and qualitative meaning (1986: 87–90, 95–101).

As this brief survey suggests, there is no shortage of theoretical reflection on the significance of the facial close-up in narrative cinema. One of the key contrasts that emerges, moreover, is that between the subjective/expressive aspect of such images and their objective/significatory aspect. The close-up both expresses the subjectivity of a character, or a person, thereby playing a vital role in focusing, intensifying, and directing emotional engagement in narrative film; but it also presents a significatory dimension, pregnant with aesthetic fascination and symbolic meaning, that 'depersonalises' the face and evokes other dimensions of meaning, whether aesthetic, psychological, or moral. As Mary Ann Doane points out, this duality also manifested itself at the level of film theory, with contrasting traditions emphasising the subjective expressive dimensions of the (facial) close-up (from Münsterberg to contemporary cognitivist theories of empathy) and the objective significatory dimensions of the same shots (from Balázs to Deleuzian film theorists) (2003: 91–7). The fascination of facial close-ups is that they can bring both dimensions together in complex ways, both expressing the subjective feeling or emotions of a character and articulating powerful forms of aesthetic or symbolic meaning that go beyond the shot's immediate or indexical character.[1]

On the one hand, the facial close-up is the paradigmatic way in which emotion or feeling is expressed in narrative cinema, the magnification of, and intensive focus on, the face providing a powerful means of communicating emotional expression. On the other hand, theorists have long noted the 'artificial', stylised, distorting effects of the close-up, the manner in which isolating the face or its elements (eyes, mouth, and so on) can fragment or distort it in ways that are both fascinating and alienating. The expressive power of the facial close-up is connected with these subjective and objective dimensions of meaning, the simultaneous subjective/expressive and objective/distorting effect of both magnifying in scale and holding in time moving images that capture the face's communicative powers. In both respects, however, the facial close-up has typically been associated with narrative fiction film, as one of cinema's most distinctive features and powerful means of expression.

Documentary or non-fiction film, however, also uses the close-up to powerful effect, even though this has been somewhat neglected within the history of film theory. Nonetheless it has been used to characterise documentary subjects and elicit spectator engagement throughout the history of documentary, from

Robert Flaherty and direct cinema to contemporary 'hybrid' practitioners. As Ib Bondebjerg notes, emotion has remained a largely neglected topic in documentary theory, including cognitivist theories, which have tended to focus on narrative fiction film (2018: 21–37). Where documentary theorists have tackled questions of emotion, they have done so primarily in terms of psychoanalytic and phenomenological theories, or via the emphasis on questions of identity and cultural-political themes (Bondebjerg 2018: 24–5). They have also tended to adhere to the standard opposition between fiction as the 'genre of narratives, emotions and imagination' and documentary as the 'genre of direct representation of reality, rhetoric and rational arguments' (Bondebjerg 2018: 24). As against narrative cinema's discourse of emotional and imaginative play, documentary belongs to what Bill Nichols famously called the 'discourse of sobriety' (1991: 29), concerned more with rational or rhetorical persuasion than with imaginative engagement or emotional expression. As Bondebjerg (2018) and Carl Plantinga (2018) argue, however, we should resist this dichotomy and consider the full range of meaning, expression, and communication to be found in documentary film: the ways in which it combines elements of the discourse of imagination and emotional expression with the discourse of rational persuasion or evidentiary documentation.

To this end, I propose to consider the use of the facial close-up in documentary as a mode of *doubled presentation*, a mediated *and* performative act, on the part of both filmmaker *and* subject, involving both subjective/expressive and objective/significatory elements. The subject attempts to present him- or herself in an appropriate, persuasive, convincing, or desirable light, whereas the filmmaker – depending on the nature of the interview and role of the subject in the documentary – either may have the same ends in mind, accentuating or enhancing the subject's self-presentation, or may attempt to question, challenge, ironise, or undermine the subject's self-presentation. This doubled process of presentation involves an exchange between both filmmaker and subject, where the play between the filmmaker's characterisation of a documentary subject as attempting to reveal their truth or authenticity (or to expose their deceptiveness or inauthenticity) can clash with the subject's own attempts to convey a certain image or control the narrative, whether as interviewee, testimonial witness, or documentary subject. This is particularly important in documentaries that eschew conventional forms of sobriety and embrace contemporary forms of experimentation.

As Carl Plantinga points out, emotional engagement and imaginative involvement can be as relevant in documentary as in fiction film but they also raise important ethical issues concerning the characterisation of social actors on-screen (2018: 115–17). Techniques of eliciting either sympathy or antipathy (or as we shall see, eliciting both in a complex interplay) involving facial close-ups and interview sequences are essential to how such films are composed. As

Leger Grindon argues (2007), we should therefore consider more carefully the poetics of the interview within documentary film, exploring how such techniques can be used for evidentiary purposes, as supporting an argument, case, or point of view, but also for eliciting varying forms of emotional engagement and moral evaluation (involving sympathy, empathy, or ambivalence). From this perspective, we should consider also the performative aspect of the documentary face as both revealing and concealing, expressing and obscuring the veracity and authenticity of a documentary subject, often blending the related aspects of truthful presentation and fictionalising performance.

The Close-up and Facial Expressiveness

How do close-ups work? Why do scale, amplification, and facial focus generate affective and emotional responses? There are varying accounts of the relationship between facial and emotional expression, with naturalistic psychological and evolutionary accounts competing with sociological and cultural-historicist accounts (see Ekman 1992; Werth 2006). All agree, however, that the scaling and amplification of the human face, coupled with sustained focus over time on facial expressiveness, will tend to elicit powerful affective and emotional responses. These range from affective mimicry or emotional contagion responses to complex forms of emotional 'mind-reading' and moral evaluation of the sincerity or veracity of the emotional expressions on display. The question of facial expressiveness became particularly pertinent with the rise of photography and cinema, two media eminently suited to the depiction of the human face and physical movement. Modernity itself, moreover, has given the face a privileged position as locus of cultural of meaning, scientific object of study, and psychological means of manifesting the inner life of individuals within a technologically mediated environment (Werth 2006). As the great German sociologist Georg Simmel noted at the turn of the last century, 'the face was a means of studying the forms of human social life as they appeared in the "mirror" of the face, reflecting modern "inner life"'; Simmel linked the face's mobility to his emphasis 'on modernity's relativity and restless desirousness, its ceaseless flux' ([1901] 1965: 278–9, quoted in Werth 2006: 85). Such an emphasis, however, is hardly confined to Western modernity, even if technological media such as photography and cinema gave the face a privileged arena of artistic expression and cultural communication. In addition to cultural and social reasons for the focus on the face, coupled with the possibilities for facial close-ups afforded by the cinema, it is the central role of the face in the expression, communication, and elicitation of emotional response that makes it so important for film.

Although debate still persists concerning the cross-cultural universality versus specificity of facial expression, there is no doubt concerning the emotional expressivity of the face and its power to communicate as well as elicit emotional responses. Paul Ekman and his collaborators, for example, have defended the view that emotional expression has a biosocial basis – drawing on both evolutionary history and social-cultural development – and that basic emotions such as anger, fear, joy, sadness, and disgust have a universal dimension as well as a cross-cultural aspect (primarily concerning display rules regarding the degree and kind of emotional expression that is deemed appropriate within certain social situations) (Ekman 1998).[2] He cites evidence concerning the cross-cultural recognition of basic emotions and their consistency across widely differing groups or communities (Western and non-Western, literate and pre-literate), as well as evidence that many animals share similar kinds of basic emotional expression (Ekman and Keltner 1997). Basic emotions tend to occur in emotion families sharing related features or traits and are shaped by contextual features such as emotional 'plots' and social scripts (Ekman 1992). Basic emotions also have identifiable characteristics such as rapid onset, short duration, unbidden occurrence, automatic appraisal, and coherence among responses (Ekman 1992). One of the important features of basic emotions is that they have distinctive 'universal' or shared signals, most commonly recognisable facial expressions that can be modified or even feigned. Smiles, for example, are typically identifiable as either genuine expressions of joy (the Duchenne smile[3]) or variants that are to a large extent voluntary or feigned (for example, smiles expressing a social signal or social dominance).[4]

In short, the face retains a primacy in cinematic representations of emotion, whether fictional or non-fictional, precisely because of the interplay between shared or universally intelligible features of emotional expression and culturally specific display rules and customs. This also includes the standing possibility of deception, manipulation, and feigning of emotional states, which are surely universal across cultural and historical contexts as well. These elements come to the fore in the use of documentary interview sequences, particularly involving what I shall call the doubling of performative self-presentation and cinematic mediation, where documentary subjects strive to present a curated or stylised self-image, sometimes conflicting with the filmmakers' attempts to expose the subject to scrutiny or critical reflection.

THE CLOSE-UP IN DOCUMENTARY FILM

One of the most common phenomena associated with the close-up is that of affective mimicry or emotional contagion, the mirroring or mimicry of affected and emotional responses observed on-screen. Close-ups have long been recognised as the ideal means of communicating emotional expression via the face, which when sustained over time create ideal circumstances for what Plantinga (1999) has called 'scenes of empathy'. The latter are typically defined as sequences that involve explicit use of close-ups, well framed and contextualised in narrative terms, that are sustained over time, encouraging emotional engagement, and play a key role of generating moral sympathy (or antipathy) for characters. For these reasons they are most effective in inducing involuntary forms of affective mimicry and emotional contagion, which are also important in cueing and sustaining emotional engagement and thereby facilitating empathetic and sympathetic responses. The amplification and scaling involved in the close-up, providing rich and detailed depictions of the face, coupled with the affective cueing provided by music, lighting, and other sound and visual effects, typically sustained over time, make the facial close-up the favoured means of soliciting, sustaining, expressing, and communicating emotional responses. This has long been recognised as essential to narrative film but it has only recently become the object of theoretical reflection in the case of documentary or non-fiction film.

Carl Plantinga points out that documentaries typically engage in characterisation of social actors – providing a selective or stylised presentation of their qualities, personality, or attitudes – in ways that can be more or less truthful or veracious, more or less ethically justifiable (2018: 118–21). Characterisation involves many decisions concerning how to shoot, edit, and contextualise the presentation of an actual social individual. This means that such characterisations are not simply direct depictions of who they are, but rather a particular, contextualised *interpretation* of the individual depicted that has been selected and shaped for cinematic, dramatic, or rhetorical ends. It involves, as Plantinga remarks, the *characterisation* of documentary subjects: '[t]he necessity of selection and omission, emphasis, emplotting and point of view', which implies that 'the documentary filmmaker's characterisation of that person is a construction' (2018: 116).

This does not mean, however, that in using various cinematic techniques in order to characterise individuals in certain ways, documentaries are therefore akin to fictional narratives. Rather, it means that documentary filmmakers have a moral or ethical responsibility to characterise individuals in ways that are justifiable or that respect their 'dignity, identity, and right to privacy or self-determination' (or where this is not the case, that there are reasons justifying why an individual is presented in a morally questionable light) (Plantinga 2018: 116). At the same time, these ethical obligations on the part of filmmakers are also significant in respect of how audiences engage with such characters: how the presentation of individuals, especially during interview sequences, can be more or less truthful or representative, or can serve rhetorical, argumentative, or ethico-political ends.

Characterisation is intimately linked with character engagement, which is another similarity fictional and non-fictional cinematic works share, even though the expectations concerning fictional and non-fictional characters are quite different in each case. So how does such characterisation, especially where this involves the use of facial close-ups, differ in the case of documentary or non-fiction film? The most obvious difference concerns the differences between fictional characters and non-fictional persons (what Nichols (2001: 5) calls 'social actors'): spectators hermeneutically frame, contextualise, or index films as fictional or non-fictional, and thereby bring different expectations, assumptions, and evaluative criteria to each. I participate imaginatively in the fictional world of the film and engage emotionally with fictional characters, while at the same time being able to admire or enjoy the artistic value of the actors' performances (what Ed Tan (1996) calls 'artefact emotions', directed at the film or aspects of it as an artefact, as distinct from fictional emotions, directed at the narrative events or characters within the fiction).[5] In a non-fiction film, by contrast, I adopt a more critical evaluative stance, taking individuals depicted on-screen to be actual persons articulating their own experiences, views, or beliefs, while evaluating their utterances, claims, and demeanour for their sincerity, veracity, or plausibility. While I may admire Russell Crowe's performance as whistleblower Jeffrey Wigand in *The Insider* (1999, dir. Michael Mann), and become emotionally gripped and morally appalled at his plight, I would not take the same aesthetic or imaginative approach to such an individual within a whistleblower documentary. Indeed, while I may admire the moral courage and sympathise with the plight of Edward Snowden or Julian Assange, evaluating their testimony for sincerity, veracity, and plausibility, I would not be given to admiring the artistry of their on-screen performance, or moved to adopt an aesthetic attitude towards their impressive ability to portray (fictional) emotions. I can of course admire the way a documentary on such a subject is composed, such as Laura Poitras's *Citizenfour* (2014) on Snowden, or the remarkable transformation that occurs in filmmaker, documentary subject, and the relationship between filmmaker and subject in Bryan Fogel's *Icarus* (2017) (on Russian sports medicine doctor Grigory Rodchenkov and his role in the Russian state-sponsored sports doping programme). But in these cases – as in Morris's works – I am adopting a reflective attitude (and experiencing artefact emotions), admiring the manner in which a documentary is made, how the filmmaker presents his/her subject, or the relationship that unfolds between them, rather than adopting an aesthetic perspective on how charismatic, appealing, or convincing a given (social) actor might be on-screen.

There are, clearly, different aesthetic, imaginative, and epistemic attitudes taken towards fictional characters and documentary social actors. A screen actor, at one level, is a different entity from the character she portrays (Marilyn Monroe as Sugar Kane Kowalczyk in *Some Like It Hot* (1959, dir. Billy Wilder)); a documentary on an actor (for example, *Love, Marilyn* (2012, dir. Liz Garbus)), by contrast, presents the actor as its subject, who in this case is both Marilyn Monroe and Norma Jeane Baker/Mortenson. We can also have actors portraying actors in dramatised biopics (Michelle Williams as Marilyn in *My Week with Marilyn* (2011, dir. Simon Curtis)), which can cross over between fictional and documentary modes in interesting ways. In a narrative fiction, I imagine a fictional character, want to know what their actions, expressions, and utterances mean in narrative terms, and can admire the quality of the actor's performance in portraying the character. In a documentary, where we are dealing with non-fictional situations and historical contexts, I can imagine what the subject's situation is like, evaluate whether their testimony is truthful or sincere, mendacious or misleading, informative and illuminating, or ambiguous and perplexing, but do not generally take an aesthetic attitude regarding their performance on-screen. It is true that I may be impressed or appalled, fascinated or repulsed by the attitudes, views, or mode of self-presentation that he or she may adopt (for example, the state-sponsored gangster-killers in Joshua Oppenheimer's *The Act of Killing* (*Jagal*, 2012)). Or I may be impressed, puzzled, or disturbed by the filmmaker's strategies or directorial decisions and reflect upon the ethical meaning and implications of his or her approach to their documentary subjects.[6] In either case, the fact that documentaries involve characterisation, narrativisation, and dramatisation, along with aesthetic techniques used for rhetorical purposes, does not mean documentaries are fictional, even though they may have elements in common with fictional narratives.

This is because there are always background claims to truth, veracity, authenticity, or factuality that remain pertinent, a set of hermeneutic commitments or assumptions that remain essential, for evaluating the critical claims made by non-fiction films precisely *as non-fictional*. Such films, to put it simply, refer not to fictional worlds but to real individuals, events, or social, historical, or political situations pertaining to our shared actual world. Fiction films generally do not solicit such attitudes as the predominant mode of engaging with what the narrative depicts (although they may be pertinent in the case of historical fictions), while documentary films generally do not solicit aesthetic attitudes as the predominant mode of evaluating the film's claims (although they may play a role in more subjective, experimental, performative, and poetic modes of documentary, without, however, neutralising their underlying claims to truthfulness, veracity, or plausibility).

These contrasting modes of evaluation, and the possibility of their interplay, are what make 'fake' documentaries or 'mockumentaries' so compelling or intriguing. The fake documentary is parasitic upon the claims to veracity, truthfulness, and plausibility of genuine documentary but adopts the techniques and modes of documentary address in a 'fictional' mode. Such works simulate a documentary style that solicits epistemic and evaluative attitudes typically associated with documentary, while being based upon the aesthetic, dramatic, and imaginative attitudes we typically adopt towards fictional narratives (given that we are generally contextually cued as to the fictional character of the documentary once it has been 'indexed' that way in terms of its reception) (see Plantinga 2018: 116). One can have simultaneous aesthetic and imaginative responses to a well-crafted or convincing fake documentary, entertaining the imaginative possibility or idea of such a scenario (Could something like this really have happened? What would that have been like?) while at the same time admiring the skill, artistry, and plausibility of the fake documentary itself.[7]

Although boundaries between fictional and non-fictional works may be porous, and techniques pertaining to both can overlap, and attitudes typically adopted towards each can be manipulated, there nonetheless remain important differences between the two that are not to be ignored, especially concerning the epistemic and hermeneutic attitudes we bring to understanding such films. To sceptically dismiss a Holocaust documentary – say, the remarkable *Auschwitz Untold: In Colour* (2020, dir. David Shulman) – as failing to be able to make historical, epistemic, scientific, moral, or political claims to truthfulness or plausibility simply because no documentary can lay claim to 'absolute truth' (in this example, because black-and-white footage of the victims in the camp has been colourised) or, as a corollary, point out errors, distortions, or falsehoods, would be dogmatic and nihilistic scepticism of the worst kind.[8] The fact that we can distinguish between 'true' and 'fake' documentaries presupposes such a distinction between them. It also suggests that, notwithstanding the prevailing scepticism towards claims to truth in respect of documentary film, we do presuppose that documentaries can make truthful claims, or expose falsehoods and (ideological) distortions, for otherwise there would be no grounds for distinguishing fake from true documentaries. This remains true even when theorists mistakenly claim that any complexification of the truth/falsity distinction means that objectivity is unavailable, hence that 'there is no truth': the difficulty of attaining truth, or the fallibility of our knowledge claims, or the challenges of attaining objectivity, does not mean that there is no truth or that we can never know anything.[9]

DOCUMENTARY SELF-PRESENTATION AND PARADOXICAL CANDOUR

What happens, however, when documentaries focus on the truthfulness or deceptiveness of a social actor or real individual, using extended sequences involving facial close-ups in order to both reveal and scrutinise the individual's testimony or mode of self-presentation? I shall address this question by considering examples of documentary self-presentation where the question of the truth, veracity, or authenticity of the subject's testimony, discourse, and manner of self-presentation are at stake. This will enable me to consider the question of truthfulness (and deceptiveness), and the key role played by facial close-ups, in both presenting and examining the social actors in question. This in turn opens up broader questions of truth, performance, and appearance when presented via the medium of cinema.[10]

As with social interaction more generally, documentary self-presentation involves both subjective and intersubjective ('objective') aspects, which we could also call *performative* and *evidentiary* aspects. Any act or process of intersubjective communication involves a subjective aspect (one's perceptions, beliefs, attitudes, and intentions) and an intersubjective aspect (what the other party perceives, interprets, understands of the interaction, and the social context as shaped by tacit rules or norms of communicative engagement). There are also complex perspectival dimensions at play. There is what I intend to say or communicate, how I take myself to be as a person, what I take the other person to be, as well as what I take the other person to take me as being, and so on. The same is true of the other party in the interaction, so the possibilities for ambiguity, error, misunderstanding, and miscommunication are considerable. All such interactions are shaped, constrained, and structured, moreover, by social norms of communication and interaction as well as ideological prejudices and implicit biases.

Once this complex hermeneutic communicative situation is modified or extended via the addition of a camera, say in a documentary interview situation, the possibilities multiply even further. If I am the subject of a documentary interview, there is what I bring to the interview situation, how I take myself to be, what I intend to communicate on-screen, as well as what I take the filmmaker to want, how they are as an interlocutor, what they want to get out of the interview, how they regard me and the reason for my being interviewed, and so on. For the filmmaker, the same applies, with certain asymmetries. There is what the filmmaker brings to both film and interview situation, the beliefs or attitudes they bring to the interview, how they take the interview subject to be as far as personality or character is concerned, what they intend the interview to achieve, how they take the interview subject to be approaching the interview and the filmmaker him- or herself, and how the interview footage will be treated in post-production, perhaps the most important part of the documentary exchange.

To this we must add the same kinds of hermeneutic conditions and meaning constraints that apply in the reception of the film, what audiences bring to, draw on, and make of the film or interview sequences, how these are interpreted in light of viewer 'prejudices' (hermeneutic assumptions, standing beliefs, normatively constrained ways of understanding), and so forth. This brief sketch of the hermeneutic complexities of the interview situation – a conventionalised communicative performance staged and recorded on camera and shaped into an argumentative, rhetorical, epistemic, as well as dramatic component of the film – suggests that we need to examine more closely how the questions of truth, veracity, and authenticity are performed within documentary interviews.

Indeed, as I discuss below, this complex hermeneutic situation itself becomes the very question posed by a documentary focusing on a significant or ambiguous social actor or historical individual.

What are the evidentiary and performative aspects of the documentary interview situation, particularly those involving extended sequences of facial close-ups? On the one hand, as Bill Nichols remarks, every documentary, including individual shots or sequences, presents an evidentiary aspect (2016b: 99–110): 'documenting', so to speak, that such and such an individual was filmed at such and such a time and location, that he or she communicated certain things, presenting him- or herself in certain ways, gave a certain kind of testimony or responses to questions, and so on. Or that certain kinds of documentary footage capture a profilmic reality that takes on a primary evidentiary character that shares certain features with eyewitness footage or CCTV camera footage (for example, the infamous Rodney King police beating footage or concealed camera footage). Evidentiary documentary interview footage retains a strongly 'realist' character, showing the interview subject's appearance and demeanour, recording their speech, expressions, and gestures, and depicting them as trustworthy or dubious, sincere or insincere, convincing or suspicious, depending on the context, subject, and circumstances.

On the other hand, such sequences also have a *performative* dimension involving what I have called a doubled presentation of self on-screen. By this I mean the manner in which both filmmaker and documentary subject aim to portray either themselves, an issue, an argument, a perspective, an event, or a situation, in a particular light for the intended audience of the documentary. A filmmaker, for example, might intend to present evidence supporting a point of view, an account of events, or a broader argument or case, and the interview subject in this respect will offer testimony, evidence, eyewitness corroboration, or narrative elaboration supporting the intended thesis or claims (for example, the former SeaWorld employees turned whistleblowers in Gabriela Cowperthwaite's *Blackfish* (2013), an exposé of the unethical practices behind SeaWorld orca and dolphin entertainment shows, and exploring the conditions behind the death of Dawn Brancheau, killed by Tilikum, the abused orca at the centre of the documentary). Or the filmmaker may intend to show the unreliability, falseness, or inauthenticity of the interview subject, perhaps editing the footage in such a way as to suggest their untrustworthiness or moral dubiousness, for instance, Michael Moore's editing of such interview or attempted interview footage in *Roger and Me* (1989). The performative aspect of documentary interview, by contrast, involves the subject's attempts to present themselves as honest or sincere, truthful or trustworthy, believable or authoritative, as the case may be, and the correlated attempts of the filmmaker either to enhance these impressions or else question them, depending on the context and subject matter at hand.

PARADOXICAL CANDOUR

These are the two most common scenarios in documentaries that use extended or intimate interview sequences in order to characterise their interviewees in particular ways and thus to foster the claims or point of view that the documentary aims to convey. There is, however, a third alternative. In some cases, the complex dialectical interplay between these perspectives, the doubled presentation of self that occurs on-screen – the attempted self-presentation of the subject and the mediated representation of that subject's self-presentation by the filmmaker – becomes a key focus of the exchange in its own right. This is what I am calling the 'paradoxical candour' on display in certain documentary exchanges, which involves the subject striving to present themselves in a convincing light, and the filmmaker attempting to cast critical light on that very self-presentation, resulting in an ambiguous contest or struggle for hermeneutic or narrative control. The filmmaker, for example, may want to 'catch out' the interviewee by exposing their mendacity or unreliability, whereas the interviewee might aim to outwit, control, or even mislead the filmmaker, using the interview format to present a certain image of themselves or manage the narrative account of events or claims in question, steering it in their preferred direction. The television media interview, particularly those involving high-profile political figures answering accusations, is a familiar example. In such cases, however, the interviewee has only limited capacity to 'control' or direct the manner in which their self-presentation is rendered on camera, let alone how the footage will be used after the interview has concluded. The extended interview sequences, however, found in documentaries such as Errol Morris's *The Fog of War* (2003, on Robert P. McNamara) or *The Unknown Known* (2013, on Donald Rumsfeld), offer more complex and interesting cases of the dialectical dance between filmmaker and interviewee. For these performative interview sequences feature extended struggles between filmmaker and subject for hermeneutic control over the narrative perspective and affective orientation of the interview and how it may figure in the documentary's overall argument.

What such sequences reveal is the complex interplay of perspectives between filmmaker and subject: the dialectic of disclosure and deception, of involuntary self-expression and intentional modulation or manipulation of self-expression that characterises their exchanges on-screen. The interplay of these contrasting and often conflicting points of view gives these documentary sequences their fascinating quality of being at once candid and constructed, revealing and concealing their subjects in an ambiguous manner. They offer a penetrating critical exposé and a demonstration of deception, making the hermeneutic struggle between filmmaker and subject in search of the truth, or attempting to elude it, the dramatic as much as ethical focus of the film.[11] This is what I am calling the 'paradox of candour' evident in documentaries featuring extended interview sequences: the more the subject reveals him- or herself, the more ambiguous or inscrutable he or she becomes; the more the interview subject aims to modulate or control his or her self-presentation on camera, the more undecidable, or, on the other hand, revelatory, the interview can become. In doing so, these sequences inadvertently reveal the subtle forms of concealment or manipulation of self-disclosure that contribute to the filmmaker's aims of 'catching' the subject in the act of deception, or controlling the hermeneutic battle for truth at play between them.

There are many recent (and not so recent) documentaries where this paradox of candour is evident. These are films that focus on the interplay of candour and concealment, self-disclosure and self-deception, transparency and opacity, sincerity and stylisation, openness and subterfuge, authenticity and inauthenticity that unfolds between filmmaker and subject. Consider, for example, 'Little Evie' in the Maysles Brothers' *Grey Gardens* (1975), Timothy Treadwell in Werner Herzog's *Grizzly Man* (2005), Robert P. McNamara in *The Fog of War*, Anwar Congo in *The Act of Killing*, Donald Rumsfeld in *The Unknown Known*, Inong and Amir Sirhaan in *The Look of Silence* (2014, dir. Joshua Oppenheimer/ Anonymous), and Elizabeth Holmes in Alex Gibney's *The Inventor: Out for Blood in Silicon Valley* (2019), among many others.

Morris's 'Interrotron' Interviews

Errol Morris's recent works – *The Fog of War* (2003), *Standard Operating Procedure* (2008), and *The Unknown Known* (2013) – offer fascinating case studies in the paradox of candour, focusing on high-profile individuals within the government and the military, most of whom played a direct role in important historical and political events. Both *The Fog of War* and *The Unknown Known* focus on major American political figures (Robert P. McNamara and Donald Rumsfeld, respectively), using extended interview sequences, coupled with stylised graphics and found footage, as well as imaginative audiovisual sequences accompanying but also commenting on the interview sequences. So far this conforms to most standard expository-style documentary but Morris's works go several steps further. Their aim is more ambitious than to simply chronicle historical events by drawing on commentary offered by key historical players. Rather, Morris undertakes the much more demanding exercise of presenting a 'political psychology' (Pippin 2013) that not only examines and scrutinises the moral psychology and subjective self-presentation of the interview subject but examines the psychological perspectives, moral-political beliefs, and ideological horizons of these individuals and what they represent. Key to linking both aspects – moral psychology and political psychology – is examining the manner in which ethical attitudes and political beliefs are imbricated with each other, along with the way that emotional self-display is intertwined with emotional self-control, the manner in which the subject performs both candour and concealment, self-disclosure and self-deception, in attempting to narrate and justify their historical and political actions and decisions. These are films that meticulously document and cinematically foreground the protagonists' performative projection of a carefully curated self-image coupled with their unintentional self-revelation of how political power is intertwined with moral and emotional self-fashioning (see Ricciardelli 2010).

One of the primary ways in which these elements are articulated in the film is via extended interview sequences using Morris's famous 'Interrotron' device (which allows the interviewee to gaze directly at the interviewer's image projected on a screen affixed to the camera, thus giving an uncanny direct address effect as the interviewee addresses Morris's image and thereby appears to address us as viewers). The effect is to enable direct facial close-ups to be captured during long-take interview sequences that offer extraordinarily open access to the interviewee's facial expressions and intonations sustained over time. In both *The Fog of War* and *The Unknown Known*, the faces of McNamara and Rumsfeld provide the anchoring points of the film, commanding our attention and demanding our scrutiny as to their sincerity and veracity. Morris also composes both films as structured as a series of 'lessons' or 'chapters' on what we could construe as a historical chronicle or non-fictional 'novel' featuring McNamara and Rumsfeld as first-person narrators of the historical events and political situations in which they participated, both as protagonists and as observers.

Indeed, Morris has remarked that his inspiration in non-fiction filmmaking focusing on particular individuals is 'the metaphor of Nabokov's "self-deceived narrators"' (quoted in Druick 2007: 208). The question posed to the viewer is therefore whether these 'narrators' – offering first-person accounts of tumultuous political events in American history such as the Vietnam War or the Iraq War – are trustworthy and reliable or unreliable and manipulative. That McNamara and Rumsfeld, two skilled and seasoned media performers and highly experienced political figures, agreed to Morris's extended Interrotron interview format suggests that they were confident they could control or direct the interview sessions, steering the narrative where they preferred. At the same time, Morris's Interrotron interviews strive to capture their gaze directly addressing the camera/spectator, revealing their facial expressions in minute detail. The result is to create a fascinating interplay between Morris as offscreen interviewer (frequently heard as he poses questions to his subjects), found historical and political media images and footage, atmospheric musical accompaniment, and Morris's signature artful visual vignettes, using objects, symbols, and graphics in ways that both illustrate as well as question the verbal accounts that both McNamara and Rumsfeld give concerning their roles in key political events.

ROBERT SINNERBRINK

The opening sequence of *The Unknown Known* is a case in point. Morris's voice can be heard asking if we can 'put up the next memo', against a background drone of informational static. This is followed by a close shot of Rumsfeld against a neutral dark background, slightly off-centre but gazing directly at us, asking, 'Do you want me to read this?' As he does so, we cut to a close shot of the typewritten memo: 'February 4, 2004': 'SUBJECT: What You Know'. What follows is Rumsfeld's most famous quotation from the period, each sentence – or rather key phrase – given its own close shot, illuminating the words fringed with shadows: 'There are known knowns. There are known unknowns. There are unknown unknowns. But there are also unknown knowns. That is to say, things you think you know that it turns out you did not.' The sequence gives way to a shot of the ocean surface, taken from a great height, as the title appears on-screen ('The Unknown Known'). This brief sequence captures well the intriguing interplay of perspectives, both cooperative and conflictual, between filmmaker and subject, which becomes more pronounced as the film unfolds, and to which Morris and Rumsfeld return at the end, the Interrotron interview sequences providing a performative elaboration of the meaning of the enigmatic phrase 'unknown knowns'.

Indeed, the entire film can be understood as a meditation on this memo, with its intriguing epistemological subtleties. It refers not only to the difficulty of making weighty political decisions amidst tumultuous political conflicts, but to the enigmatic character of Rumsfeld himself, whose combination of candour and deceptiveness, interweaving arrogant self-justification and occasional selective self-reflection, makes him such a compelling documentary interviewee. Morris and Rumsfeld work together, developing an intriguing relationship, Morris directing Rumsfeld to read his own memo, Rumsfeld immediately showing what a skilled media and political performer he is – his demeanour and voice perfectly calibrated to deliver the lines with steely authority and precision, while his face retains its familiar air of resolute purpose and amused irony.

This opening exchange sets the stage for the rest of the film, which focuses on deciphering a sample of Rumsfeld's thousands of political memos ('snowflakes') dictated over the course of many decades in the White House – a remarkable historical and political archive as well as a fascinating source of evidence to decipher the ideological and political 'mindset' of both Rumsfeld as a political figure and the American government administrations that he represented. The battle between filmmaker and interviewee – Morris providing Rumsfeld with a platform to explain his political decisions while also pressing him to reveal his subterfuges and deceptions, with Rumsfeld aiming to maintain control over the narrative, justifying the Bush administration's prosecuting of the 'War on Terror' – becomes the central drama of the film, which ends on the same note of epistemic and moral ambiguity on which it began.

Towards the end of the film, Rumsfeld returns to the 'Unknown Knowns' memo we encountered at the beginning of the film, ruminating on another possibility or reinterpretation than the one he originally gave. Rumsfeld remarks that there is actually a fourth epistemic possibility, a missing hermeneutic perspective, namely: 'Things that you may possibly know, that you don't know you know.' At this point, Morris interjects from offscreen, remarking that the original memo does not say that we know more in this case but rather that we know less than we think we do. Rumsfeld seems perplexed, asking to see the memo again, then remarks, after rereading the line in a measured manner, that he still thinks the memo should have stated the reverse of what it does: namely, that 'unknown knowns' are things that we may know but do not know that we do. The fact that these could be taken as two slightly different senses regarding the same point – that things we may know but without any certainty could also be things that we think we know that turn out to be wrong – seems to trouble or perplex him; he is far more inclined, in retrospect, to emphasise the possibility that we may be right, without knowing it, rather than that we may be wrong, without knowing it.

It is clear throughout this exchange, moreover, and many others punctuating the film, that Morris and Rumsfeld are referring in the end to the US government's claim that Saddam Hussein had stockpiled weapons of mass destruction (WMDs), and so needed to be deposed and his regime dismantled. This clearly qualifies as a paradigmatic case of an 'unknown known': Rumsfeld and the Bush administration thought that they knew Hussein had WMDs but it turns out that he did not, which Rumsfeld in retrospect prefers to construe as the US possibly knowing that Hussein had such weapons without knowing (for sure) that he did so. This subtle and ambiguous shift – from thinking we know something but being proven wrong to possibly knowing something without knowing with certainty that we do – exemplifies that complex game of truth, power, and historical revisionism being conducted through the Morris–Rumsfeld exchanges in *The Unknown Known*.

What becomes clear, moreover, in both *The Fog of War* and *The Unknown Known* is that Morris's focus on their faces not only contributes to characterising McNamara and Rumsfeld, but also enables us to submit their testimony and commentary to critical scrutiny. One intriguing issue the Interrotron interviews raise is that of sympathy/empathy: does the use of extended facial close-ups, and particularly direct address responses, including episodes of emotional display – both McNamara and Rumsfeld become visibly upset and emotional recounting anecdotes concerning fallen soldiers or soldiers recovering from injury – encourage a sympathetic/empathetic response to these candid and controversial interviewees? Indeed, some critics have opined that, given the exclusive focus on McNamara and Morris (whose interviews occupy the entirety of the film), and particularly the extensive use of direct address facial close-ups, Morris ends up inviting a sympathetic understanding of his subjects and so must therefore, at some level, share his subjects' political views.

What these films show, however, is that close-ups do not always equate with the generation of sympathetic responses, as is typically the case with their use in fiction film: much like the debate over point of view shots and central versus acentral imagining, context, characterisation, and other cinematic cues shape the meaning and significance of the use of close-ups in fiction as well as non-fiction film.[12] Indeed, it is difficult to engage emotionally with either McNamara or Rumsfeld given the context of their interviews, the political history of which they were a part, the otherwise opaque facial expressions and measured, precise, articulate manner of their speech. This is even before we get to the often shocking, chilling, or confronting content of their discussions.[13] Rather, their mask-like physiognomies invite critical fascination as well as distanced scrutiny: instead of emotional engagement, Morris's use of direct address close-ups prompts emotional estrangement and critical reflection in these intensive and stylised interview sequences. The scaling and focus on their faces that would ordinarily elicit sympathetic engagement is, in these instances, paradoxically strained: the interviewees' unnervingly direct gaze into the camera means that the spectator simultaneously occupies the position, if not role, of the interviewer/filmmaker, that is, interlocutor/addressee, while also occupying the more conventional position of observer/spectator both beholding and reflecting upon the visages directly addressing us.

Morris's Interrotron interviews involve the interplay of evidentiary and performative aspects of self-disclosure presented and performed by his politically powerful interviewees. His use of direct address facial close-ups comprising extended interview sequences, positioning the spectator in the place of interlocutor/addressee as well as spectatorial observer, thus solicits an ambiguous and ambivalent mode of engagement that I have described as the paradox of candour: the more 'intimate' the depiction of the subject, the more distanced they become from the spectator, who is encouraged to shift from sympathetic engagement or moral allegiance to a more critical scrutiny and ethical questioning of the veracity, authenticity, and plausibility of the interviewees' discourse. These documentaries represent a very particular form of this paradox, which is evident in works that seek to expose their subject but has a quite different effect in cases where the intimacy revealed during filmed interviews has an alternative purpose (such as revealing the state of mind of the subject).[14]

This dialectical tension between truthful self-presentation and modulated/manipulated performance is powerfully present in Morris's Interrotron interviews, which evoke psychological/emotional candour and moral/psychological ambiguity at once. This ambiguity of both interviewees' modes of self-disclosure and their ambivalent accounts of the political-historical events they justify lie at the core of these two documentary 'moral' experiments. They do not show, contra standard sceptical views in documentary theory, that truth is impossible to reach or merely relative to historical context or subjective perspectives, but rather that the truth of the subject – in this case historical and political subjects who attempt to both reveal and control the narrative perspective on events in which they took part – is at once ambiguous and opaque, pluralistic and political, demanding careful critical scrutiny as well as moral-political reflection. In these remarkably ambiguous examples of performative cinematic self-disclosure, we are left to ponder the many 'unknown knowns' that Morris's paradoxically candid Interrotron interviewees represent.

NOTES

1. Consider the extraordinary close-ups of Maria Falconetti in Carl Theodor Dreyer's *The Passion of Joan of Arc* (1928) as expressing both these dimensions very powerfully (affective subjective expression and symbolic or transcendent meaning).
2. For a critique of universalist accounts of facial expression, see Gendron et al. (2018). Critics of the universalist position argue that evidence of cultural variation in the expression and interpretation of emotion refutes claims that emotional expression can be universally shared. It is worth pointing out, however, that the display rules and other forms of cultural modification of emotional expression presuppose the kind of universal intelligibility and social communicability of emotional expression at issue (otherwise there would be no need or basis for feigning, modulating, or moderating such expressions in particular contexts).
3. The Duchenne smile, named after nineteenth-century French neurologist Guillame Duchenne, involves both the zygomatic major muscle (which raises the corners of the mouth) and the orbicularis oculi muscle (which contracts the cheek and other muscles around the eyes), resulting in the characteristic wrinkling or 'crows' feet' around the eyes. In the majority of people, these muscles cannot both be activated at will, hence these signs used as indicators of a smile expressing genuine pleasure or joy rather than signalling approval or friendliness.
4. Interestingly, much of the research on the expression and intelligibility of basic emotions has used photographs or in many cases video recordings of individuals, which raises the interesting question as to what extent in situ expressions of emotion can be equated with filmed (or acted) versions of emotional display.
5. See also the debate concerning emotional responses to fictional characters, sparked by Radford (1975) on the 'irrationality' of responding emotionally to fictional characters that we know do not exist. See Carroll (1990); Dadlez (2010); Currie (1995); Plantinga (2009a); Thomson-Jones (2008); Walton (1990).
6. See, for example, Bill Nichols's (2016a) critique of Morris's focus on the perpetrators of the Abu Ghraib abuses interviewed in *Standard Operating Procedure* (2008).
7. A good example is William Karel's remarkable demonstration of how easily media conspiracy theories can be generated, *The Dark Side of the Moon* (*Opération Lune*) (2002), a fake documentary on build-up to the 1969 moon landing, which, as urban legend has it, was 'faked' in a secret studio by Stanley Kubrick.

8. Morris's fascinating and unnerving study of capital punishment expert turned Holocaust denier, Fred A. Leuchter, in *Mr. Death: The Rise and Fall of Fred A. Leuchter, Jr.* (1999) is a case in point.
9. See Renov (1993) and Winston (1993) for representative renderings of the critique of objectivity and scepticism towards attaining truth in documentary. See the early essays by Carroll (1983, 1996) and Plantinga (1997) for critical responses to this pervasive scepticism concerning documentary truth claims. For more recent versions of this debate, see Renov (2004) and Plantinga (2005, 2009b).
10. See MacDougall (1999) for an interesting discussion, from a visual anthropologist's perspective, of the challenges facing ethnographic filmmakers who reflect upon their practice and involvement in the documentation of individuals from diverse cultures.
11. Werner Herzog's films on prisoners facing execution – *Into the Abyss* (2011) and the *On Death Row* television series (2012) – offer compelling but related contrast cases. Unlike Morris's attempts to 'catch out' his subjects, Herzog's uncannily direct question-and-answer interviews appear to create a space in which to draw out their subjects, inviting them to reveal their state of mind candidly in ways that might otherwise not be possible.
12. Consider, for example, the extreme facial close-ups used in the encounter between Clarice Starling and Hannibal Lecter in Jonathan Demme's *Silence of the Lambs* (1991): in Clarice's close-ups the effect is to generate sympathetic emotional engagement and moral allegiance; with Lecter's close-ups, on the contrary, it is to present his face as a disturbing opaque mask, devoid of particular expression, thus generating emotional estrangement and moral-cognitive dissonance. Suffice to say that Rumsfeld's image, in particular, is closer to the Lecter close-up than the Starling close-up.
13. McNamara, who adopts a more reflective historical perspective on the 'lessons' drawn from his political career, does not shy away from bluntly describing his role in the incendiary bombing raids on Tokyo that killed '100,000 civilians' in one night during World War II, and other atrocities that he admits would count as 'war crimes', whereas Rumsfeld, without the benefit of historical distance or reflective distance, prefers to avoid direct acknowledgement of such crimes and reverts to euphemism, colloquialisms, and other rhetorical means of downplaying, justifying, or relativising the deaths and destruction caused by the Bush administration's prosecuting of the 'War on Terror' and disastrous occupation of Iraq.
14. As remarked, one could productively contrast Herzog's use of related techniques in documentaries such as *Into the Abyss* or the carefully composed and 'annotated' use of found footage by Timothy Treadwell in *Grizzly Man*.

REFERENCES

The Act of Killing (Jagal). Documentary. Directed by Joshua Oppenheimer, Anonymous, and Cynthia Cynn. UK, Denmark, Norway: Final Cut for Real, 2012.
Auschwitz Untold: In Colour. TV series. Directed by David Shulman. USA, UK: Fulwell 73, 2020.
Blackfish. Documentary. Directed by Gabriela Cowperthwaite. USA: CNN Films, 2013.

Bondebjerg, Ib. 2018. 'A Documentary of the Mind: Self, Cognition and Imagination in Anders Østergaard's Films.' In *Cognitive Theory and Documentary Film*, edited by Catalin Brylla and Mette Kramer, 21–37. Cham: Palgrave Macmillan.

Carroll, Noël. 1983. 'From Real to Reel: Entangled in Nonfiction Film.' *Philosophic Exchange* 14.1: Article 1. <http://digitalcommons.brockport.edu/phil_ex/vol14/iss1/1> (last accessed 22 March 2021).

Carroll, Noël. 1990. *The Philosophy of Horror; or, the Paradoxes of the Heart*. London and New York: Routledge.

Carroll, Noël. 1996. 'Nonfiction Film and Postmodern Skepticism.' In *Post-Theory: Reconstructing Film Studies*, edited by David Bordwell and Noël Carroll, 283–306. Madison: University of Wisconsin Press.

Citizenfour. Documentary. Directed by Laura Poitras. USA, Germany, UK: Praxis Films, 2014.

Currie, Gregory. 1995. *Image and Mind: Film, Philosophy, and Cognitive Science*. New York: Cambridge University Press.

Dadlez, Eva M. 2010. 'Seeing and Imagination: Emotional Response to Fiction Film.' *Midwest Studies in Philosophy* 34: 120–35.

The Dark Side of the Moon (*Opération lune*). Documentary. Directed by William Karel. France: ARTE, 2002.

Deleuze, Gilles. 1986. *Cinema 1: The Movement-Image*, translated by Hugh Tomlinson and Barbara Habberjam. Minneapolis: University of Minnesota Press.

Doane, Mary Anne. 2003. 'The Close-Up: Scale and Detail in the Cinema.' *differences: A Journal of Feminist Cultural Studies* 14.3 (Fall): 89–111.

Druick, Zoe. 2007. 'Documenting False History: Errol Morris and *Mr. Death*.' *Studies in Documentary Film* 1.3: 207–10.

Eisenstein, Sergei. 1949. *Film Form: Essays in Film Theory*, edited and translated by Jay Leyda. San Diego: Harcourt.

Ekman, Paul. 1992. 'An Argument for Basic Emotions.' *Cognition and Emotion* 6.3/4: 169–200.

Ekman, Paul. 1998. 'Afterword: Universality of Emotional Expression? A Personal History.' In Charles Darwin, *The Expression of Emotion in Man and Animals*. 3rd edition, 363–93. New York and Oxford: Oxford University Press.

Ekman, Paul, and Dacher Keltner. 1997. 'Universal Facial Expressions of Emotion: An Old Controversy and New Findings.' In *Nonverbal Communication: Where Nature Meets Culture*, edited by Ullica Segerstråle and Peter Molnár, 27–45. Mahwah, NJ: Lawrence Erlbaum Associates.

Epstein, Jean. 1977. 'Magnification and Other Writings', translated by Stuart Liebman. *October* 3 (Spring): 9–25.

The Fog of War: Eleven Lessons from the Life of Robert S. McNamara. Documentary. Directed by Errol Morris. USA: Sony Pictures Classics, 2003.

Gendron, Maria, Carlos Crivelli, and Lisa Feldman Barrett. 2018. 'Universality Reconsidered: Diversity in Making Meaning of Facial Expressiveness.' *Current Directions in Psychological Science* 27.4: 211–91.

Grey Gardens. Documentary. Directed by Ellen Hovde, Albert Maysles, David Maysles, Muffie Meyer. USA: Portrait Films, Maysles Films, 1975.

Grindon, Leger. 2007. 'Q&A: Poetics of the Documentary Interview.' *The Velvet Light Trap* 60 (Fall): 4–12.

Grizzly Man. Documentary. Directed by Werner Herzog. USA: Lions Gate Films, Discovery Films, 2005.

Icarus. Documentary. Directed by Bryan Fogel. USA: Alex Productions, 2017.

The Insider. Film. Directed by Michael Mann. USA: Touchstone Pictures, 1999.

Into the Abyss. Documentary. Directed by Werner Herzog. USA, UK, Germany. Creative Differences Projects, Skellig Rock, Spring Films, 2011.

The Inventor: Out for Blood in Silicon Valley. Documentary. Directed by Alex Gibney. USA: HBO Documentary Films, 2019.

The Look of Silence. Documentary. Directed by Joshua Oppenheimer, Anonymous, Cynthia Cynn. Denmark, Indonesia, Finland, Norway, UK, Israel, France, USA, Germany, Netherlands: Anonymous, Britdoc Foundation, Final Cut for Real, 2015.

Love, Marilyn. Documentary. Directed by Liz Garbus. USA, France: Diamond Girl Productions, 2012.

MacDougall, David. 1999. *Transcultural Cinema*, edited with an introduction by Lucien Taylor. Princeton, NJ: Princeton University Press.

Metz, Christian. 1974. *Film Language: A Semiotics of the Cinema*, translated by Michael Taylor. Oxford and New York: Oxford University Press.

Mr. Death: The Rise and Fall of Fred A. Leuchter, Jr. Documentary. Directed by Errol Morris. USA, UK: Independent Film Channel (IFC), 1999.

Münsterberg, Hugo. 2002. 'The Photoplay.' In *Hugo Münsterberg on Film. The Photoplay: A Psychological Study and Other Writings*, edited by Allan Langdale, 43–162. New York and London: Routledge.

My Week with Marilyn. Film. Directed by Simon Curtis. USA, UK: The Weinstein Company, 2011.

Nichols, Bill. 1991. *Representing Reality: Issues and Concepts in Documentary*. Bloomington: Indiana University Press.

Nichols, Bill. 2001. *Introduction to Documentary*. Bloomington: Indiana University Press.

Nichols, Bill. 2016a. 'Letter to Errol Morris: Feelings of Revulsion and the Limits of Academic Discourse.' In *Speaking Truths with Film: Evidence, Ethics, Politics in Documentary*, 181–90. Oakland: University of California Press.

Nichols, Bill. 2016b. 'The Question of Evidence: The Power of Rhetoric and the Documentary Film.' In *Speaking Truths with Film: Evidence, Ethics, Politics in Documentary*, 99–110. Oakland: University of California Press.

The Passion of Joan of Arc. Film. Directed by Theodor Dreyer. France: Société générale des films, 1928.

Plantinga, Carl. 1997. *Rhetoric and Representation in Nonfiction Film*. Cambridge: Cambridge University Press.

Plantinga, Carl. 1999. 'The Scene of Empathy and the Human Face on Film.' In *Passionate Views: Film, Cognition, and Emotion*, edited by Carl Plantinga and Greg M. Smith, 239–55. Baltimore and London: Johns Hopkins University Press.

Plantinga, Carl. 2005. 'What a Documentary Is, after All.' *Journal of Aesthetics and Art Criticism* 63: 105–17.

Plantinga, Carl. 2009a. *Moving Viewers: American Film and the Spectator's Experience.* Berkeley: University of California Press.

Plantinga, Carl. 2009b. 'Documentary.' In *The Routledge Companion to Philosophy and Film*, edited by Paisley Livingston and Carl Plantinga, 494–504. London and New York: Routledge.

Plantinga, Carl. 2018. 'Characterization and Character Engagement in the Documentary.' In *Cognitive Theory and Documentary Film*, edited by Catalin Brylla and Mette Kramer, 115–34. Cham: Palgrave Macmillan.

Pippin, Robert B. 2013. *Hollywood Westerns and American Myth: The Importance of Howard Hawks and John Ford for Political Philosophy.* New Haven, CT: Yale University Press.

Radford, Colin. 1975. 'How Can We Be Moved by the Fate of Anna Karenina?' *Proceedings of the Aristotelian Society*, Supplemental Volume 49: 67–80.

Renov, Michael. 1993. 'Introduction: The Truth about Non-Fiction.' In *Theorizing Documentary*, edited by Michael Renov, 1–11. New York and London: Routledge.

Renov, Michael. 2004. *The Subject of Documentary.* Minneapolis: University of Minnesota Press.

Ricciardelli, Lucia. 2010. 'Documentary Filmmaking in the Postmodern Age: Errol Morris and *The Fog of Truth*.' *Studies in Documentary Film* 4.1: 35–50.

Roger and Me. Documentary. Directed by Michael Moore. USA: Dog Eat Dog Films, Warner Bros., 1989.

Silence of the Lambs. Film. Directed by Jonathan Demme. USA: Strong Heart, Demme Productions, Orion Pictures, 1991.

Simmel, Georg. [1901] 1965. 'The Aesthetic Significance of the Face [1901]', translated by Lore Ferguson. In Georg Simmel et al., *Essays on Sociology, Philosophy and Aesthetics*, edited by Kurt H. Wolff, 276–81. San Francisco: Harper and Row.

Some Like It Hot. Film. Directed by Billy Wilder. USA: Ashton Productions, The Mirisch Corporation, 1959.

Standard Operating Procedure. Documentary. Directed by Errol Morris. USA: Participant, Sony Pictures Classics, 2008.

Tan, Edward S. 1996. *Emotion and the Structure of Narrative Film: Film as an Emotion Machine*, translated by Barbara Fasting. Mahwah, NJ: Lawrence Erlbaum.

Thomson-Jones, Katherine. 2008. *Aesthetics and Film.* London and New York: Continuum.

The Unknown Known. Documentary. Directed by Errol Morris. USA: History Films, Moxie Pictures, 2013.

Walton, Kendall L. 1990. *Mimesis as Make-Believe: On the Foundations of the Representational Arts.* Cambridge, MA: Harvard University Press.

Werth, Margaret. 2006. 'Modernity and the Face.' *Intermédialités: histoire et théorie des arts, des lettres et des techniques/Intermediality: History and Theory of the Arts, Literature and Technologies* 8: 83–102.

Winston, Brian. 1993. 'The Documentary Film as Scientific Inscription.' In *Theorizing Documentary*, edited by Michael Renov, 37–57. New York and London: Routledge.

7. *MINDHUNTER*: THE POSSIBILITY OF KNOWING EVIL

Damian Cox

INTRODUCTION

In the first episode of the Netflix series *Mindhunter* (2017–), two protagonists discuss the possibility of understanding people who murder compulsively and repeatedly. They are Holden Ford (Jonathan Groff) and Bill Tench (Holt McCallany), FBI officers about to embark upon a long-term study of the psychology of serial killers. Tench has a word of warning:

> Tench: Let me tell you something about aberrant behaviour Holden, it's fucking aberrant. If we understood it, we'd be aberrant too. Fortunately, it is not incumbent upon us to write a dissertation.
> Ford: Well, maybe we should.

What does it take to understand evil? How does one hunt a mind that is broken in a seemingly inaccessible way? What would it be to capture such a mind and what are the moral hazards of such a venture? The questions are posed in a clear and forthright way in the first series of *Mindhunter* (they mostly disappear from view in the second series). Over ten episodes, the first series draws out the epistemological struggle of its protagonists and gives it both structure and depth. There are three protagonists: Tench and Ford are soon joined by a civilian psychologist, Wendy Carr (Anna Torv), and they each represent a different epistemological position. The conflict between them dramatises the philosophical question of the possibility of knowing evil.

CRIMINAL PROFILERS

Mindhunter is based upon a 1995 book by John Douglas and Mark Olshaker: *Mindhunter: Inside the FBI Elite Serial Crime Unit* ([1995] 2017). Douglas is a well-known FBI criminal profiler and Olshaker is a popular author. The book is both Douglas's memoir and a justification of his methods and their effectiveness. It chronicles the development of criminal profiling techniques at the Behavioural Sciences Unit of the FBI, housed at Quantico. Douglas, along with Robert Ressler and Roy Hazelwood, developed techniques for investigating violent crime using crime scene analysis (a hermeneutic attempt to 'read' the scene of a crime), forensic psychology, and behavioural science. The actual-world investigative value of criminal profiling is widely disputed (e.g. Snook et. al. 2008), but in many fictional worlds, criminal profilers carry all before them.

In the book *Mindhunter*, Douglas puts the case for criminal profiling in the starkest possible terms. He and Olshaker write:

> In every horrible crime since the beginning of civilisation, there is always that searing, fundamental question: what kind of person could have done such a thing? The type of profiling and crime scene analysis we do at the FBI's Investigative Support Unit attempts to answer that question.
>
> Behaviour reflects personality.
>
> It isn't always easy, and it's never pleasant, putting yourself in these guy's shoes – or inside their minds. But that's what my people and I have to do. We have to try to feel what it was like for each one.
>
> Everything we see at a crime scene tells us something about the unknown subject – or UNSUB, in police jargon – who committed the crime. By studying as many crimes as we could, and through talking to the experts – the perpetrators themselves – we have learned to interpret those clues in much the same way a doctor evaluates various symptoms to diagnose a particular disease or condition. And just as a doctor can begin forming a diagnosis after recognising several aspects of a disease presentation he or she has seen before, we can make various conclusions when we see patterns start to emerge. (Douglas and Olshaker [1995] 2017: 14)

Notice that Douglas switches between two very different epistemological tasks within the one passage. On the one hand, his job is to 'get inside the minds' of serial killers. On the other, it is to be a pattern recogniser: observing behaviour from the outside and identifying patterns that will lead to the identification of external features of the UNSUB. The task is to identify such things as his age, race, marital status, habits, and observable peculiarities, whether he owns a dog, has a lisp, is organised or opportunistic, whether he is sexually confident and aggressive or sexually inadequate and prone to over-compensating for it, and so on. Some of this is common-sense deduction; some of it is won through hard study; some of it is intuitive psychological hypothesising.

The task of understanding serial killers is formidably complex. It involves a phenomenological task of understanding the lived experience of the UNSUB (predominantly misogynist serial killers), which includes knowledge of how he experiences women, how he interprets their behaviour, what it is like for him to prey on women, and so on. The task of pattern recognition is categorical. It involves identifying external marks of the killer and his life, things that may or may not be part of his lived experience. Understanding serial killers also requires successful explanation of them. This is announced by the blurb on the back of the Douglas and Olshaker book, which screams (in giant red block letters) 'What makes a serial killer?' It is a causal explanatory question rather than a phenomenological or categorical one. The three tasks – phenomenological, categorical, and explanatory – produce distinct epistemological perspectives and investigative approaches, and the conflict between them plays out in a vital and productive way in the Netflix series. In the book, Douglas offers little more than cherry-picked success stories and illustrations of how the process is supposed to go. Epistemological conflict is buried deep in his text. The makers of the series *Mindhunter* brought it to the surface.

The First Season

The showrunner for the first season of *Mindhunter* is the Australian playwright Joe Penhall. He wrote seven of the episodes. Although the series is based on the Douglas and Olshaker book, Penhall chose to fictionalise Douglas's character. In a nod to the now defunct Australian car industry, he named the chief protagonist Holden Ford. Ford is a much more complicated and conflicted character – a very much more interesting character – than that which emerges from Douglas's memoir. Penhall opens up the memoir by including a fictional account of Ford's private life. The series is framed by his relationship with a graduate student of sociology, Debbie Mitford (Hannah Gross). We follow the arc of this relationship from the charm and energy of its inception to its awkward and dispiriting ending. The other protagonists are Bill Tench, who is based – again loosely – on Robert Ressler; and Wendy Carr, who is based – even more loosely – on Ann Wolbert Burgess.

The season portrays a succession of interviews with serial killers in jail, mixed in with a series of police investigations, the private lives of three protagonists (a relationship arc for Ford, liberation from a domineering lover for Carr, a struggling marriage for Tench), added together with a portrait of the political struggle to form and advance the Behavioural Sciences Unit in Quantico. This does not sound like promising material for tight, serial storytelling. But Penhall manages to do just this. He does it by structuring the series around a philosophical clash. The series is a struggle between its three main protagonists, but this struggle is primarily epistemological. They have the task of developing a knowledge base about serial killers to facilitate their capture early in their careers. But how does one do this? And what are the moral hazards of doing it?

THE STUDY

Ford's founding insight is to turn to the best resource for understanding serial killers: the killers themselves. This is a brilliant move for dramatic purposes, but it faces some obvious epistemological hurdles. First, serial killers are, by and large, manipulative, self-serving liars. So even if they do have something to tell the investigators, they are more than likely to wrap it in distortions and self-serving mythologising. Breaking through that to the truth is a devil of a business. Second, serial killers are generally inarticulate and unreflective characters. Centring the study on an unusually articulate and reflective serial killer (Ed Kemper in the first season) biases the study towards a certain kind of killer. Third (Ed Kemper points this out to a bemused Ford in the fifth episode of the second season), interviewing serial killers in jail biases the sample towards serial killers who got caught: to the unintelligent, disorganised, self-destructively boastful, or, as in Kemper's case, to those who weary of the business and effectively give themselves up. The most dangerous serial killers, Kemper observes, are still at large. These three problems constitute one kind of challenge to the study.

A second, more daunting, challenge is philosophical. The study requires clarity about its goals and clarity about the ethics of its methods. I discuss the ethics of the study below, but for now I concentrate on philosophical questions about the goals of the study. What are Ford, Tench and Carr after? Very roughly: they are looking for psychological knowledge of serial killers that will help catch them. But what is this knowledge? How is it to be organised? How is it to be validated? How is it to be pressed into practical service? The first of these questions – what is this knowledge? – is the most basic and most intractable. It constitutes the main point of contention between the three protagonists.

Ford, Tench, and Carr come to represent three distinct epistemological approaches. Ford's first and central task is to understand serial killers from the inside. Carr's approach is to identify salient features of the subjects, categorise them, and use this to form and test inductive hypotheses. Ultimately, this is the sort of information that will help catch killers. For example, if most misogynist serial killers had controlling and hypercritical mothers (a position the team settles upon in the first season), then one might use this information to help profile suspects. Investigative priority would then be given to suspects whose mothers were controlling and hypercritical.

Tench's goals are more modest than those of either Carr or Ford. As illustrated in the scene quoted at the beginning of this chapter, he is initially sceptical of both the validity and pragmatic value of Ford's idea that they mine convicted serial killers for insights into their characteristics, motivations, and experience. When Ford first proposes that they interview convicted serial killers, Tench is dismissive. Tench chooses to play a lonely round of golf rather than join Ford in an interview of Ed Kemper. (At this early stage, before Carr joins the team, interviews are held without official permission and on Tench's and Ford's days off.) When Ford furnishes an enthusiastic report about his interview with Kemper, Tench claims that Kemper is playing him: manipulating him with self-serving lies in the hope of extracting privileges. Ford, however, is doggedly persistent and eventually Tench joins in on the third interview of Kemper. The interview persuades Tench of the possible merits of the study. This is in keeping with Tench's pragmatic approach.

Kemper is a lucky find. He is intelligent, articulate, talkative, self-knowing, theoretical. Had Ford first interviewed a less forthcoming and reflective convict, say Richard Speck, the whole study may not have got off the ground. (At least it would have taken very high levels of self-belief to press forward.) Kemper's apparent self-insight encourages the two to seek official permission to carry on the study. At no point in future serial killer interviews, through both Season One and Season Two, do the team interview someone who gives them such clear access to his lived experience, mindset, and motivations. The interview with Kemper encourages Tench, and especially Ford, to apply their findings to ongoing cases. Carr remains resolutely unimpressed by their premature rush to application. In Episode Three, shortly after hearing from Kemper that his misogyny originated in the humiliations visited upon him by his mother, Tench and Ford consult on a case of an elderly woman murdered in Sacramento. Tench hypothesises that the killer is white and has a maternal relationship much like Kemper's. This insight leads almost immediately to a suspect, who quickly confesses. In the span of two episodes, we move from serial killer interview to result.

Early success encourages Ford and Tench to over-value cases where their insights bear fruit and under-value cases where they do not. That is to say, it sets up a habit of confirmation bias in their work. Somewhat mixed results are produced by future investigations, including the extended portrayal of the Atlanta murders of 1979–81 in Season Two. But the investigative momentum of Episode Three casts a long shadow over the series. It establishes a standing conviction that these people are onto something important and that their insights have invaluable investigative potential – even when the investigation itself proves difficult to resolve. Nonetheless, there is much more going on under the epistemological surface than this.

Ford's epistemological project is to understand the mind of a serial killer from the inside (I discuss this in greater depth below), and Tench's more pragmatic approach is aimed at learning just enough about serial killer habits and characteristics to inform his investigations. Both of them are in the business of solving crimes and securing convictions, so they rush their initial findings into practice. However, Carr's entry into the show in Episode Three transforms the study. This is Carr's first speech to Tench and Ford, the two amateur social scientists:

> You obviously need to put this onto a more formal footing. It is going to take a lot of time and energy to expand it into a larger project with a specific questionnaire; like their family histories, what their thoughts were on why they did it, when they were aroused during the killings, that sort of thing. Then contrast, compare and publish.
>
> You know why it took me nearly a decade to publish my book? Because narcissists don't go to the doctor. Psychopaths are convinced that there is nothing wrong with them, so these men are virtually impossible to study. And yet you have found a way to study them in near perfect laboratory conditions. That's what makes this so exciting and so potentially far-reaching.

Carr's laboratory conditions turn out to be chimerical. The first employment of Carr's carefully crafted questionnaire ends in interview disaster. Interviewing Jerry Brudos, the standardised interview first bores Brudos and then alienates him. He stonewalls, insisting upon his innocence. Initially Tench, and then Ford, abandon the questionnaire and re-interrogate Brudos to elicit a confession. This fails. They also learn that their serial killer subjects had somehow been communicating with each other (Kemper had let Brudos know of the FBI duo and their naïve interest in the inner workings of the serial killer mind). Carr is surprisingly sanguine at this outcome, even excited. Recall that she is primarily concerned with categorisation: the task of identifying patterns of behaviour, background, triggers, and so on that will help her draw up a systematic and evidence-based picture of the phenomenon of serial killing. Now she has a new category by which to sort convicted serial killers: post-conviction admission. It is hard to see the investigative point of the new category, but this is the writer's (Penhall's) point. At this early stage, Carr is studying the phenomenon simply to understand it.

Carr never loses this commitment to the goal of developing categorical knowledge of the serial killer phenomenon. Causal knowledge – what leads to this behaviour? What triggers it? – emerges from categorical knowledge. Phenomenological knowledge – what shapes and structures the serial killer's lived experience? – is merely a supplement, a possible source of categorical insight, but little more. From Carr's perspective, once an offender's behaviour is sorted into a complex typological matrix, its trigger points and pathological origins may be better understood. The fundamental object of study is the typological matrix. First, we need to identify *what* (if anything – another categorical distinction to observe) immediately triggers murder. Then we can join this dot to others. We join all the dots, as it were, and tell a story about why they murder.

The clash between Ford's intuitive and phenomenological approach and Carr's categorical approach is key to a number of dramatic scenes in the series. For example, in order to achieve a breakthrough with Brudos, Ford hits upon the idea of bribing him with a pair of women's shoes (Brudos's fetish). It appears to work extraordinarily well. Carr, however, is unimpressed. She admonishes them: 'This is a scientific study, not a locker-room hazing.' Her enthusiasm for the standardised interview returns and the heart of the epistemological struggle begins to take form, as shown in this extended dialogue from Episode Seven:

Carr: You threw our questionnaire right out the window.

Tench: *Your* questionnaire, which wasn't working.

Carr: All you wanted to do was force him to admit that he wears women's clothes.

Ford: Yeah, get under his disguise.

Tench: Cross-dressing is part of his psychology, his fixation on women's clothes, women's bodies; wanting to own them, to inhabit them. If we can understand that, we can recognise it in another killer.

Carr: Cross-dressing is not an antecedent to homicidal behaviour.

Tench: I didn't say that.

Carr: For most people it is a harmless form of expression.

Ford: Most people?

Carr: Those who do it.

Tench: It is usually sexual, right, and we know sex drives our subjects.

Carr: Sometimes sexual. Transvestism has been practised in every era and human culture.

Tench (getting up to leave): If you want to teach a class, go back to Boston.

Carr: You weren't speaking his language. You were persecuting him about something that challenges your masculinity.

Tench: What?

Carr: That interview was personal.

Tench (returning): No. This is personal. You're being irrational. Where's this coming from?

Carr: I don't know. Maybe shock at your total lack of objectivity.

Tench: We were supposed to be objective? Because I seem to remember you urging us to use our families to get to him. How objective is that?

Ford (interjecting): We have to use strategies.

Carr: I said to use fake information as long as you establish rapport . . .

Tench: That's not what you said, and it is not possible. It is not possible to communicate with someone like Brudos and be fake. We can either hassle him or open up to him, but either option has a cost.

In this exchange, both Carr and Tench have a point. Tench is right on a number of points: the questionnaire is not working; faking it with characters like Brudos is a dead end; given the task, and its circumstances, the goal of robust objectivity is elusive. Carr is also right. Tench's implicit bias has led him to a comprehensive categorising error. Cross-dressing is not a promising category in this context; something more relevant to pathology is required.

This exchange represents the emergence of different goals between the team members. Carr is after categorical knowledge. Tench is after familiarity. Fittingly – given his pragmatic sceptical orientation – he wants to develop an informal, intuitive familiarity with types of serial killers, one that he can count on in their investigation and prosecution. He expects, at this stage probably unconsciously, to develop the *art* of criminal profiling more than the science of it. It is to be part and parcel of the *art* of criminal investigation in general. (Of the three, Tench is the one who works the physical evidence most assiduously in all their consultations; he is also the one most sceptical of the overuse of categorical theory in investigations. He is prepared to use it, but with a sceptical reserve – an implicit acknowledgement that there is always more to the art or skill of criminal profiling than following the criminal profiler's rulebook.) To develop intuitive familiarity requires interactions in which one gets under the skin of the killer, becoming familiar with the sort of moves they make under pressure, the sort of self-serving lies and obfuscations they turn to, the cadence of their behaviour. It is not something one can capture in a standardised interview; it does not match easily to evidence-based typological matrix generation. It is something one eventually gets a feel for, but only after long experience with the real thing. It is also quite compatible with the unobjective moral disdain Tench feels and rarely hides in his interactions with convicted killers.

Ford is after something else again. He is after understanding. Roughly, he wants to know what it is like to be a serial killer from the inside in the hope that this capacity for mental simulation will bear investigative fruit. For that, he has to be able to assume a distinct sort of objectivity: one that nullifies his own moral consciousness in his efforts at empathetic interactions with the killers and in his striving to understand the crime from the perpetrator's point of view. This ambition, and the interview technique that most emphatically demonstrates it, is on vivid display in his interview with Richard Speck in Episode Nine. The interview begins in the accustomed formal, standardised fashion. Ford recites protocol statement:

Ford: Mr Speck, we are conducting interviews with people who have been convicted of violent crimes. We will be asking you about your family history, antecedent behaviour, and thought patterns surrounding the crime.
Speck: Fuck you, Hoover boys.

Ford: Our goal is to publish a statistical analysis that will not include your name.

Speck: You fucking better know my name.

Ford: I beg your pardon?

Speck: 'Beg your pardon.' Fuck you.

Ford: We know your name. Everybody knows your name.

Ford immediately switches from distant FBI interviewer to fanboy. He asks to see Speck's tattoo. His projected attitude is one of boyish awe in the face of celebrity. (It is not entirely feigned; something that emerges through many interviews, most vividly in the second season interview he and Tench conduct with Charles Manson.) Tench carries on with the Speck interview along pre-established, standardised lines and utterly fails to elicit a meaningful response from Speck. At this point Ford intervenes. He leans towards Speck and begins a repellent misogynist conversation with him about the women he murdered. It is a conversational gambit so repellent that, on Tench's advice, Ford doctors the record of the interview to omit it. I discuss the ethics of Ford's methods below, but there are two main points about this passage relevant to my interpretation of the show's handling of epistemological questions.

The first is how superficially successful it is: Speck immediately opens up about his crime and how he experienced it. Eventually, though, Ford turns the conversation to Speck's moral consciousness. Did he ever think about why he did it? (Answer: no.) But why then did he try to kill himself? (Self-delusional response: it didn't happen.) Threatening Speck's self-image in this way leads to a tantrum (Speck throws a small bird he had been nursing into a fan, killing it) and a rapid end to the interview. The radical departure from the interview procedure and technique insisted upon by Carr had an immediate payoff, but the result is not entirely satisfactory from a categorising point of view. Speck opens up when Ford switches from fanboy to fellow traveller; but when Ford turns his moral intelligence on him like a surgical tool, Speck's overreaction shuts the interview down. The Speck interview is productive if one's aim is to learn the 'feel' of a misogynist killer: what it is like to be with him as he boasts, as he cowers from the truth, as he explodes in rage when confronted with humiliating revelation, and so on. It is also, perhaps, a useful experience for someone trying to acquire the skill of misogynist killer empathy. It furnishes relatively paltry categorical insight.

The second significant feature of the passage is Ford's technique. Recall that, in Episode Seven, Tench insisted on the unproductivity of 'faking it' with convicted killers. In the Episode Nine encounter with Speck, Tench remains true to this conviction, but Ford seems to play Speck like a violin. Is he faking it? In one very clear sense he is. There is no filmic evidence that Ford harbours the sort of misogynist attitudes on display in his discussion with

Speck. His relationship with his female partner is breaking down – largely because of his obsessive self-concern, his jealousy of her relationship with a fellow graduate student, the hubris he is gradually acquiring from his professional success, and the fact that he is starting to bore her – but none of this involves misogyny.

Ford is playing a role in the Speck interview. But there are several ways of playing such a role. One is to recite expected lines and mimic expected behavioural cues. This is a matter of self-consciously copying a misogynist: their habits of speech, choice of words, opinions, and so on. The other way of faking it is through mental simulation: imaginatively taking on a target persona from the inside (Currie and Ravenscroft 2002). In simulation, one uses one's cognitive and affective capacities to run through a proffered scenario. The run-through is both temporary and offline. It is offline in the sense that it is insulated from deeper convictions and attitudes (it does not turn one misogynist) and from elaborate intentions and behaviours (it does not lead one to plan or carry out misogynist actions). When successful, the consequences of the simulation are felt and expressed bodily in a way that is closely analogous to the real thing. When Ford leans in to Speck and exchanges misogynist victim-insults with him, his emotional experience is somewhat analogous to that of a misogynist. The misogynist judgements he expresses remain unendorsed, but they are also experienced with much of the emotional character of actual misogynist judgement. He simulates, not bare belief, but a rich affective field of experience: bitterness, disguised inadequacy, contempt, and so on. Adam Waytz and Jason Mitchell (2011) usefully distinguish between two kinds of mental simulation: mirroring and self-projection. Mirroring is a form of empathy and self-projection is a form of imaginative recreation. They argue that the two processes dissociate and have distinct neural bases. Ford is play-acting, and this involves a form of self-projection. My contention is that play-acting in situations like Ford's can generate a mirroring effect out of self-projection. In projecting himself into the affective, normative landscape of Richard Speck, Ford comes to experience aspects of what it is to live in such a landscape.

A related aspect of Ford's interview is projected sympathy. Ford projects a sympathetic, non-judgemental attitude towards Speck and a sympathetic interest in his crime. It emerges naturally from his initial fanboy approach to Speck and has Speck fooled until the interview takes a forensic turn. Sympathy, understood in this colloquial sense, is distinct from empathy. In empathic experience one partially adopts the point of view of another, both cognitively and affectively (see Coplan and Goldie 2011). In sympathy one projects, not approval and endorsement, but reassurance that the subject behaviour is understandable. It is perhaps regrettable, but not a fitting object of negative reactive attitudes: anger, disgust, contempt, pity, and so on.[1] Sympathy is not merely non-judgemental interest; that might be merely forensic and entirely unconcerned with the moral quality of the behaviour. Sympathy is a reassuring projection of good company. Roughly, a typical script goes: 'This is a bad thing, but you are not contemptible, you are not evil, you are as deserving of respect as anybody else. You have made a mistake, for which you must bear the consequences, but it was a mistake, not an irremovable taint and it didn't make you a fitting object of hate.' It is not an act of forgiveness but is a likely precursor of forgiveness.

Ford fakes sympathy. He shares none of these accommodating attitudes towards serial killers. For example, in Season One, Episode Ten, Carr tries to convince District Attorney Esther Mayweather (Rhoda Griffis) not to impose the death penalty on Gene Devier, who had been apprehended earlier in the episode. Ford accompanies her but is entirely indifferent to her plea on Devier's behalf. He cuts her off in the midst of her argument against the death penalty. He simply fails to see a problem, either moral or strategic, with allowing serial killers caught through the unit's work to be executed by the state. Sympathy is, as he says in another context, merely a 'strategy'. Convincing fake sympathy is difficult to sustain without mental simulation. To convince another of one's sympathy, one has to project the bodily cadence of someone genuinely non-judgemental and understanding of that person's actions, and the easiest way to do that is to fall into a shared pattern of affect and cognition with them. This means simulating their mental state sufficiently well to produce agreeable body and vocal inflections in one's response to them. And this is just what Ford achieves.

The entire skill set – mental simulation to align with the interview subject, cognitive and affective empathy with them, projection of sympathy towards them – is put to use in Ford's interviews with suspected serial killers. In Episode Ten, Ford puts the entire skill set to use in his interview with Devier, eventually extracting a confession from him. In her summary of the interview to Mayweather, Carr says: 'Agent Ford assembled a psychological sketch of Mr Devier based on our research which was used to secure a confession.' This is an oversimplification. Ford used the profile to identify an interview trigger point: the dramatic uncovering of the murder weapon mid-interview. The interview's success, however, depended upon Ford's psychological manipulation of Devier; and much of that depended on an elaborate and utterly convincing charade of sympathy and fellow feeling. Ford (and Tench) have assembled not so much a theory with which to identify potential suspects and interview them, but a skill set. By Episode Ten, they have become apparently very good at the interview part of it.

Ford and Tench have been acquiring a new set of skills, or refining an old one, through the study. But they understand themselves to be doing something else. They are developing a theory of serial killers – a knowledge base with which to understand them from both the outside and inside and through which they will be able to profile, identify, interview, and help prosecute serial killer suspects. What epistemic value does mental simulation bring to this task? Apart from role-playing in interviews, its value is that it affords phenomeno- logical insight. When tuned to the mental lives of others – rather than to an imagined persona – mental simulation affords empathy, both cognitive empa- thy (in which one understands the cognitive state of another approximately as it appears to them) and affective empathy (in which one understand the affec- tive state of another by sharing something analogous to it). Phenomenological knowledge is not the mere registering of cognitive and affective empathy – phenomenological knowledge is descriptive, critical, and structural. Nonetheless, it would be barely possible – perhaps not possible at all – to acquire phenom- enological knowledge of a misogynist killer without building on a foundation of cognitive and affective empathy with them. This is its fundamental value for Ford. If I am right, Ford's epistemological goals do not align neatly with those of his colleagues. Where Carr is looking for categorical knowledge and Tench is becoming familiar with serial killers (learning what they are like to be around), Ford is learning what it is like to be one of them. In his interviews with serial killers, Ford is deploying his capacity for mental simulation both as an interview technique and as path to phenomenological knowledge. Ford may not fully understand the demands of this epistemic goal, but he is pursuing it relentlessly. He wants to know what it is like to be a serial killer even if he is unlikely to understand just how complex and elusive such knowledge must turn out to be.

Knowing the Mind of a Killer

What is knowledge of other minds? There can be greater or lesser knowledge of them, of course, so the question is not quite as categorical as it seems. There can also be partial knowledge of other minds in the following sense. I can know another mind in one mode or aspect without knowing it in another. For example, I might be able predict how another will respond to an event without knowing what it means to them. (Do they see it as a thoughtless insult or a betrayal? I don't know. All I know is that they are going to throw a fit.) There are both aspects and degrees of knowledge of other minds. This is very much in evidence when our goal is to know the minds of people who are very differ- ent from ourselves; often we can achieve no more than a partial understanding of them.

The hypothesis that I will now work from is an integrative hypothesis about knowledge of other minds. I claim that there are four modes of knowledge of other minds: causal theoretic modelling, hermeneutic story-building, phenom- enological analysis, and mind simulation.[2] To gain knowledge of another mind, it is necessary to integrate all four modes of understanding. Consider knowl- edge of a person's action, φ.

To know (really know) why a person has φ'd, one must:

1. Have a justified causal theoretic model of the origin of the behaviour (at some level).
2. Make sense of the behaviour, where it is amenable to sense-making, by giving a reason-based interpretation of it.
3. Know the fundamental character and structure of the lived experience of the person φing.
4. Empathetically adopt (to an approximate degree of accuracy) the cognitive and affective point of view of the person φing.
5. Bring these four modes of understanding under one coherent knowledge structure.

The idea is that failure to realise any one of these modes of understanding will generate only partial knowledge, and failure to integrate them into a coherent package will generate only a confused grasp of reality. We never know others completely – we never know ourselves completely – but there is a difference between incomplete knowledge and partial knowledge. Partial knowledge misses a fundamental and ineliminable aspect of the phenomenon in question. It is a failure to properly understand, not just a failure to completely understand.

Consider the example of Devier's murder of Mary Stoner. To understand Devier's act one must be able to say something substantial (although not complete) about the causes of it. Causal theoretic modelling of events can take various forms, but the aim in all of them is to identify the confluence of factors that led – if not predictably, then tractably – to the murder. In Douglas's terms, this would be a matter of identifying categories of his pathology and triggering incidences that led to the killing. It is not robust causal knowledge because it is profoundly incomplete. Whatever factors one might identify, and whatever triggers one may hypothesise, they will be shared by many incidences that are innocent of murder. It may even be necessarily incomplete, there being nothing that necessitates action given the kind of causal knowledge available to us. However, without some causal knowledge, the murder will remain mysterious to us. We will fail to connect it to our causal grasp of human affairs. It will be an arbitrary, unexplained event in these affairs.

Causal knowledge, no matter how complete, is insufficient to know another's action. In addition, we need to understand the action hermeneutically. This means, at a minimum, being able to explicate the action in terms of reasons. What reasons did Devier respond to when he decided to kill Mary Stoner? How did he understand himself? What reasons (as opposed to blind impulses) moved him? This is the fundamental difference between an action and an event. Events have causes; actions have reasons.[3] The hermeneutical grasp of an act consists in the articulation and interrogation of its reasons, including interrogation of their grounding in the actor's worldview, the actor's culturally mediated self-understanding, the self-deceptive strategies and motivated irrationality which sustained this worldview, and so on.

Again, hermeneutic knowledge is insufficient for knowing other minds. Actions have mental causes, and exist in a world of reasons, but they also exist as lived experience. So, to know another's mind is to know something of the structure and nature of their consciousness. What do they fixate upon? What dreams disturb them? What consciousness of time settles upon them as they fixate upon a fugitive desire? Devier was working as a tree-lopper in Mary Stoner's neighbourhood. He saw her leave for school in the morning in her band outfit. He saw her return from school. She sometimes waved at him. How did he experience the wave? How did he spend the time – did tree-lopping allow his mind to wander? – between the sight of her? How did his repellent desire grow within him: gradually or with overwhelming suddenness? She was twelve years old. How did he experience her age: as false, as irrelevant, as an object of desire? We do not know the mind of Devier (perhaps we do not want to know) without some such knowledge as this.

Finally, phenomenological knowledge is also insufficient for knowledge of other minds. This is because phenomenological knowledge, as it is understood in the phenomenological tradition of philosophy, is general and structural. It is not merely having acquaintance knowledge of an experience; it involves understanding the structure and character of an experience. We come to know Devier's choice situation phenomenologically, for example, by describing the structure and content of relevant parts of his consciousness. But acquaintance knowledge is nonetheless important in fully understanding the mind of another. It is important to know approximately what it is like for them. One way to put this is to say that knowledge of another's mind consists, in part, of first-person acquaintance with this mind. Mental simulation is a necessary feature of such knowledge. To know Devier's mind is, at least in part, to be able to occupy its cognitive and affective landscape. It is to not just describe, map, or causally track relevant features of that landscape, but to be intimately acquainted with something like it. It is to have been there, if only in imagination.

This integrative model of knowledge of other minds sets the bar to knowledge high: but it is high with respect to modes of knowledge (all modes must be accounted for) rather than level of knowledge. We must always know others incompletely – as we must know everything about the world incompletely – but our aim in coming to know another mind is to reduce this incompleteness and to ensure that our knowledge is not merely partial.

MINDHUNTER: IT ALL FALLS APART

Is integrative knowledge of the mind of a serial killer possible? Is there such an epistemic object at all? Perhaps there is nothing which it is to know such a mind because such minds are not integratable in the sense I have set out. There may be minds which are profoundly inaccessible to us, not because we lack the imagination and information to know them, but because the very act of coming to know them in one mode undermines the possibility of coming to know them in another. This possibility is illustrated in *Mindhunter*'s tenth episode.

This episode, which concludes the first season, sets up a number of tensions and failures for the three protagonists, especially Ford. The investigation of a doctored interview tape (Ford's interview with Speck) comes to a head after the tape is sent anonymously to internal investigators. Ford's arrogant, dismissive, and uncooperative response to the investigation jeopardises his career. He breaks up with his partner, Debbie, very much at her initiative. Throughout the episode Ford, buoyed by his success with Devier, becomes irrationally hubristic and grandiose. He then gets a phone call from the California Medical Facility informing him that Ed Kemper has named him as medical proxy. Without telling anyone, Ford flies to California to see Kemper. Their encounter leads to Ford's emotional and mental collapse.

The nature of the encounter is revealing. Kemper wants to know his criminal profile and Ford obliges. He is an 'organised killer', of which Ford gives a brief, facile rundown. Kemper's response shows Ford how empty his epistemological boasts really are. Kemper becomes threatening and spouts self-serving nonsense about his victims becoming his spirit wives. Standing toe-to-toe with Ford, he says: 'I could kill you now pretty easily. Do some interesting things before anybody showed up, then you'd be with me in spirit.' He then embraces Ford in an intense and one-sided hug of friendship. This precipitates Ford's breakdown.

Several things are happening in this climactic scene. Ford is overwhelmed by a concatenation of issues, including the collapse of his relationship and, seemingly, his career. But at its core this is an epistemological collapse. Ford's epistemic confidence, and with it his hubristic epistemic self-conception, breaks down. The primary source of his insights – Ed Kemper – has effectively repudiated the validity of his approach, demonstrating to Ford how little insight has come from his dealings with the killer. He has called Ford's bluff on the pretence that he is merely faking friendship, that his sympathy is a disguise, that his powers of empathetic engagement with inaccessibly broken people are yielding theoretical insights, that he has any real insight at all into Kemper's mind. At best Ford has learned some psychological party tricks to play on unsuspecting suspects in interview.

The complexity of Ford's overall epistemic task – integrating causal, hermeneutic, phenomenological, and acquaintance knowledge – has overwhelmed his sense of mission. To gain third-person knowledge of a person one is in some kind of relationship with (that is, causal, hermeneutic knowledge of their mind and phenomenological insight into the character and structure of their consciousness) one needs to stand at some distance from a subject, at a place where observation leaves the observer fundamentally intact and unaltered. To gain first-person knowledge, by contrast, one must be in an epistemic space where pretence and affection, mental simulation and sympathy become entangled. One must become an intimate of the subject: to be, in a sense and on occasion, of one mind with them. One can only do both sorts of thing in the same epistemic space if the knower and the known occupy roughly analogous moral and emotional landscapes. When investigators share a moral and emotional landscape with the subject of their investigation, they can move between first person and third person investigation without one undermining the other. Otherwise, they must adopt a stance in the first person which they repudiate in the third person. They must see the apparent value and point of a thing in one stance, and the unyielding moral truth of it in the other. This muddies their capacity to form robust integrated judgements of a subject's actions. To be intimate with a serial killer in the way Ford wanted to be, to understand them from the inside, one is likely to become unfit for the task of understanding them from the outside. And vice versa. Kemper's effortless toying with Ford in this scene shows Ford the incoherence of what he has been up to.

I have contrasted three epistemic projects on display in the first season of *Mindhunter*: Carr's categorical/explanatory project, Tench's familiarity project, and Ford's mindhunting. It is Ford's project that fails so spectacularly in the final episode. The other two projects remain intact, but neither of them is strictly speaking a form of mindhunting. In Season Two, Ford returns as a much-diminished figure, one who sticks closely to the Carr model of applied theoretical insight. Indeed, by Season Two, whether through insight gained from his breakdown or as an unreflective reaction to the pain of his failure, Ford has largely given up the task of putting himself inside the mind of a serial killer. Tench had it right in the first episode (Episode One, 55.50): 'Let me tell you something about aberrant behaviour Holden, it's fucking aberrant. If we understood it, we'd be aberrant too.'

THE ETHICS OF MINDHUNTING

There seems to be nothing ethically wrong, as such, with the project of coming to understand the mind of a serial killer. Yet the behaviour on display in the first season of *Mindhunter* is ethically problematic in various ways. Convicted criminals, even those guilty of horrendous crimes, have not lost their standing as persons owed respect. Such respect entails that they be interviewed in a non-deceptive and minimally manipulative way. Ford and Tench start out dealing honestly with the participants in their study – it is a relatively easy task with the affable and forthcoming Ed Kemper – but they soon descend into crass manipulation: bribing Jerry Brudos; play-acting sympathy with Richard Speck. These are relatively minor ethical concerns, however, primarily because the level of potential harm to Brudos and Speck is low. It is wrong to treat such people disrespectfully, but not so wrong, perhaps, as to shut down the show. Ford's manipulative and ugly interview technique also leads him into dishonest dealing with his colleagues: lying about an interview, doctoring records. This is a more serious, if very familiar, ethical failure.

The more vivid ethical concern here is aretaic in nature. In aretaic reflection, one examines actions in light of their significance for character. I have argued that Ford's project is epistemically illegitimate, but what does its pursuit mean for his character? Is he being merely foolish – trying to square a psychological circle, as it were – or is he acting in a way that undermines his integrity? The project does in fact undermine Ford's integrity: his breakdown at the conclusion of Season One is primarily a crisis of integrity. But need it have done this? Might one seek to understand evil fully and intimately, in the first person as well as the third person, without undermining one's integrity? As I noted above, such a project requires that we adopt a stance in the first person which we fully repudiate in the third person. Imagine a virtuous person taking up this task. The virtuous inquirer mentally simulates a form of experience which they do not merely reject but find hard to withstand and which they react to as repulsive and degrading. In the first person, they simulate the experience without repulsion. (One cannot accurately capture the perspective of evil whilst holding one's nose.) In the third person, they give full expression to their repulsion. In the first person, they effectively subtract their capacity for empathetic identification with victims. In the third person, they feel the full force of the horror of this. To achieve all this without undermining their integrity, an inquirer must possess unusual powers of self-projection. They must have an accomplished actor's capacity to pretend – to themselves as to others – without this pretence diminishing them. This seems to be conceptually possible, and if valuable, not wrong. One might acquire the semblance of such a thing by consuming fiction: as one is led through the inner lives of awful people by a storyteller skilled at manipulation. But in the fictional world of *Mindhunter*, Ford is not in the hands of a storyteller: he is an investigator coming intimately to grips with actual people: broken moral personalities with terrible crimes to their name. And they do a number on him.

Notes

1. This is an account of the ordinary language meaning of what it is to adopt a sympathetic attitude. When philosophers and psychologists discuss sympathy as a psychological process and its relation to empathy, they come up with a range of distinctions. For a review of these distinctions, see Switankowsky (2000).

2. The literature on this question is very large. I propose an integrative model, but much philosophy of social science has sought to prioritise one mode over another. For a clear overview of the various modes, the contest between them, and their varying relations to empathy, see Stueber (2019).
3. There is a long-standing philosophical debate about whether reasons are themselves causes or not. Michael Levine and I defend the actions are causes thesis and describe the structure of hermeneutic explication of action in Cox and Levine (2018).

References

Coplan, Amy, and Peter Goldie (eds). 2011. *Empathy, Philosophical and Psychological Perspectives*. Oxford: Oxford University Press.

Cox, Damian, and Michael Levine. 2018. 'Agency, Explanation and Ethics in International Relations.' In *The Routledge Handbook of International Relations and Ethics*, edited by Brent Steele and Eric Heinze, 78–89. New York: Routledge.

Currie, Gregory, and Ian Ravenscroft. 2002. *Recreative Minds: Imagination in Philosophy and Psychology*. Oxford: Oxford University Press.

Douglas, John, and Mark Olshaker. [1995] (2017). *Mindhunter: Inside the FBI Elite Serial Crime Unit*. New York: Gallery Books.

Snook, Brent, Richard M. Cullen, Craig Bennett, Paul J. Taylor, and Paul Gendreau. 2008. 'The Criminal Profiling Illusion. What's Behind the Smoke and Mirrors?' *Criminal Justice and Behaviour* 35.10: 1257–76.

Stueber, Karsten. 2019. 'Empathy.' In *The Stanford Encyclopedia of Philosophy*, edited by Edward N. Zalta. Fall 2019 edition. <https://plato.stanford.edu/archives/fall2019/entries/empathy/> (last accessed 13 April 2021).

Switankowsky, Irene. 2000. 'Sympathy and Empathy.' *Philosophy Today* 44.1: 86–92.

Waytz, Adam, and Jason P. Mitchell. 2011. 'Two Mechanisms for Simulating Other Minds: Dissociations between Mirroring and Self-Projection.' *Current Directions in Psychological Science* 20.3: 197–200.

PART THREE

POLITICS

8. INTERACTIVE DOCUMENTARY, NARRATIVE SCEPTICISM AND THE VALUES OF DOCUMENTARY FILM

Ted Nannicelli

The ostensible topic of this chapter is a relatively recent form of documentary known as interactive documentary or 'i-doc'. My twofold aim is to critically assess a number of the claims that have been made about interactive documentary's putatively special capacity to yield a variety of values – epistemic, ethical, political, and so forth – and, in relation, to defend a moderately pessimistic view of interactive documentary's ability to realise *any* of those values in a way that is superior to traditional, narrative documentary film. The second of my objectives stems from the fact that the bolder claims for interactive documentary's special status usually make the corollary claim, at least implicitly, that there is something(s) retrograde about traditional linear narratives – something(s) that interactive form is able to surmount. The narrative scepticism that putatively bolsters the buoyant claims for interactive documentary's special values is a cluster or amalgam of unsound ideas that has risen from the dead again and again to haunt theorising about film and media. I will at least attempt to put the final nail in the coffin.

The plan for the chapter is as follows: first, I will give a brief overview of what interactive documentary is, noting, where relevant, different categories and subcategories of the form. The reason for doing so is partly for conceptual clarity and partly because my pessimism about the value of interactive documentary is limited to *some* sorts of i-docs. Second, I will review the extant claims regarding the putative values interactive documentary is specially equipped to realise by virtue of its form, as well as the corollary claims about linear narrative's *inability* to realise these values. Third, I will offer a sustained critique of these claims, attempting to show how and why they are fundamentally unsound. Finally, I will attempt to close on a more positive note by highlighting the various virtues narrative documentary can realise at its very best.

The Nature of Interactive Documentary

My discussion here will be brief in part because there is now a cottage industry dedicated to canvassing and assessing definitions and typologies of interactive documentary. Readers who are keen to pursue more detailed discussions would do well to consult Nash (2012), O'Flynn (2012), Aufderheide (2015), and Aston et al. (2017). A reasonable start at a rough-and-ready definition of interactive documentary – and one that is frequently cited – can be found in Judith Aston and Sandra Gaudenzi's introduction to a special issue of *Studies in Documentary Film* dedicated to interactive documentary. According to Aston and Gaudenzi, an interactive documentary is 'any project that starts with an intention to document the "real" and that uses digital interactive technology to realize this intention' (2012: 125). Clearly, various elements of this definition would require further elaboration in other contexts. For the moment, we can restrict our focus to the matter of 'digital interactive technology'.

An emphasis on digital interactive *technology* can help avoid difficult questions about how to characterise interactivity per se. As Dominic McIver Lopes points out, 'the trouble with "interactivity" isn't that it's meaningless [but that] it means too much – it means so many different things in different situations that it's hard to come up with a one-size-fits-all definition' (2010: 36). In addition, digital interactive technology is often, if not always, the characteristic or prototypical feature that people have in mind when something is described as an 'interactive documentary'. More specifically, documentaries that are interactive in a technological sense are well described by Siobhan O'Flynn as typically 'designed as databases of content fragments, often on the web, though not always, wherein unique interfaces structure the modes of interaction that allow audiences to play with documentary content' (2012: 142). Furthermore, documentaries that are interactive in this technological sense tend to be implicitly committed to a more general conception of interactivity 'as characterised by a need to engage physically: touching, clicking, moving, typing, and so on' (Nash 2014: 53–4).

Rather than attempting to further flesh out the concept of 'digital interactive technology', let us now proceed with this rough-and-ready description of it and suppose, for the sake of argument, that with some more work we could sufficiently describe it in a way that clearly distinguished it from 'non-interactive technology' (digital or otherwise). The practical advantage of conceiving of interactive documentary as prototypically involving digital interactive technology is that doing so allows us to identify the sorts of projects that are characteristic or representative of the category of interactive documentary as it is discussed in the literature. Paradigmatic examples include *Public Secrets* (2006, dir. Sharon Daniel), *Gaza/Sderot: Life in Spite of Everything* (2008, dir. Khalil Al Muzayyen and Ayelet Bachar), *Highrise* (2009–present, dir. Katerina Cizek), *Prison Valley* (2009, dir. David Dufresne and Phillipe Brault), *Bear 71* (2012, dir. Jeremy Mendes and Leanne Allison), and *Points of View* (2014, dir. Zohar Kfir). In each of these cases, a proper engagement with the documentary requires the user to act in ways that shape the presentation of the audiovisual content in one or more of a set of possibilities given by the overall design of the work.

Some scholars who write about interactive documentary have in mind a more expansive notion of interaction. In particular, it is worth mentioning that, for some scholars, a documentary can be interactive by virtue of being *participatory*. 'Participatory' suffers from the same trouble as 'interactivity': it means a wide variety of different things in different contexts. Traditionally, it has been understood in cinematic contexts as referring to a process of documentary filmmaking – often ethnographic filmmaking – that is marked by the collaboration of the ostensible subjects of the film and the ostensible filmmaker in the creation of the film itself. To the best of my knowledge, the anthropologist and filmmaker David MacDougall first used 'participatory cinema' in this sense in his 1975 essay 'Beyond Observational Cinema', writing of it:

> Here the filmmaker acknowledges his or her entry upon the world of the subjects and yet asks them to imprint directly upon the film aspects of their own culture [. . .] By giving them access to the film, they make possible the corrections, additions, and illuminations that only the subjects' response to the material can elicit. Through such an exchange a film can begin to reflect the ways in which its subjects perceive the world. (MacDougall [1975] 1998: 134)

Perhaps the best-known examples of this sort of participatory cinema are the ethno-fictions of Jean Rouch (e.g. *Chronicle of a Summer* (1961) and *Jaguar* (1967)), who, like MacDougall, traces the origins of participatory cinema to Robert Flaherty (Rouch [1973] 2003). The term 'participatory cinema' has since achieved wider currency as one of the 'modes' of documentary theorised by Bill Nichols, who uses it in a somewhat more expansive sense (2010).

For reasons that I do not have space to explore at present, I think that both interactive and traditional documentaries that are participatory in the above sense often do have ethico-political value by virtue of being collaborative. Readers who are interested in interactive documentary in *this* sense may consult recent work by Jon Dovey (2014), Liz Miller and Martin Allor (2016), and Mandy Rose (2017) for a start. But for now what is important is just that *this* sense of the term 'participatory' is quite distinct from the sense in which, say, Henry Jenkins ([1993] 2003) uses it in his conception of 'participatory culture' or Janet Murray uses it in her claim that, by their nature, 'digital environments are participatory' ([1997] 2017: 90).[1] And this is worth mentioning because although it may be the case that interactive documentaries are often 'participatory' in the broad sense that they are forms of so-called participatory media, they are not necessarily – perhaps rarely – participatory in the ethically meritorious sense MacDougall has in mind. (And, of course, much cinema that is participatory in *his* sense, such as Rouch's, is not interactive in the sense of relying upon digital interactive technology.) I mention this because I suspect that a confusion or conflation of these various senses of 'participatory' is partly behind some of the stronger claims for the ethical and political value of interactive cinema, which I hope we can agree, for the present purpose, is best characterised in terms of its use of digital interactive technology to afford the possibility of user interaction in the sense described above.

The Claims for Interactive Documentary

The starting point, from which all of the claims I shall explore here begin, is the observation that interactive documentaries typically eschew a single, linear narrative structure that is designed by the documentarian(s). An interactive documentary like *Welcome to Pine Point* (2011, dir. Michael Simons and Paul Shoebridge) or *Bear 71* might have a narrative structure, but, en route from the start to the end of the narrative, the user has a number of opportunities to interact with the work in a way that temporarily forks off from the narrative. This could involve clicking through a series of still photographs, listening to an audio recording, watching an embedded video, or exploring a map. Importantly, interactive documentaries *prescribe* that the user pause and temporarily diverge from the central narrative (where there is one) in this way. This is what distinguishes the user's exploration of narrative tangents or embedded narratives in interactive documentary from one's skipping around on a DVD menu to 'interact' with a traditional documentary film. For it is an appreciative norm of traditional documentary filmmaking that the audience should engage with the work by watching it from start to finish in the (sole) temporal order established by the filmmaker.

Less linearly structured interactive documentaries are certainly possible – and, as we shall soon see, in fact tend to be held in higher critical regard. *Life Underground* (2018, dir. Hervé Cohen) is a recent, representative example of interactive documentary's ability to embrace multi-threaded storytelling. In *Life Underground*, the user chooses one or more cities from around the world to 'visit' for the purpose of virtually riding the local subway. Once the ride begins, the user has the option of listening to the stories of up to three fellow passengers. But although *Life Underground* embeds linear narratives, its overall form is non-linear and non-narrative. Sometimes interactive documentaries that allow the user to explore select stories, in the order of their choosing, from amongst a range of possibilities, are referred to as database documentaries. Some scholars, following Lev Manovich (1999), regard database structure and narrative structure as fundamentally opposed. Yet, although a completely non-narrative database documentary would appear to be a conceptual possibility, it seems clear that database form can and sometimes does abet storytelling in interactive documentary.[2] Indeed, even one of the creators of the Korsakow software, which allows filmmakers to produce 'database-driven' documentaries, takes issue with Manovich's claim, noting that within the Korsakow System the content that comprises the database – the building blocks of the overall film – are referred to as the 'smallest narrative units' (Soar 2014: 162).[3]

On the other hand, the comments of one of the other creators of the Korsakow System, Florian Thalhofer, provide a useful starting point for exploring the sorts of bold claims that have been made for interactive documentary – and made by drawing a sharp contrast to linear narrative film. The gist of Thalhofer's claim is that non-linear interactive documentaries like those produced with the Korsakow software are inherently better able to represent the complexity of reality – and that this is an essential condition for creating a more tolerant society. As Thalhofer puts it:

> Computer-based narration can celebrate complexity and create awareness of the multi-dimensional nature of reality in ways that might in fact be transcending our obsession with story. Whatever the case, computer-based narration can definitely help us to better understand how things influence, as opposed to cause, each other – which is central to our understanding and acceptance of complexity. I am convinced that this is the direction towards a more tolerant world [. . .] (Thalhofer et al. 2018: 111)

By 'computer-based narration', Thalhofer means the sort of non-linear, database structure that Manovich also champions. Also, like Manovich, Thalhofer sees the non-linear structure afforded by computer-based systems like Korsakow as essentially opposed to linear narrative, and we will return to Thalhofer's narrative scepticism presently.

We can think of Thalhofer's comments as making a claim for interactive documentary's special epistemic value and ethico-political value. Such claims are mirrored in the writing of numerous scholars. For example, according to Ryan Watson:

> In interactive documentaries that critically engage with radical political movements, the impact of the evidence presented, both affective and effective, is amplified due to its vast accumulation and can thus potentially

operate more forcefully on the viewer/user in the service of engagement with the political claims presented, moving the viewer/user into broader movements of militant activism [. . .] The interactive documentary form engenders an expansive, deep, and transformative witnessing: an affective knowing that demands action. (Watson 2017: 604)

Explicitly drawing upon Manovich's conception of the database as a digital archive, Watson asserts that 'interactive documentaries function as archival interfaces' that are more emotionally moving and politically efficacious by virtue of their unique capacity to accumulate evidence (2017: 603).

Consider one more example: in an article published in the same issue of *Alphaville: Journal of Film and Media* as the above-cited interview with Thalhofer, Patricia R. Zimmerman asserts:

Polyphony is a useful theoretical construct to understand the significant shifts in new media practices from a single authorial vision to a multiplicity of voices that come together to generate and activate new understandings of subjects and events [. . .] Together, these voices can articulate and unravel complex political and social issues [. . .] A polyphonic model [. . .] dismantles the unified linear three-act and genre-derived structures embedded in some feature-length documentaries and most mass cultural forms. Polyphonic new media projects avoid causal and explanatory recountings to create architectures for layered multiple temporalities that unlock new ways to consider complex interconnected social and political issues. (Zimmerman 2018: 11)

In this passage, Zimmerman succinctly articulates a number of the key ideas underlying the brief of the special issue, which is titled 'I-Docs as Intervention: The Poetics and Politics of Polyphony': inasmuch as interactive documentary offers the possibility of non-linear forms that eschew causal explanations in favour of the intermingling of different perspectives, it is said to more capably represent the complexities of reality, to be a more equitable form of discourse, and to destabilise hierarchies of power.

The concept of 'polyphony', taken up from Mikhail Bakhtin's discussion of the plurality of distinct voices in Dostoyevsky's novels is, in this context and in much of media and cultural studies, thus held to imbue the artwork or cultural product in which it appears with particular epistemic and ethico-political value. According to the editors of this special issue of *Alphaville*, 'through the use of interactive digital media we are able to create documentary experiences that capture multiple visions of reality [. . .] In other words, the multiplicity of reality helps us to generate a dialogical sense of truth by presenting a multilayered reality' (Aston and Odorico 2018: 75). That is the epistemic claim; it is, in turn, marshalled as putative support for the further, ethico-political claim: 'This commitment to polyphony [is] a means through which to enact democracy' (Aston and Odorico 2018: 72).

Because my critique of this cluster of claims for interactive documentary's value will partly involve criticism of its proponents' assumptions about the form with which they contrast it – that is, linear narrative – I want to now briefly examine their narrative scepticism before proceeding. Again, it will be useful to begin with a quote from Korsakow creator Florian Thalhofer because, although he is a software designer and entrepreneur, he is also involved with the scholarly research groups working on interactive documentary and, moreover, the narrative scepticism he expresses is of the same sort found in various corners of academia. According to Thalhofer:

> Linearity leads to exaggeration and this produces a distorted view of reality [. . .] The organising principle of film is simple: one thing after another. A leads to B, B leads to C, and so on. Because film is so popular, it has shaped the minds of billions of people, who are now thinking according to this principle. Nature sometimes, but not often, works like this. Most frequently, things don't *cause* each other, they *influence* each other [. . .] Linear stories, by nature of the format, come to a conclusion [. . .] And so linear stories have a strong tendency to develop a 'truth'. Truth is a bullshit concept and should be avoided by any means, when trying to achieve a better understanding of reality. (Thalhofer et al. 2018: 106–7)

Moreover, Thalhofer claims, there are socio-political implications:

> If someone happens to know the 'truth', that person naturally feels superior to people that don't know it. Therefore, in the linear world of the truth, there is a hierarchy, and anyone who sees things differently is considered to be worth less. If you imagine a society where every member is aware that there are different ways to look at things and that there is not only one 'true' way, this awareness would create a more tolerant society. (Thalhofer et al. 2018: 107)

Lest one get the erroneous impression that views like Thalhofer's are not seriously held within film and media studies and other corners of academia, consider another claim of Zimmerman's, which echoes his: 'Poststructuralist and postcolonial historiographers argue for polyphony as a strategy to turn away from causality, linearity, and unity, those elements often linked to hegemonic power that minimises difference' (2018: 13). This quote from Zimmerman is especially helpful inasmuch as it succinctly identifies the crux of the conceptual opposition to linear narrative and points to its origins.

One of the key reference points in the poststructuralist turn in historiography is the work of Hayden White, which has had a lasting impact across a number of humanities fields. In one well known essay, White claims:

> historians themselves [. . .] have transformed narrativity from a manner of speaking into a value, the presence of which in a discourse having to do with real events signals at once its objectivity, its seriousness, and its realism. I have sought to suggest that this value attached to narrativity in the representation of real events arises out of a desire to have real events display the coherence, integrity, fullness, and closure of an image of life that is and can only be imaginary. The notion that sequences of real events possess the formal attributes of the stories we tell about imaginary events could only have its origin in wishes, daydreams, reveries. (White 1981: 23)

As W. J. T. Mitchell pithily observes in his introduction to the collection in which White's essay appears, the implication of White's argument is that 'narrativity *as such* tends to support orthodox and politically conservative social conditions and that the revolt against narrativity [. . .] is a revolt against the authority of the social system' (1981: viii). Mitchell's statement more or less encapsulates the understanding of narrative that underlies much scepticism towards it that can be found across the humanities over the past forty years right up to contemporary theorising about the epistemic and ethico-political value of non-narrative, non-linear interactive documentary.

A Moderate Pessimism about Interactive Documentary and a Critique of Narrative Scepticism

Now that the various claims for the particular value of interactive documentary have been canvassed and the narrative scepticism that underlies those claims has been summarised, it is time to appraise both. By way of a summary review, let me begin by briefly outlining the claims considered above regarding the values of interactive documentary:

1. Interactive documentary possesses a distinctive *affective* value; it has a special capacity to move viewers/users affectively.
2. Interactive documentary possesses a distinctive *persuasive* value; it has a special capacity to persuade viewers/users.[4]
3. Interactive documentary possesses a distinctive *epistemic* value; its form more closely approximates the complexity of reality than other forms.
4. Interactive documentary possesses a distinctive *political* value; it has a special capacity to spur viewers/users to take action that effects social change.

5. Interactive documentary possesses a distinctive *ethical* value; insofar as it eschews the single voice or structuring authority of a sole author in favour of polyphony, it is a more inclusive form that is more likely than other forms to promote tolerance.

As we saw above, these claims can be combined in various ways. For example, Watson's (2017) argument for (4) tacitly employs (1), (2), and (3) as premises. And many other examples are possible. Rather than critiquing a specific argument that makes use of one or more of these claims, however, I want to assess each on its individual merits.

Let us consider claims (1) and (2) as a subset because they are straightforward, empirical claims. By this, I mean that they make claims whose approximate truth, falsehood, or plausibility can be determined by empirical inquiry. The claim that interactive documentary is particularly good at generating affective responses from viewers is *empirical* because it is a claim that can, in principle, be confirmed or falsified by going out into the world and discovering whether viewers really do have more affective responses, more intense affective responses, and so forth, to interactive documentary than to traditional documentary. 'Discovering' should not be taken to mean 'discovering once and for all'; yes, there is a fact of the matter about whether an empirical claim like this one is true, but our understanding of whether it is true or not is subject to revision in light of further investigation and evidence.

As it happens, there is so little evidence in support of the claim that interactive documentary possesses a special affective value that it is hard to see why anyone would think it is true. Watson makes the claim, but presents no evidence in favour of it. My own review of the literature turned up nothing except for a recent study that found that for one interactive documentary, at least, interactive elements seem to have *lessened* viewer engagement (Ducasse et al. 2020). More specifically, 'data collected on the web portal show[ed] a decrease in the number of user[s] every time they had to click on one interactive element' (Ducasse et al. 2020: 21).

At this point, the proponent of the claim could respond that, despite the lack of empirical evidence, we might still find conceptual support for the claim by positing some sort of hypothetical spectator whose responses to interactive documentary we can reasonably infer based on what we know about the general emotional responses of actual spectators. Appealing to a hypothetical spectator is a controversial gambit in some corners of film and media studies, but it is one that I think is entirely reasonable. Yet the claim still faces another problem, which is that there is lots of conceptually sound theorising, bolstered by empirical research on actual spectators, that clearly indicates that, in fact, motion picture *narratives* have an impressive capacity for eliciting strong affective responses from viewers.

One highly plausible and influential account of emotion conceives of familiar emotions like anger, fear, happiness, sadness, surprise, and disgust as partly defined by their function as appraisal mechanisms – that is, as 'tools' for evaluating a situation or object in relation to one's own interests or goals.[5] (My anger is elicited by the revelation that another child has been bullying my son; my fear is elicited by the knowledge that a loved one has been exposed to COVID-19.) Emotive appraisals are thus, as Noël Carroll puts it, 'relative to certain criteria [. . .] [e.g.] perceived danger is a criterion for fear' (2010: 4). Narrative cinema (fiction and nonfiction), which is clearly in the *business* of offering powerful emotional experiences, is designed to be 'criterially prefocused' for viewers – it is 'structured [so] that the descriptions and depictions of the pertinent objects of our attention in the movie clearly and decisively satisfy the criteria for the emotional state intended by the creators of the moving picture' (Carroll 2008: 159). In other words, if we are not laughing at a comedy, not scared by a horror film, not saddened by a melodrama, or not sympathetic to a film's hero, something has gone very wrong because these are the aims of filmmakers, and the success of their movies largely depends upon them successfully eliciting the emotions they intend.

As numerous theorists have described, film narrative (along with its constituent features) is a key mechanism for filmmakers to cue viewers' emotions (e.g. Tan 1996; Grodal 1997; Carroll 2008; Smith 2003; Plantinga 2009, 2018). In particular, mainstream narrative films often rely on so-called paradigm scenarios – that is, in Ronald de Sousa's words, 'a situation type, a kind of original drama that defines the roles, feelings, and reactions characteristic of [a particular emotion]' (quoted in Plantinga 2009: 80). 'Drama' is an apposite choice of word, for these paradigm scenarios work so well in narrative cinema in part because they have the form of mini-narratives. As Plantinga puts it, 'Narrative form is not simply a matter of the organisation of cues to facilitate story comprehension; it also encourages a chronological pattern of emotional response' (2009: 91). Numerous empirical studies support the idea that not only is narrative form in motion pictures designed to 'encourage a chronological pattern of emotional response', but it often succeeds in this effort both in fictional and non-fictional contexts (e.g. Lang et al. 2003; Green et al. 2004; Zillman 2006; Busselle and Bilandzic 2009).

In fact, it is precisely because narrative has the capacity for so powerfully stirring our emotions that scholars from diverse perspectives commonly attribute to narrative a special power of persuasion. Currently, narrative persuasion is a thriving area of research in communications and media psychology, and recent work has begun to illuminate the role of emotion in contributing to a narrative's persuasive effects (Appel and Richter 2010; Nabi and Green 2015; Alam and So 2020). But, of course, the intuition that narrative has a special persuasive value by virtue of its ability to stir our emotions has been around for a long time, and it has been formalised and reformulated periodically over the years – sometimes to emphasise the socio-political or ethical potential of narrative (Nussbaum 1990; Carroll 2001; Stadler 2008; Kozloff 2013; Sinnerbrink 2016; Plantinga 2018) and sometimes to reveal narrative's supposed penchant for perpetuating pernicious ideology or abetting ethical wrongs (e.g. Wollen [1972] 2004; White 1981; Presser 2018).

This is not to say that claim (2) about interactive documentary's special persuasive value is false. But it is to say that its advocates have a significant burden of proof to shoulder because narrative's special capacity for persuasion is widely accepted by its champions and its sceptics alike. Are there reasons to think that interactive documentary possesses a similar, let alone greater, capacity for persuasion? Again, Watson offers no evidence to think that it does. The extant empirical research suggests that there may be some grounds to think that interactive media (not specifically documentary) *might* have persuasive effects, but the research is limited and in early stages (for discussion, see Sundar and Oh 2020).

However, there are also some good conceptual reasons for remaining sceptical of (2). In particular, as Charles Forceville notes, 'the freedom of the user in interactive documentary comes at the price of proportionally reducing the maker's power to argue, and considerably increases the risk that the user will prematurely stop engaging with the documentary [cf. Ducasse et al. 2020]' (2017: 225). The 'freedom of the user', Forceville observes, has at least two important aspects: one is the freedom to manipulate the documentary's temporality in a way that eschews narrative, linearity, and causality; the second is the resulting freedom to eschew a narrative or authorial point of view on the represented events. And although this is what numerous interactive documentary champions ostensibly advocate, it is very difficult to imagine how interactive documentary could persuade anyone of anything if causality and point of view are evacuated in this way.

It is also important to note the implications of accepting the counter-claim (2*) that narrative has a special capacity for persuasion.[6] Accepting (2*) makes it hard to defend the sort of thoroughgoing scepticism about narrative's inherent political or ethical perniciousness. Why? Because, evidently, the political or ethical valance of narrative's persuasive effects will depend on the content of the narrative; it will depend upon what the narrative is designed to persuade viewers *of*. And this is crucial because it undermines the narrative scepticism that ostensibly motivates claims (4) and (5) regarding interactive documentary's special political and ethical values.

It is hard to see, for example, why we should be sceptical of the political or ethical value of a linear, narrative documentary like *Strong Island* (2017, dir. Yance Ford), which tells the story of a young Black man's death at the hands of a white man who later walked free. Directed by the victim's brother, Yance

Ford, *Strong Island* embraces linear, narrative form (and a distinct, authorial perspective) to relay this tragedy in a way that is designed to elicit our moral indignation and persuade us of the plausibility of the filmmaker's contention that at least a distal, if not proximate, cause of it is the systemic racism of American society. Moreover, the idea that a film like this one (and it is easy to think of many analogous examples) could, in principle, be better politically or ethically simply by virtue of eschewing narrative form in favour of interactive form borders on perversity. For it is crucial to the film's political and ethical value that the viewer's moral indignation be elicited, which in turn partly depends upon the viewer perceiving the story from the perspective of the victim's brother and the viewer apprehending the causal links between American society's structural racism and the miscarriage of justice in this particular case. Indeed, affording a viewer/user the means to rearrange the story in a way that evacuated the linear narrative, the authorial perspective, or these causal links would not only deprive the film of its political and ethical force, but could actually be politically and ethically pernicious.

Moreover, offering a viewer/user such interactive affordances in a case like *Strong Island* would misrepresent the facts of the case; it would be inaccurate and could potentially mislead a viewer/user about the truth of the incident. Here we arrive at the thorniest issue at stake – namely, the question of epistemic value and documentary's relationship to it. Obviously, I will have to gloss over a number of rather complex matters. First, the question of 'truth'. Is 'truth' a 'bullshit concept' as Thalhofer claims? It is actually hard to see how truth could not be involved in what Thalhofer describes as 'a better understanding of reality' since one cannot make much sense of *that* idea unless there are some true facts about reality that one can understand to a greater or lesser degree. Surely, coming to a better understanding of reality is nothing more than arriving at a more approximate truth about reality – say, moving from the false view that African Americans receive equal justice in the American legal system to a view of the truth, which is that they do not.

Perhaps this seems uncharitable to Thalhofer. Is there a better way to construe his view? One might suppose a better way for him to phrase things could be along the lines Aston and Odorico advocate – 'a dialogical sense of truth by presenting a multilayered reality' (2018: 75). However, this phrasing seems to me simply a prolix way of saying that the truth about reality is that it is multilayered, multifaceted, complex, or whatever. And I gather that this is related to what Thalhofer has to say about the prominence of 'influence' over 'causality'. But the 'influence'/'cause' dichotomy is surely a false one that has been created by an implausibly narrow conception of causality. Indeed, it is not clear how we are to understand the concept of 'influence' *without* some concept of causality. The point we should grant is that causality, like reality, is complex. Causality can be indirect, multiple, diffuse, distal, and so forth. But it is a concept we need to retain because it is an essential part of the 'folk' conceptions (upon which we all rely) of the way the universe works.[7]

Thus far, I have tacitly been focusing on claims about what we might call the truth about the 'world out there'. What I have in mind here is something like truth in the sense of a proposition's correspondence to some fact or state of affairs in the world (see, for full accounts, Alston 1996; Fumerton 2002). On one formulation of this sort of conception of truth,

> What it takes to render a statement true is something that is objective vis-à-vis that statement, namely, a fact involving what that statement is about. The truth value of the statement depends on how it is with 'the world' 'beyond' the statement rather than on some feature of the statement itself. (Alston 2001: 41)

The reason for thinking about truth in this way – at least in relation to propositions about the 'world out there' – is that this is most plausibly the tacit, 'folk' conception of truth operative in our everyday lives. Indeed, claims about the socio-political value of interactive documentary – or, more broadly, about polyphony – actually depend upon this concept of truth. Clearly, for example, to 'articulate and unravel complex political and social issues' (to use Zimmerman's words) requires there to be some approximate truth that can be arrived at in the process of unravelling complex issues; it is not that there is no truth, but just that it is complex. And if, of course, there were no truth, it would be very hard to see the point of discussing, articulating, debating, trying to unravel complex political and social issues. What would the end goal of those processes be if not to glean a better understanding of those issues, which, as we saw above, in turn depends upon there being some truth about them?

Matters are even less straightforward, however, with regard to ethics. Are there moral facts to which moral claims may or may not correspond? Or is there no 'truth' to a moral claim beyond its expression of an attitude on the part of the speaker? Nobody really knows, and the debate will not be settled anytime soon. And of course, aside from the difficult meta-ethical questions, there are tricky questions about normative ethics. There are multiple, sometimes incompatible or conflicting ethical values at stake in our informal communities (think about the debates about gay rights in churches) and our local communities (is protesting the police virtuous or disrespectful?), not to mention within and across societies and cultures. So, perhaps the most charitable way that calls for polyphony or 'a dialogic' sense of truth can be understood is as a step beyond a *recognition* of the plural and heterogeneous values to which people are committed – as, rather, an embrace of the idea that none of these values (or value systems) has a greater claim to truth than another; they are equally 'true' for the people or communities who hold them.

Even in that case, however, there are still reasons to be sceptical about the coherence of the claims for polyphony. In the first place, clearly even the writers who ostensibly advocate for polyphony in this sense of value pluralism cannot fully embrace polyphony in practice. For Thalhofer, tolerance is a good that should be promoted; for Aston and Odorico, democracy is a good to be promoted; for Zimmerman, polyphony is a good. The point is not that these are implausible claims, but rather that at some point they need to be grounded upon a claim about what constitutes value – or at least, the sorts of things that *are* valuable – that these authors think is *right* regardless of what the multiplicity of voices surrounding them says about it. Aston and Odorico, at least, acknowledge this, but do not seem to recognise the implications of their view being self-defeating.

There is another point, which Aston and Odorico deserve commendation for at least acknowledging, which is that it is hard to accept the rather buoyant claims for polyphony (and, more broadly, pluralism about truth in the context of value[8]) given that it entails introducing prejudiced, bigoted, and hateful voices into dialogue (on 'equal footing', to mix metaphors) with tolerant, open-minded (dare I say 'liberal'), and loving voices. Polyphony puts democracy into dialogue with totalitarianism, feminism into dialogue with patriarchy, Black Lives Matter into dialogue with white power. All well and good, one might think, if it results in a better understanding on the part of the fascists, bigots, and the like. But that is not what polyphony or value pluralism promises. Indeed, the equal dialogue – the 'heteroglossia' – of these distinct views is something that, by their very nature, value pluralism and polyphony are committed not only to accepting by virtue of their epistemic commitments, but, as a logical consequence, to celebrating as politically and ethically virtuous. And this should be regarded as an unpalatable result.

Let us return now to documentary, specifically. Should interactive documentary's eschewal of linear narrative and affordance of polyphony be regarded as an epistemic virtue?[9] We certainly should not accept that claim for the reasons given by Thalhofer et al. or Zimmerman: we should reject the idea that interactive documentary, by virtue of abandoning linearity, authorial point of view, and/or causality, necessarily offers viewers/users a more accurate picture of reality. Conceptual points aside, this ought to be clear enough by reflecting for just a moment on the interactive documentary *Life Underground*: if a white supremacist decides to interact with that documentary by *only* engaging with the stories of white subway passengers, is that going to afford him a more accurate picture of reality than if he were to watch *all* of the stories in a linear fashion – in the form of a traditional documentary? Surely not. We should reject the idea that, by virtue of its capacity for polyphony, interactive documentary necessarily offers viewers/users better understandings of complex socio-political issues. Again, the example of *Strong Island* should make this clear enough aside from all the conceptual points: should we think that supplementing Yance Ford's perspective on structural racism in the United States with the perspective of ignorant white supremacists will afford viewers/users a better understanding of the phenomenon simply because a plurality of voices are represented? Surely not.

Watson's argument for the epistemic value of interactive documentary has more to recommend it. There is certainly some plausibility to the idea that the accumulation of a greater amount of facts and information afforded by a database documentary could yield epistemic advantages. But, again, it is unlikely the interactive technology *alone* – say, solely the database form of the documentary – could be the source of epistemic value. An analogy might be instructive here: there is little reason to think that a physical archive, on its own, yields epistemic gains. You could show up at the Library of Congress or the Academy Film Archive, poke around aimlessly for a week, and not be much better off epistemically. Why? Because your access of the information in the archives lacks a structure, a context, a navigating force. However, if you befriend a good archivist – someone who can help you navigate the archive – you could be much better off epistemically at the end of your trip. It is plausible that database documentaries are like archives in this way: perhaps they have the capacity to let you access more facts and information than a traditional feature-length documentary might, but that alone is insufficient to make them sources of epistemic value.

CONCLUSION: ON NOT GIVING UP ON NARRATIVE DOCUMENTARY

This brings us back to the question of narrative. In the same way that there is a long history of suspicion of narrative's political and ethical value because of its particular capacity for eliciting emotions and persuading, there is also a long history of suspicion of narrative's epistemic value for these and additional reasons. In an illuminating overview, Paisley Livingston (2009) describes a number of these reasons that have parallels in statements of narrative scepticism in the context of documentary. The one that is relevant here is the idea that narratives are 'unsound by virtue of selectivity or closure' (Livingston 2009: 26).[10] This is a claim we encountered above – one that ostensibly motivates the championing of polyphony, which avoids selecting or privileging a single viewpoint, as well as the database, which is accumulative rather than selective. But just as we saw that the privileging of a single viewpoint is not necessarily the source of an epistemic flaw or an ethical flaw, we should now recognise that neither is the selection and organisation of *some* facts and information necessarily the source of an epistemic flaw (see Plantinga 1997: 198–200). *Knock Down the House* (2019, dir. Rachel Lears) is a traditional, linear narrative that tells the story of four female, Democratic candidates who ran for Congress in 2018. But there is no reason to think that it is inaccurate, biased, false, misleading, or otherwise epistemically deficient by virtue of selectively presenting the Congressional race from the perspective of only four candidates, of only female candidates, or of only Democratic candidates.

On the contrary, narrative documentary's capacity to select particular facts, information, and events, and to organise their presentation, can be the source of epistemic value.[11] One possibility here is that the selection and organisation of facts, information, and events in the form of a linear narrative offers the best representational approximation of an actual situation or event. Sometimes the best explanation for how or why something happened takes the form of a narrative because that form is closer than any other to the structure of the event itself. If you want to know why I was late to class yesterday, the best explanation – that is, the one that most accurately represents the actual event and its associated causes – is that I woke up late, which meant that my kids were up late, which meant that we left the house later than normal, which meant we got stuck in heavier traffic than normal, all of which together resulted in me arriving to class late. There were other aspects to the event that I could mention – we listened to Nick Cave in the car – but they would not be relevant to the explanation. Thus, selectivity is warranted to the extent that it highlights *salient* facts, events, and so on – that is, those facts and events that actually had a causal influence on the event that needs explaining.

A second possibility for narrative documentary's selectivity and organisation to yield epistemic value is closely related to the case of *Strong Island*: it involves the way narrative's presentation of causality can lead a viewer to a better understanding of an event or situation. Consider, briefly, two documentaries that are both about incarceration – perhaps less charitably, the prison industry – in the United States: the interactive documentary *Public Secrets*, by Sharon Daniel, allows viewers/users to click through a computer interface in a way that allows them to listen to audio recordings of women incarcerated in the California Correctional Women's Facility; the linear, narrative documentary *13th* (2016), by Ava DuVernay, offers a historical narrative of the origins on the prison industrial complex that identifies America's structural racism as a key cause.

Both *Public Secrets* and *13th* possess a number of epistemic, not to mention politico-ethical merits – most notably in terms of the ways in which they illuminate the structural inequality that underlies mass incarceration and the prison industry in the United States. I do not mean to in any way denigrate *Public Secrets*, which I think to a large extent successfully realises Daniel's aim to bring to light the 'public secret' that is mass incarceration and her aim to give a platform for expression to a group of people whom society normally silences. I understand her claim that

> where one voice, an individual story, is intended to stand in for a class of subjects, there is a dangerous and disabling tendency to identify the subject as a case of a tragically flawed character or unusually unfortunate

victim of aberrant injustice – rather than one among many affected by structural inequality. (Daniel 2012: 217)

But I disagree that this is necessarily the case (again, think: *Strong Island*), and I further disagree that 'to understand and empathize, to hear and accept, a listener must be moved beyond the logic of cause and effect and into the realm of affect' (Daniel 2012: 225).

On the contrary, not only are cognition and affect compatible, but it is our comprehension of the inveterate structural *causes* of mass incarceration – racism and other forms of inequality – that yields the best understanding of the phenomenon and elicits our moral indignation *at the system* as well as our empathy for its victims. The narrative form of *13th*, which identifies and traces the roots of these causes, seems to offer viewers a fuller explanation and better grasp of the *why* the United States has the prison-industry complex it does, *how* it came to have it, and *why* it is unfair and morally unacceptable.[12]

At their best, narrative documentaries like *13th* harness all of the features of narrative that have been the sources of scepticism towards it at one time or another – its capacity to elicit emotion, its capacity to persuade, its capacity to yield understanding – and use them in conjunction to achieve politically and ethically salutary aims. Manohla Dargis's *New York Times* review of *13th* describes this well:

> Powerful, infuriating and at times overwhelming, Ava DuVernay's documentary '13th' will get your blood boiling and tear ducts leaking. It shakes you up, but it also challenges your ideas about the intersection of race, justice and mass incarceration in the United States [. . .] By the time her movie ends, Ms. DuVernay has delivered a stirring treatise on the prison industrial complex through a nexus of racism, capitalism, policies and politics. It sounds exhausting, but it's electrifying [. . .] With few exceptions, the movie's voices [. . .] speak in concert [. . .] Even with its surprise guests [e.g. Newt Gingrich] the movie isn't especially dialectical; it also isn't mainstream journalism. Ms. DuVernay presents both sides of the story, as it were (racism versus civil rights). Yet she doesn't call on, say, politicians who have voted against civil rights measures for their thoughts on the history of race in the United States. She begins from the premise that white supremacy has already had its say for centuries. (Dargis 2016)

Those comments, I think, nicely summarise, with a concrete example, not only why we might reserve praise for interactive documentary simply for being interactive, non-linear, polyphonic, and so forth, but also why we are still right to think that, at its very best, narrative documentary can elicit our moral emotions, inform, and persuade in ways that are politically and ethically vital.

Acknowledgements

I am grateful to Alex Bevan, Marguerite La Caze, Paisley Livingston, and Carl Plantinga for helpful comments on earlier versions of this chapter. None of them are responsible for whatever errors or other infelicities it contains (especially not Alex).

Notes

1. In fact, a remark from Murray helps explain to some extent how and why the terms 'interactivity' and 'participatory' are often conflated in discussions of digital technology: 'the primary representative property of the computer is the codified rendering of responsive behaviours. This is what is most often meant when we say that computers are *interactive*. We mean that they create an environment that is both procedural and participatory' ([1997] 2017: 90).

2. Manovich's argument is not very good, but worth reproducing for readers to see his thinking: 'As a cultural form, the database represents the world as a list of items which it refuses to order. In contrast, a narrative creates a cause-and-effect trajectory of seemingly unordered items (events). Therefore, database and narrative are natural "enemies". Competing for the same territory of human culture, each claims an exclusive right to make meaning out of the world' (1999: 85).

3. Matt Soar offers a useful description of the relevant differences of the Korsakow System: 'Unlike [many other] authoring tools, and the works produced with them (which one might compare in terms of structure to Choose Your Own Adventure books), the [smallest narrative units] in a Korsakow film are not connected together with fixed paths. Rather, they are contextually articulated to one another using two sets of keywords (tags), what we might think of as metadata [. . .] For filmmakers who already work with production software, perhaps the most vivid clue to Korsakow's uniqueness is that the application interface does not have a timeline (unlike, say, Final Cut Pro, iMovie, After Effects, Flash, Pro Tools, Audacity). This is a definitive reminder that, in a Korsakow film, story elements are not triggered based on a fixed "master" sequence, but by hidden, iterative, keyword searches' (2014: 162).

4. Another way to put this would be to say – as Carl Plantinga does – that (screen-based) narrative has a special rhetorical power (2018: 13), but I am wary of that phrasing in the current context because of the multiple, often conflicting senses in which 'rhetoric' is understood in different disciplines.

5. I want to remain agnostic on the right account of emotions, but what I have in mind here is some sort of hybrid cognitive–perceptual account, according to which emotions are 'embodied appraisals' (Prinz 2004), 'concern-based construals' (Roberts 2003), or something of the sort.

6. One could accept (2*) without necessarily accepting an analogous counter-claim (1*) to the effect that narrative has a special capacity to elicit emotion, though I think, as a matter of fact, (1*) is an important part of explaining (2*).

7. This way of phrasing things is meant to indicate my agnosticism (and ignorance) about the question of whether causality exists at the level of fundamental physics. For discussion, see Field (2003).

8. I would rather call this 'value-relativism' but the term has so many connotations that I am afraid I will be accused of attacking a straw man if I use it.

9. There is a parallel here to the way 'reflexivity' has been championed in the literature on documentary film, as well as to Carl Plantinga's (1997: 214–18) critique of it.

10. Other statements of scepticism regarding narrative's epistemic value which have parallels in the literature on documentary include the ideas 'that narratives or stories tend, by virtue of their narrativity, to be: (1) pseudo-explanatory: narratives embody or encourage the fallacy of *post hoc ergo propter hoc*; (2) pseud-justificatory: the persuasive appeal of stories is disproportionate to their real evidential support or reliability; (3) misleading: stories encourage the error of *pars pro toto*; (4) seductive: a story's narrativity is likely to lead to a "hot" irrationality through its strong or even "irresistible" emotional appeal, which is obtained at the price of cognitive shortcomings' (Livingston 2009: 25).

11. For a sustained, illuminating discussion of these issues, see Plantinga (1997), especially chapters 5 and 7.

12. Since completing this chapter, I discovered that the historical argument advanced by *13th* has been disputed by some historians (e.g. Scott 2020). The case I make here for *13th* assumed the veracity of that argument and, indeed, my point about the epistemic and ethical values of narrative documentaries is restricted to those narrative documentaries that, indeed, are also accurate, truthful, etc. My *general* claim is thus not undermined even if it turns out that *13th*'s historical argument is flawed, misleading, or plainly wrong.

References

13th. Documentary. Directed by Ava DuVernay. USA: Netflix, 2016.

Alam, Nizia, and Jiyeon So. 2020. 'Contributions of Emotional Flow in Narrative Persuasion: An Empirical Test of the Emotional Flow Framework.' *Communication Quarterly* 68.2: 161–82.

Alston, William P. 1996. *A Realist Conception of Truth*. Ithaca, NY: Cornell University Press.

Alston, William P. 2001. 'A Realist Conception of Truth.' In *The Nature of Truth: Classic and Contemporary Perspectives*, edited by Michael P. Lynch, 41–66. Cambridge, MA: MIT Press.

Appel, Markus, and Tobias Richter. 2010. 'Transportation and Need for Affect in Narrative Persuasion: A Mediated Moderation Model.' *Media Psychology* 13: 101–35.

Aston, Judith, and Sandra Gaudenzi. 2012. 'Interactive Documentary: Setting the Field.' *Studies in Documentary Film* 6.2: 125–39.

Aston, Judith, Sandra Gaudenzi, and Mandy Rose (eds). 2017. *I-Docs: The Evolving Practices of Interactive Documentary*. New York: Columbia University Press.

Aston, Judith, and Stefano Odorico. 2018. 'The Poetics and Politics of Polyphony: Towards a Research Method for Interactive Documentary.' *Alphaville: Journal of Film and Screen Media* 15: 63–93.

Aufderheide, Pat. 2015. 'Interactive Documentaries: Navigation and Design.' *Journal of Film and Video* 67.3–4: 69–78.

Bear 71. Documentary. Directed by Jeremy Mendes, Leanne Allison. Canada: National Film Board of Canada, 2012.

Busselle, Rick, and Helena Bilandzic. 2009. 'Measuring Narrative Engagement.' *Media Psychology* 12: 321–47.

Carroll, Noël. 2001. 'Art, Narrative, and Moral Understanding.' In Noël Carroll, *Beyond Aesthetics*, 270–93. Cambridge: Cambridge University Press.

Carroll, Noël. 2008. *The Philosophy of Motion Pictures*. Malden, MA: Blackwell.

Carroll, Noël. 2010. 'Movies, the Moral Emotions, and Sympathy.' *Midwest Studies in Philosophy* 34: 1–19.

Chronicle of a Summer. Documentary. Directed by Jean Rouch and Edgar Morin. France: Argos Films, 1961.

Daniel, Sharon. 2012. 'On Politics and Aesthetics: A Case Study of "Public Secrets" and "Blood Sugar".' *Studies in Documentary Film* 6.2: 215–27.

Dargis, Manohla. 2016. 'Review: "13th," the Journey from Shackles to Prison Bars.' *The New York Times*, 29 September. <https://www.nytimes.com/2016/09/30/movies/13th-review-ava-duvernay.html> (last accessed 19 March 2021).

Dovey, Jon. 2014. 'Documentary Ecosystems: Collaboration and Exploitation.' In *New Documentary Ecologies: Emerging Platforms, Practices, and Discourses*, edited by Kate Nash, Craig Hight, and Catherine Summerhayes, 11–32. Basingstoke: Palgrave Macmillan.

Ducasse, Julie, Matjaž Kljun, and Klen Čopič Pucihar. 2020. 'Interactive Web Documentaries: A Case Study of Audience Reception and User Engagement on iOtok.' *International Journal of Human-Computer Interaction*. Advance article, online. <https://doi.org/10.10 80/10447318.2020.1757255> (last accessed 19 March 2021).

Field, Hartry. 2003. 'Causation in a Physical World.' In *The Oxford Handbook of Metaphysics*, edited by Michael J. Loux and Dean W. Zimmerman, 435–60. Oxford: Oxford University Press.

Forceville, Charles. 2017. 'Interactive Documentary and its Limited Opportunities to Persuade.' *Discourse, Context & Media* 20: 218–26.

Fumerton, Richard. 2002. *Realism and the Correspondence Theory of Truth*. Lanham, MD: Rowman & Littlefield.

Gaza/Sderot: Life in Spite of Everything. Documentary. Directed by Khalil Al Muzayyen, Ayelet Bachar. France, Israel, Palestine: Arte France, Bo Travail!, Upian, 2008.

Green, Melanie C., Timothy C. Brock, and Geoff F. Kaufman. 2004. 'Understanding Media Enjoyment: The Role of Transportation into Narrative Worlds.' *Communication Theory* 14.4: 311–27.

Grodal, Torben. 1997. *Moving Pictures: A New Theory of Film Genres, Feelings, and Cognition*. Oxford: Clarendon Press.

Highrise. Documentary. Directed by Katerina Cizek. Canada: National Film Board of Canada, 2009–present.

Jaguar. Documentary. Directed by Jean Rouch. France: Les Films de la Pléiade, 1967.

Jenkins, Henry. [1993] 2003. *Textual Poachers: Television Fans and Participatory Culture*. Updated twentieth anniversary edition. New York: Routledge.

Knock Down the House. Documentary. Directed by Rachel Lears. USA: Artemis Rising Foundation, 2019.

Kozloff, Sarah. 2013. 'Empathy and the Cinema of Engagement: Reevaluating the Politics of Film.' *Projections: The Journal for Movies and Mind* 7.2: 1–40.

Lang, Annie, Deborah Potter, and Maria Elizabeth Grabe. 2003. 'Making News Memorable: Applying Theory to the Production of Local Television News.' *Journal of Broadcasting & Electronic Media* 47.1: 113–23.

Life Underground. Documentary. Directed by Hervé Cohen. France: La Huit, 2018.

Livingston, Paisley. 2009. 'Narrativity and Knowledge.' *The Journal of Aesthetics and Art Criticism* 67.1: 25–36.

Lopes, Dominic McIver. 2010. *A Philosophy of Computer Art.* London: Routledge.

MacDougall, David. [1975] 1998. 'Beyond Observational Cinema.' In David MacDougall, *Transcultural Cinema*, edited by Lucien Taylor, 125–39. Princeton, NJ: Princeton University Press.

Manovich, Lev. 1999. 'Database as Symbolic Form.' *Convergence: The International Journal of Research into New Media Technologies* 5.2: 80–99.

Miller, Liz, and Martin Allor. 2016. 'Choreographies of Collaboration: Social Engagement in Interactive Documentaries.' *Studies in Documentary Film* 10.1: 53–70.

Mitchell, W. J. T. (ed.). 1981. *On Narrative.* Chicago: University of Chicago Press.

Murray, Janet. [1997] 2017. *Hamlet on the Holodeck: The Future of Narrative in Cyberspace.* Updated edition. Cambridge, MA: MIT Press.

Nabi, Robin L., and Melanie C. Green. 2015. 'The Role of Narrative's Emotional Flow in Promoting Persuasive Outcomes.' *Media Psychology* 18.2: 137–62.

Nash, Kate. 2012. 'Modes of Interactivity: Analysing the Webdoc.' *Media, Culture, and Society* 34.2: 195–210.

Nash, Kate. 2014. 'Clicking on the World: Documentary Representation and Interactivity.' In *New Documentary Ecologies: Emerging Platforms, Practices, and Discourses*, edited by Kate Nash, Craig Hight, and Catherine Summerhayes, 50–66. Basingstoke: Palgrave Macmillan.

Nichols, Bill. 2010. *Introduction to Documentary.* 2nd edition. Bloomington, IN: University of Indiana Press.

Nussbaum, Martha C. 1990. *Love's Knowledge: Essays on Philosophy and Literature.* Oxford: Oxford University Press.

O'Flynn, Siobhan. 2012. 'Documentary's Metaphoric Form: Webdoc, Interactive, Transmedia, Participatory, and Beyond.' *Studies in Documentary Film* 6.2: 141–57.

Plantinga, Carl. 1997. *Rhetoric and Representation in Nonfiction Film.* Cambridge: Cambridge University Press.

Plantinga, Carl. 2009. *Moving Viewers: American Film and the Spectator's Experience.* Berkeley, CA: University of California Press.

Plantinga, Carl. 2018. *Screen Stories: Emotion and the Ethics of Engagement.* New York: Oxford University Press.

Points of View. Documentary. Directed by Zohar Kfir. Canada, Israel, Palestine: B'Tselem, 2014.

Presser, Lois. 2018. *Inside Story: How Narratives Drive Mass Harm.* Berkeley, CA: University of California Press.

Prinz, Jesse J. 2004. *Gut Reactions: A Perceptual Theory of Emotion.* New York: Oxford University Press.

Prison Valley. Documentary. Directed by David Dufresne, Phillipe Brault. France: Arte France, Upian, 2009.

Public Secrets. Documentary. Directed by Sharon Daniel. USA, 2006.

Roberts, Robert C. 2003. *Emotions: An Essay in Aid of Moral Psychology.* Cambridge: Cambridge University Press.

Rose, Mandy. 2017. 'Not Media About, But Media With: Co-creation for Activism.' In *I-Docs: The Evolving Practices of Interactive Documentary*, edited by Judith Aston, Sandra Gaudenzi, and Mandy Rose, 49–65. New York: Columbia University Press.

Rouch, Jean. [1973] 2003. 'The Camera and Man.' In Jean Rouch, *Ciné-Ethnography*, edited and translated by Steven Feld, 29–46. Minneapolis, MN: University of Minnesota Press.

Scott, Daryl Michael. 2020. 'The Social and Intellectual Origins of 13thism.' *Fire!!!* 5.2: 2–39.

Sinnerbrink, Robert. 2016. *Cinematic Ethics: Exploring Ethical Experience through Film.* New York: Routledge.

Soar, Matt. 2014. 'Making (with) the Korsakow System: Database Documentaries as Articulation and Assemblage.' In *New Documentary Ecologies: Emerging Platforms, Practices and Discourses*, edited by Kate Nash, Craig Hight, and Catherine Summerhayes, 154–73. Basingstoke: Palgrave Macmillan.

Smith, Greg M. 2003. *Film Structure and the Emotion System.* Cambridge: Cambridge University Press.

Stadler, Jane. 2008. *Pulling Focus: Intersubjective Experience, Narrative Film, and Ethics.* New York: Continuum.

Strong Island. Documentary. Directed by Yance Ford. USA, Denmark: Yanceville Films, 2017.

Sundar, S. Shyam, and Jeeyun Oh. 2020. 'Psychological Effects of Interactive Media Technologies: A Human–Computer Interaction (HCI) Perspective.' In *Media Effects: Advances in Theory and Research.* 4th edition, edited by Mary Beth Oliver, Arthur A. Raney, and Jennings Bryant, 357–72. New York: Taylor and Francis.

Tan, Ed S. 1996. *Emotion and the Structure of Narrative Film: Film as an Emotion Machine.* Mahwah, NJ: Lawrence Erlbaum Associates.

Thalhofer, Florian, Judith Aston, and Stefano Odorico. 2018. 'Enacting Polyphony: An Interview with Florian Thalhofer.' *Alphaville: Journal of Film and Screen Media* 15: 106–12.

Watson, Ryan. 2017. 'Affective Radicality: Prisons, Palestine, and Interactive Documentary.' *Feminist Media Studies* 17.4: 600–15.

Welcome to Pine Point. Documentary. Directed by Michael Simons, Paul Shoebridge. Canada: National Film Board of Canada, 2011.

White, Hayden. 1981. 'The Value of Narrativity in the Representation of Reality.' In *On Narrative*, edited by W. J. T. Mitchell, 1–24. Chicago: University of Chicago Press.

Wollen, Peter. [1972] 2004. 'Godard and Counter Cinema: *Vent d'Est.*' In *Film Theory and Criticism*, edited by Leo Braudy and Marshall Cohen, 525–33. New York: Oxford University Press.

Zillmann, Dolf. 2006. 'Dramaturgy for Emotions from Fictional Narration.' In *Psychology of Entertainment*, edited by Jennings Bryant and Peter Vorderer, 215–38. Mahwah, NJ: Lawrence Erlbaum Associates.

Zimmerman, Patricia R. 2018. 'Thirty Speculations Toward a Polyphonic Model for New Media Democracy.' *Alphaville: Journal of Film and Screen Media* 15: 9–15.

9. WON'T SOMEBODY PLEASE THINK OF THE CHILDREN! ON THE MORALISATION OF VIDEO GAME VIOLENCE

Grant Tavinor

VIDEO GAMES AND MORAL PANIC

The sociologist Stanley Cohen begins his seminal work on public moralisation by noting that

> Societies seem subject, every now and then, to periods of moral panic. A condition, episode, person or group of persons emerges to become defined as a threat to societal values and interests; its nature is presented in a stylized and stereotypical fashion by the mass media; the moral barricades are manned by editors, bishops, politicians and other right-thinking people; socially accredited experts pronounce their diagnoses and solutions [. . .] (Cohen 2002: 1)

Cohen's focus was the Mods and Rockers phenomenon of 1960s Britain, but his description is filled with resonance for the issue of the public reception of violent video games. The disparity between the force with which the moral case against video games has been pursued, and what can be demonstrated about the connection between video games and harm, might lead one to think that this issue is just such a moral panic. Indeed, this claim has occasionally been made in the psychological literature on violent video games (Ferguson 2008; Kutner and Olson 2008; Sternheimer 2007).

If this evaluation is accurate, one might also enquire into the question of why the moralisation of games with violent content has been so enduring. The moralisation of video games has been a persistent and predictable reaction to the medium, from its initial appearance in the early days of gaming in the 1970s concerning games such as *Death Race*, to a resurfacing in the 1990s in the wake of the Columbine shootings and in Dave Grossman and Gloria DeGaetano's moralist screed *Stop Teaching Our Kids to Kill* (1999), to its invocation by Donald Trump in August 2019 as the United States was again beset by a wave of mass shootings.

The concern has often presented video games as a threat to children and society. During her failed run for the Democratic nomination in 2005, Hillary Clinton drew from the scientific literature regarding games to claim that 'Playing violent video games is to an adolescent's violent behavior what smoking tobacco is to lung cancer. [. . .] This isn't about offending our sensibilities – it is about protecting our children' (CBS News 2005). Talk show host Dr Phil McGraw was rather less reserved:

> common sense tells you that if these kids are playing video games, where they're on a mass killing spree in a video game, it's glamorized on the big screen, it's become part of the fiber of our society. You take that and mix it with a psychopath, a sociopath or someone suffering from mental illness and add in a dose of rage, the suggestibility is too high. And we're going to have to start dealing with that. (Quoted in Kutner and Olson 2008: 197)

In this chapter I will suggest that this moralism is at least partly sustained by the political capital inherent in the moralisation of entertainment forms such as violent video games. Middle-class moralists of many kinds have lined up against the perceived threat of gaming; we will find that this moralism frequently betrays the class-based aesthetics of its adherents, that it employs children as a proxy for advocating regulative responses that would be impossible if it were just adults playing the games, and that the moralism may act as a distraction – perhaps intentional – from other significant social dangers. One other note is important here as I begin. This chapter is not concerned with the morality of the content of violent video games, nor with the production or enjoyment of this fictional 'violence'. There has already been a great deal written on these topics (Bartel 2015; Briggle 2012; Patridge 2011; Tavinor 2009). Rather this chapter focuses on political and moral aspects of the social reception of such games.

Not just any social moral disturbance or disagreement constitutes the unnecessary or problematic moralism of a moral panic. The moral concern with the recent opioid crisis, for example, seems entirely warranted. The issue of mass shootings itself clearly deserves the moral concern it receives, and nothing that I say in this chapter is intended to claim otherwise. According to the sociologists Erich Goode and Nachman Ben-Yehuda (1994), the distinguishing features of a genuine moral panic are an acute level of concern in the public about an issue and its societal impact or harm, hostility towards the behaviour that comprises the issue or those involved in it, a relative consensus within some group that the issue is a societal problem, and a disproportionate moral weighting of the issue and the proposed response. Goode and Ben-Yehuda found that these distinguishing features could be used in a relatively objective way to identify a moral panic (1994: 41).

Thus, to establish if the concern with video games is *merely* a moral panic, we need to examine the wider details of their impact on social and personal well-being to settle whether the response is proportionate to the actual danger. Almost twenty years ago, during the height of the public concern with game violence, many of the scientists at the centre of the debate seemed quite certain that video games caused aggression in their players, and that this aggression was a significant cause of real-world violence. In their influential work on games and aggression, the psychologists Craig Anderson, Douglas Gentile, and Katherine Buckley concluded that the debate about media violence and aggression 'is over [. . .] and should have been over 30 years ago' (2007: 4). A meta-analytic literature review of the effects of game violence conducted by Anderson and his colleague Brad Bushman found the real-world effect to be significant when they concluded that 'These results clearly support the hypothesis that exposure to violent video games poses a public health threat to children and youths, including college-age individuals' (2001: 358). Anderson, Gentile, and Buckley would also claim that 'If society reduced the amount of exposure children have to violent videogames and other violent media, there would probably be a tremendous social impact' (2007: 143–4).

However, it is no longer as clear that the empirical case really does align with the strength of the moralist concerns with video games, as this earlier work has been subjected to an increasing amount of scepticism (Tavinor 2018). Lawrence Kutner and Cheryl Olson of the Harvard Medical School Center for Mental Health and Media conducted a large federally funded study into the effects of video games in which they decided to look more closely into the Anderson and Bushman meta-analytic review, going back to the original studies which it aggregated, finding numerous faults which made them very sceptical of the results (2008: 79). The psychologist Christopher Ferguson notes that, in terms of the theory that video games cause aggression, 'Meta-analytic studies of media violence effects have consistently demonstrated that links between media violence exposure and increased aggression are close to zero' (2010: 43). He concludes, 'If you are curious whether media violence contributes to violent crime, the simple answer is that we really don't know' (2010: 39). And, in fact, the idea that video games are driving an epidemic of violence sits uncomfortably with the 'reality [. . .] that [. . .] as violent video games have become more prevalent, violent crimes have decreased dramatically' (Ferguson 2008: 33). Of the very limited number of correlational studies that have investigated the link between violent video games and actual violent crime, at least one study has found that there may even be a negative correlation between video game play and actual crime (Ward 2011). Even Bushman and Gentile have moderated their views in recent years. In an interview with NPR, Gentile admitted that he could not say that the elimination of video games would have an effect on the prevalence of mass shootings, and that the scale of the effects they originally expected for video games was ultimately not borne out (NPR 2018).

The consideration that some widespread cases of social moralism are warranted by real moral dangers does raise the possibility that public moralism itself may play an important function in society by setting community norms and allowing the public to frame and respond to newly perceived threats to personal and public well-being and health. Moralisation may thus provide the impetus for societies to deal with threats to the integrity, health, or order of the community, by bringing an issue within a moralistic schema. According to Paul Rozin, 'Moralisation frequently occurs in the health domain, because of a deep and pervasive link between health and moral status, a link that extends throughout history and across cultures' (1999: 218). The philosopher J. L. Mackie gives a glimpse of how this moralisation process may work at the personal level. For him, morality is a set of constraints which 'work[s] by modifying an agent's view of possible actions, by attaching to them a moral characterisation, favourable or adverse, which has prescriptive entailments, and carries with it a corresponding characterisation of the agent himself if he performs those actions' (1977: 210). Mackie principally has in mind the intentional and rational application of moral constraints by individuals, but this picture may also apply to the less consciously or individually directed changes that drive public moral change.

An effective disruption of a prevailing norm, or adoption of a moralistic schema in a previously non-moral realm, may require a purported 'crisis' to focus and motivate the moral changes. The attending conviction that the new realm of deviance is a real social threat provides the energy needed to interrupt the status quo and provide the moral gestalt shift. That this moralism sometimes misfires on a societal level is not surprising, but it suggests that to understand the ethical significance of game violence we should also investigate the forces that have propelled this case of public and personal moralism; that is, just why video games have provoked a 'crisis' that 'we're going to have to start dealing with'.

The investigation of the social forces that propel and sustain the academic, political, and media panic around media violence has been taken up by the sociology and communications theorists Tom Grimes, James Anderson, and Lori Bergen (2008) in work that investigates the intersection of ideology and the science of media and aggression. Grimes, Anderson, and Bergen are very sceptical of the science around games, thinking that because it is so saturated with ideological motivations and methodological flaws, 'there's very little left of value' once these flaws in the science are identified (2008: 220). After surveying the history of the media effects literature, they conclude:

> What this history of effects tells us is that the process is not simply a disinterested science quietly going about its business of discovering facts about the world. Historically, the actual process has begun when society has been required to accommodate a new, rapidly defusing form of entertainment. That form raises societal concerns in its own right because it is quickly connected to the ongoing and often intractable problems of that society. Politicians and their hunt for social ills they can exploit for political gain, in turn, further elevate the significance of what is now *the problem*. But happily, these politicians often provide the funding for the science that follows. That science has a mandate to solve *the problem*, and *the problem* is now a media problem. Consequently, the issue gets framed as the effects of the media. (Grimes et al. 2008: 50; original emphasis)

Thus, Grimes, Anderson, and Bergen single out at least two key sociological factors in the moral panic around games as being the activities of *politicians* and *scientists*. Leaving the discussion of the ideological and moralistic role of scientists for the end of this chapter, it will be profitable to investigate the political and more broadly social aspects of video game moralism.

MIDDLE-CLASS MORALISM

It is tempting, especially from an outsider's perspective, to attribute the moral panic around video games in the United States – where video game moralism is most evident – to a distinctive brand of American Christian conservatism. The Parents Music Resource Center's (PMRC) concern with 'porn rock' in the 1980s, and the moralism around *Dungeons and Dragons* in the same decade (Cardwell 1994), were both reasonably clear cases of this Christian conservatism, given their frequent fixation on the so-called occult and other bugbears of Christian conservatism in those moral debates. Conservative Christians were similarly active in the heyday of the moralistic debate against video games. Republican politicians such as Newt Gingrich weighed in against games, often drawing clearly religious moral connections:

> I think the fact is, if you look at the amount of violence we have in games that young people play at 7, 8, 10, 12, 15 years of age, if you look at the dehumanisation, if you look at the fact that we refuse to say that we are, in fact, endowed by our creator, that our rights come from God, that if you kill somebody, you're committing an act of evil. (Quoted in Cooper 2012)

Gingrich seemed not to have noticed that no one is really killed in the playing of video games. Nevertheless, his evident willingness to appeal to conservative Christians over the crisis of video game violence is clear enough. The attitude of failed 2012 Republican presidential candidate Mitt Romney is similarly clear:

> I want to restore values so children are protected from a societal cesspool of filth, pornography, violence, sex, and perversion [. . .] I've proposed that we enforce our obscenity laws again and that we get serious against those retailers that sell adult video games that are filled with violence and that we go after those retailers. (Quoted in Cooper 2012)

Christian moralism about games is not new. John Stuart Mill made observations in 1859 that foreshadow the current moral issue:

> Wherever the Puritans have been sufficiently powerful, as in New England, and in Great Britain at the time of the Commonwealth, they have endeavoured with considerable success, to put down all public, and nearly all private, amusements: especially music, dancing, public games, or other assemblages for purposes of diversion, and the theatre. There are still in this country large bodies of persons by whose notions of morality and religion these recreations are condemned; and those persons belonging chiefly to the middle class, who are the ascendant power in the present social and political condition of the kingdom [. . .] (Mill [1859] 1974: 154)

It would be a mistake to think that the concern with video games is merely a case of conservative Christian moralism, however. What is notable about the moral concern with video games in the United States and elsewhere is that it bridges the divide between progressives and conservatives, in that it is a moral issue that engages secular, progressive, and scientific America. In fact, much of the strongest criticism has come from liberals such as Hillary Clinton. Clinton, of course, was running for the Democratic presidential nomination when she made the statement cited earlier, and her views could hardly be labelled those of a Christian moralist. Even Barack Obama (2010) has signalled his concern with games, although perhaps his worry is that games are a distraction from more meaningful life pursuits and civil engagement, rather than an insidious moral force.

Grimes, Bergen, and Anderson argue that what the political criticisms of video games may genuinely have in common, however, is that they are *class-based*: the demographic group in question being the middle-class, middle-aged, middlebrow hump in the voting public to which the politicians cited here most want to appeal (2008: 86–9). Groups in society, differentiated by politics, gender, class, or ethnicity, have always had and always will have their characteristic moral concerns.

The moral concerns of the middle classes are often of prominence in capitalist and democratic societies given the heft this demographic has as consumers and voters. That video games have become such a trusty political talking point in the last thirty years in the United States signals that moral attitudes towards them in the middle classes are relatively entrenched.

A key part of the middle-class moralism identified by Grimes, Bergen, and Anderson is *parental concern* and the understandable desire to 'protect the children' and defend 'family values' (2008: 87–8). The sharp edge of this concern is the effect that video games might have within the family unit by causing violence and other aspects of delinquency. Parents are uniquely positioned to worry about children, and furthermore video games represent the confluence of traditional parental worries about the effects of the media and a new wave of public health concerns about the impact of new technologies. Technology is increasingly seen as a new threat to children, with video games, social media, and mobile phones currently exercising the moral sensibilities of middle-class parents: video games are making us violent, social media is destroying our real social lives, and Google is making us stupid (Carr 2008).

Conservative pundit Peggy Noonan forwarded this concern shortly after the Newtown shootings, where twenty children and six staff of Sandy Hook Elementary School were killed:

> everyone who has warned for a quarter-century now that our national culture has become a culture of death – movies, TV shows, video games drenched in blood and violence – has been correct. Deep down we all know it, as deep down we know our culture has a bad impact on the young and unstable who aren't sturdy enough to withstand and resist sick messages and imagery. (Noonan 2012)

Protecting the children is a laudable objective: there are lots of genuine threats to child safety, and prudent measures such as child restraints in cars and child-resistant bottle caps on poisons and medicines are thoroughly sensible things to have and have saved lives. Nevertheless, this usually worthy concern for the health and safety of children has sometimes itself done more harm than good. For example, in New Zealand, the number of children that cycle or walk to school has in recent years reduced dramatically, partly because of exaggerated parental fears for the safety of unaccompanied children; this has had a negative effect on the health of young people who are now increasingly sedentary (Mackie 2009).

The call to 'protect the children' is especially acute when the topic is aggressive play. Steven Pinker (2011) notes that in addition to video games, it extends to other cases of pretended and playful, but potentially violent, games, and in a way that has left us with the puzzling moralisation of the largely non-consequential, such as in the frequent ban of childhood games like dodgeball. He considers such responses as representing 'the overshooting of yet another successful campaign against violence, the century long movement to prevent the abuse and neglect of children' (2011: 381). Pinker chalks the overreaction up to 'political correctness', a term probably best avoided due to its conservative and reactionary overuse. And yet it is undeniable that the opposition to ostensibly aggressive play has led to some eye-rolling cases of prudential overreaction. In early 2013, a five-year-old girl from Mount Carmel Area Elementary School in Pennsylvania was suspended from school and given a psychological evaluation after threatening to shoot another child with a bubble gun (Newcomb 2013). As a result, 'protect the children' has become such a familiar exhortation that it is also the target of widespread satire. *The Simpsons* lampoons this moralism in the catchphrase of perpetually overwrought Helen Lovejoy: 'Won't somebody please think of the children!'

But significantly, the issues here are not solely with the care for children, but also with the potential threat those children pose. The threat of the latest generation of 'the youth' has also been a frequent feature of moral panics – it was a feature of Cohen's original study – and so a further and associated part of this middle-class moralism is a lack of sympathy for the tastes of young people and, indeed, a suspicion or fear of those tastes. A childhood preoccupation with violent video games often strikes older people, who are demographically and culturally distanced from the interests of children and adolescents, as threatening (Grimes et al. 2008: 189). This is especially the case when the children in question are not one's own, but of 'those people' (Grimes et al. 2008: 87–9). The parental concern with violent video games is not merely deciding about what one's own children should watch and play but being able to influence or decide this for others. An undoubted aspect of the parental moralism around violent games and other violent media is the suspicion that other parents are not shielding their children from these harms, and that regulation such as the labelling or age-rating of games, age limits for purchasing games, or even the outright ban of some kinds of video games, is needed to enforce moral standards on these wayward children who pose a threat to society.

That the moral panic around video games is a largely middle-class phenomenon is further illustrated by the exact choice of violent media that is the critical focus when there is a school shooting or spree killing. Violence is a staple in all kinds of art and literature, of course. As Grimes, Anderson, and Bergen half-jokingly note, 'George Bizet's 1875 opera Carmen is full of violence and sexual intrigue, and it ends with the enraged murder of a beautiful woman', but that the scientific concern with opera as a cause of violence is non-existent (2008: 86). The serious point in this, they contend, is that 'We are not concerned about opera because of our vision of its audience as highly educated, moneyed, high-class, cultured people who would never consider mugging someone on the street' (2008: 86).

Aesthetic preferences are thus another aspect of the moral panic with violent video games. An aesthetic suspicion of popular art has been a common feature of moral panics, from penny dreadfuls to gangster films and action movies of the 1980s. Violent art is certainly a taste for some, but not one that everyone enjoys or can even stomach. The aesthetic tastes of the youth, and their attraction to gratuitous violence, are clearly distasteful to many people. Thus, this middle-class moralism may partially comprise a rejection of the 'low tastes' of which video games are putatively an exemplar. Further, that video games are perceived to be pointless, trivial, or unsophisticated – hardly deserving the name 'art' (Ebert 2010) – makes them particularly vulnerable to middle-class criticism, by being representative of something that is *beneath* the more refined tastes of the critics who make such discriminations.

Hence, some of the middle-class moral opposition to video games may derive from class-based aesthetic tastes that sociologist Pierre Bourdieu theorises function as markers of 'class distinction' (1984). It may be that the moral opposition to video games is associated with, or even partially caused by, prevalent class-based aesthetic responses to games. According to Bourdieu, aesthetic taste, 'being the product of the conditionings associated with a particular class of conditions of existence [. . .] unites all those who are the product of similar conditions, while distinguishing them from all others' (1984: 56). Interestingly, Bourdieu also noted that the aesthetic tastes one does not share can prompt a 'visceral intolerance' or 'disgust' (1984: 56), a phenomenon that may explain why the distaste with video games so easily leads to moral opprobrium.

These speculations about the class-based aspect of the moral panic around media are backed up by research to some extent. Grimes, Bergen, and Anderson found that there were several features that predicted 'scholarly concern over the media', and that

> Concern over the media will be highest when the class of the audience is low (mass media are the media of the masses, after all), the cultural standing of the content is low (popular culture), the literacy requirements for engaging that content is low (any child could participate), the share of the audience is high, and the regulatory avenue is agency based [. . .] (Grimes et al. 2008: 87)

Video gaming scores high on all these fronts, and so is a natural target for class-based moralists. Furthermore, the first four of these features are effective markers that something may be a mass, popular, or lower-class taste.

This class-based moralistic response is not unique to video games, as the interaction of aesthetic and moral tastes is evident in a traditional and long-standing moralism about the arts. The philosopher Noël Carroll (1998) has argued that in the twentieth century, moralism was a frequent contributor to the academic suspicion of the 'mass arts' more generally. Many of the common criticisms of the mass arts – that they encouraged passivity in their audiences, that they are formulaic, generic, and mere *commodities* – also have an undoubted air of class concerns; especially given that the art with which the mass arts were unfavourably compared was typically the *avant garde* or high art beloved of the cultured and educated classes. Carroll notes that this 'general cultural preoccupation with the moral threat posed by mass art is also reflected in academia', and often to the extent that it can seem 'paranoid' (1998: 292).

THE POLITICISATION OF VIDEO GAMES

For these reasons, it is a reasonable conjecture that video game moralism owes a great deal to middle-class moral and aesthetic attitudes and that it is largely sustained by the political benefit achieved by speaking to these sensibilities (Grimes et al. 2008: 11). So how does this politicisation function? Moral panics are often triggered by notorious events. In Cohen's original study, the panic was prompted by a near riot in the English seaside town of Clacton on Easter Sunday 1964 (2002: 29). Tragic events such as the mass shootings at Columbine, Jonesboro, and Paducah seem to be likely candidates for the corresponding trigger for the peak of middle-class moralism about video games in the late 1990s. Their prominence in the psychological science and moral punditry around games, and their coincidence in time with the worst of the moral outrage around video games in the late 1990s, leads one to suspect that if these events had not occurred, the moral debate would have been much less contentious than it was. Columbine in particular was the poster child of this moralisation of video games, and it represented the acute end of the threat of violence to middle-class, middle-aged parental values, in posing a vivid and horrible threat to children, in a place, schools, where one should expect them to be safe. Admittedly things have now moved on, and these events are now considered, not typically as a prompt for moral panic about media violence, but as notable early examples of the phenomenon of public mass shootings that cause so much harm, and provoke so much public and political consternation to the current day.

But in addition to being responses to determinate events, moral panics involve various interested parties whose intention it is to use the triggering event to further some political or ideological project (Burns and Crawford 1999: 159). The following panic is a function of how the triggering event is employed in a larger moral and political project, including the meaning with which it is overlaid, and the objectives the interested agents use it to pursue. I have already noted that politicians frequently use violent game moralism to engage their middle-class base, and that the call to 'protect the children' is a particularly dependable political ploy because one could hardly deny that children should be protected. But, the political focus on children in the moral panic around violent games may also derive from the fact that the ostensible 'care for children' can be employed as an opening to advance paternalistic policy that affects families and hence adults. The behaviour of adults is typically thought to be partially insulated from paternalistic interference because of an adult's assumed right to freely and intentionally act in their own interests (or, frequently, *despite* their best interests). Thus, calls to regulate or control the media that adults consume can often effectively be countered by liberal considerations of personal freedom, embodied in John Stuart Mill's famous 'harm principle' that claims that the 'only purpose for which power can be rightfully exercised over any member of a civilized community, against his will, is to prevent harm to others' ([1859] 1974: 68). However, because children are not considered to be fully autonomous agents, and because of their special susceptibility to media effects, we have a special duty of care to protect them from their potentially uninformed and poor choices. But this is also seen by some to legitimise the regulative control of the adults responsible for those children. For Grimes, Anderson, and Bergen,

> Children provide a kind of natural conduit between the public realm and the private world, an entrée point for government and for other public institutions, to enter the private confines of the family. Historical examples abound of a clear pattern of intrusion by government into the realm of private lives of citizens through regulation and control of their children. (Grimes et al. 2008: 181)

This gives quite a different picture of the prominent role of children in the moral issue of game violence. Far from a simple concern with the well-being of children, the ethical concern for violent video games and children is cast as a means of governing adult moral behaviour. 'Protecting the children' may be employed as a tactic to regulate and control adults.

Related considerations also cast light on the political advantageousness of the frequent comparisons of game violence and *disease* that can be observed in the science on violent games and aggression. If even adults are not 'immune' to the aggression-fostering effects of video games, as argued by Anderson, Gentile, and Buckley (2007: 137) then their nature as free agents can be somewhat discounted when we come to consider the public health effects of game violence. Because the effects, like those of smoking on cancer, are not subject to the deliberative control of their users – especially if games are also considered addictive (Pontes et al. 2019) – game-induced violence is properly conceived of as a disease, toxin, or influence that warrants generalised public health measures. Anderson, Gentile, and Buckley end their book-length treatment of the effects of violent games with suggestions for social policy to meet this threat to public health, including regulating the labelling and availability of such games (2007: 156–9). However, the proposed regulation of violent games has frequently been unsuccessful. A bill that Hillary Clinton introduced in 2005, the Family Entertainment Protection Act, did not enter into law; it was rejected largely on constitutional considerations of freedom of speech. In June 2011, a similar attempt to regulate the sale of video games to children in California was ruled unconstitutional in the Supreme Court (United States Supreme Court 2011).

The political issue of gun control defines a further group with a vested interest in prolonging the moral panic around video games. The gun control debate seems to have played a prominent role in the continued moralisation of violent entertainment in some quarters. A week after the shootings in Sandy Hook Elementary School, the National Rifle Association's CEO Wayne LaPierre, under pressure because of the increased calls for tighter gun laws, gave a bizarre speech drawing on the now tired moralisation of violent entertainment:

> And here's another dirty little truth that the media try their best to conceal. There exists in this country, sadly, a callous, corrupt and corrupting shadow industry that sells and stows violence against its own people. Through vicious, violent video games with names like 'Bullet Storm,' 'Grand Theft Auto,' 'Mortal Kombat,' and 'Splatterhouse'. [. . .] And then they all have the nerve to call it entertainment. But is that what it really is? Isn't fantasizing about killing people as a way to get your kicks really the filthiest form of pornography? In a race to the bottom, many conglomerates compete with one another to shock, violate, and offend every standard of civilized society, by bringing an even more toxic mix of reckless behavior, and criminal cruelty right into our homes. Every minute, every day, every hour of every single year. (LaPierre 2012)

This is an extraordinary piece of moralism and is clearly a diversionary tactic that, given the high stakes of gun crime in the United States, is itself potentially unethical behaviour. In 2011, 68 per cent of all murders in the United States involved firearms (FBI 2012). Because there is credible evidence of the correlation between the prevalence of guns in a society and the murder rate in that society (Carter 1996: 3) and that gun ownership is a risk factor for homicide in the home (Kellermann et al. 1993), it is wrong to so blithely dismiss the connection with deflecting tactics. The NRA has long used such ethically cynical tactics, including successfully lobbying Congress to place a ban on funding research into gun crime by the Centers for Disease Control and Prevention (Roth 2013). Legislators in the United States have consistently failed to deal with the issue of gun control head on, and at least part of this failure could be owing to the persistence of distracting issues such as video games.

Unlike gun culture, which has the backing in the United States of a significant political demographic, gaming culture is politically vulnerable to middle-class moral panic. Children and adolescents do not vote, and young adults are less likely to do so than older age groups, so their tastes need not be taken seriously by politicians. As Burns and Crawford note concerning the persistent dubious references to video games in the immediate aftermath of school shootings,

> Juveniles are not permitted to vote in popular elections, and they are not likely to develop lobby-, or special interest groups. Thus, politicians do not fear losing juveniles' votes on election day nor any threat of opposition. Politicians also enjoy the benefit of our country's historical approach of taking our societal frustrations out upon marginal, fringe, or deviant classes, rendering juvenile delinquents prime candidates for increased punishments. (Burns and Crawford 1999: 157)

The same may also be true of the 'lower classes' who are perceived to be the biggest consumers of violent media, and who are often perceived as politically apathetic. Hence, the diagnosis that games are a moral danger to children may have been abetted by the newness of games but also by their position on the cultural and political margins; both facts mean that gamers have been largely unable to exert their political will. One prediction – if this is not already occurring – is that such political posturing as is often associated with video games will be increasingly ineffective as the generation familiar with games comes to dominate the voting public.

Ultimately, the political moralisation of video games, and the regulative proposals it leads to, such as those initiated by Clinton, can be politically and economically counterproductive, and so the moralism detailed here is not merely an academic concern. The concern with video games provides a vivid issue – and one replete with great imagery – to which one can formulate legislative proposals that appeal to a voting public, and that have the added virtue of distracting from the deeply hard issues confronting society. This can end up driving public concern, and even policy, in wrongheaded or unproductive directions. Social policy is costly to design and implement, and as Ferguson and John Kilburn (2009) note, by acting in the case of violent video games, regulators are unlikely to get 'bang for their buck'. Indeed, video game moralism and legislation may be most effective in providing an unfortunate distraction from other important issues confronting youth, such as alcohol and drug use, family violence, child abuse, and social and economic inequality. It would be truly hard to do something about the problems of domestic violence and social disadvantage, but video games and television are easy targets; moreover, and not coincidentally, they typically are not to the aesthetic tastes of the scientists, academics, politicians, and middle-class voters for which they seem like the obvious problem in society.

Moralisation and the Science of Video Game Violence

Of course, the news media have played a prominent role in this moralising process (and often, no doubt, in alliance with political moralists). Even though it was at its highpoint a decade or more ago, this moralistic exploitation of spree killings and school shootings by the news media still exists, even if one is now also likely to see media coverage sceptical of the causal link (New York Times 2019). Television news has consistently courted pundits and scientists to speak as experts on the occurrence of school shootings, who have often leapt to the conclusion that video games factored into the events. As Kutner and Olson note,

> Within hours of the shootings at Virginia Tech, pundits were on the airwaves and Internet blaming video games for Cho's behavior [. . .] It didn't matter that the police found no video games, consoles, or other gaming equipment when they searched his room. Nor did it matter that one of his college roommates told reporters that he'd never seen Cho play video games or take any interest in them; he'd spent most of his time at the computer writing. Despite all this, the supposed link between Cho's murderous behavior and violent games was assumed to be there. (Kutner and Olson 2008: 195)

This behaviour was equally evident after the events at Aurora in Colorado, where twelve people were shot and killed in a cinema complex, and those in Newtown.

This media focus on video games as a cause of violence is itself an ethically dubious tactic for several reasons. As already noted, blaming video games for these tragedies is not supported by reasonable scientific evidence. Moreover, it is a hypocritical tactic given the prevalence of fictional violence in television drama and persisting ratings-driven exploitation of *real violence* by television news shows. 'Mean world syndrome' is the phenomenon where the prevalence of violence in the mass media causes individuals to think the world to be a much more dangerous place than it is (Gerbner 2002: 297). It is well known that people are not good at estimating the extent or type of the genuine risks to their safety that exist in society; a person may be terrified of their upcoming flight as they drive to the airport, not realising, or at least not acknowledging, that driving is a far more dangerous mode of transport than flying. Of course, violent video games could add to this sense of societal danger, but the greatest contributor to this problem is surely the news media's fixated coverage of such events. Unfortunately, the perception that society is a violent place itself could influence society by eroding communal sympathy and cohesion.

Equally, the use of these school shootings and spree killings by researchers, academics, and scientists is unflattering, and it is arguable that the research into video games and aggression itself exploits the moral panic around school shootings in an unethical way. In *Stop Teaching Our Kids to Kill*, Dave Grossman and Gloria DeGaetano are patently guilty of employing school shootings as a means of ramping up fear. The school shootings act as a selling point for their moralistic vision (and their book). The claim on the cover that video games 'teach' kids to be killers is far from demonstrated in the book, but rather is a speculative provocation designed to motivate and sell their position, a task it meets spectacularly well.

Respectable scientists have also erred in a similar way. It takes Anderson, Gentile, and Buckley precisely one and a half paragraphs of their 2007 account of the science behind game violence before they mention the association between school shootings and video games, an association that seems intended to morally *prime* that connection and so motivate their following discussion (2007: 3). This is a tactic that Craig Anderson has used elsewhere (Anderson and Bushman 2001: 353) and it is a cynical move coming from social psychologists that have also developed an 'associationist' model of attitude formation that depends in part on the 'priming' of knowledge structures (Anderson et al. 2007: 41). Mass shootings are events that are worrying and are replete with powerful imagery that provokes strong moral feelings; and this seems to explain their repeated function in this scientific literature.

There may be an interesting theoretical point behind this use of school shootings to *cognitively prime* the moral importance of the science. Perhaps it is the media exploitation of the familiar cognitive biases of the *availability heuristic* and *confirmation bias* that drives much of the moralistic concern with violent video games, rather than a tangible public health concern. An availability heuristic is a cognitive bias whereby the availability to recall of an event or object leads to an over-estimation of the statistical prevalence of that thing (Tversky and Kahneman 1973). School shootings are incredibly vivid and arouse strong emotions and so when someone from outside of gaming culture thinks of gaming, this is often the kind of thing that springs to mind. I frequently meet this phenomenon when I talk to other people about their impression of games: violence, school shootings, and the other harmful aspects attributed to the medium are often the facts about games that they freely volunteer. The availability to recall of these events, and perhaps of their linguistic emblem in the form of the familiar and consonant phrase 'violent video game', may explain part of why this moralistic trope has the legs it does.

This cognitive priming may lead to a subsequent confirmation bias, a bias that involves paying much more attention to confirming instances of a theory or belief than to disconfirmations (Nickerson 1998). Because of their intuitive estimation about the prevalence of video game-driven violence, individuals may make the intuitive generalisation that games are closely associated with violence. Confirmation bias kicks in as each new potential association, no matter how tenuous, is thought to further justify the causal claim. Hence the Norwegian mass murderer Anders Breivik's mention of the video games *World of Warcraft* and *Modern Warfare* is thought to once again confirm the theory that video games bear a causal responsibility for spree killings (NY Daily News 2012). The early confused reports that Adam Lanza's brother Robert was the killer, and that he 'liked' *Mass Effect 3* on Facebook, was another sudden public confirmation of the moral conviction about games. The Australian Brenton Tarrant's cynical remarks before the Christchurch mosque killings in March 2019 are another reflexive and particularly malicious case.

One logical problem with confirmation bias is that such associations are ubiquitous. Given the prevalence of gaming in modern society, it should be all too easy to find a connection between some act of violence and a video game. But all this shows is that the coincident events can be interpreted in terms of the moral convictions around games. Karl Popper once argued that what was wrong with pseudo-sciences such as Freudian psychology or the Marxist theory of history was not that their theories could not be verified, but that they were *all too easy to verify*:

> The study of any of them seemed to have the effect of an intellectual conversion or revelation, opening your eyes to a new truth hidden from those not yet initiated. Once your eyes were thus opened you saw confirming instances everywhere: the world was full of *verifications* of the theory. (Popper 1963: 34–5; original emphasis)

Although the following risks an obvious irony, it is tempting to see this same pattern in the moral conviction around video games, and to conclude that it is based on an ideologically driven worldview in which each new violent event – a couple of mixed-up kids with access to guns and homemade bombs, a Christian terrorist killing his liberal countrymen, an autistic child whose mother bought him a rifle and taught him to fire it, a member of the Alt-Right visiting his murderous violence on a peaceful city in New Zealand – counts as a confirmation of the moral conviction.

Conclusion

As well as being provoked by events, moral panics may be reflective of wider social and political anxieties and trends. The reaction against *Dungeons and Dragons* and heavy metal music in the 1980s may have been a reflection of the growing Christian conservatism of the time. One great societal trouble in the period preceding the rise of violent media moralism in the 1980s and 1990s was, of course, the horrifying trends in violent crime rates from the 1960s through to the 1990s. While the direct stimulus for the moral panic around games may have been the dubious media and scientific fixation on and exploitation of spree killings, the distal stimulus may have been social anxieties around general societal trends in violence. But these trends were not sustained, and the early nineties proved to be a historical highpoint in violent crime in several Western nations before a subsequent 're-civilising' (Pinker 2011: 116–28). Pinker argues that the resulting politicisation of violent crime in this period led to changes in the moral norms about violence that may be one factor in the subsequent declines. He speculates that this increased moralism, when it was properly directed, had a positive effect on crime in that it led to policies – such as the famous (infamous?) 'broken windows' policies built on the contention that visible signs of crime or disorder in an area encourage more serious crime – that may be responsible for the subsequent retreat of violent crime rates in the late 1990s (2011: 123–4).

The reversal of the crime trends in the 1990s, at the exact time that video games were becoming both more popular and more graphically violent, has to some extent undermined the rationale of the moral panic around media violence. Before the events at Aurora and Newtown, crime had increasingly dropped off the political and public radar, compared with the heights of its politicisation in the late eighties and nineties. There are signs that the concern with violent media as a cause of violence in society is increasingly an anachronism: when LaPierre raised his defence of the NRA, he employed the awkward terms of the debate as it was in the 1990s. Donald Trump's recent references to video games as a cause of mass shootings also seemed tone deaf to many (New York Times 2019). Some of the sceptical research cited above is evidence of the pushback (Kutner and Olson 2008; Grimes et al. 2008; Ferguson 2008, 2010). And as noted earlier, even some of the scientists most closely associated with the thesis that video games are a cause of aggression and violence now carefully hedge their claims.

We might rightly balk at Pinker's provocative notion of a 're-civilising' process in the 1990s, but this development may itself explain the rise in violent media moralism that has been the focus here, because this period saw a moralisation of violence in all its forms. Fantasy manifestations of violence such as violent video games felt the effects of this moralism because of the blunt conceptual way that fantasy violence and played aggression are typically scientifically treated, particularly with respect to their status as entertainment and fiction (Tavinor 2017). Hence, video game moralism may be an artefact of a generalised anti-violence moralism that was an important response to societal trends from the 1960s to 1990s. Pinker also notes that the interest in violent media ultimately survived this civilising process, and even became more prominent because 'an entirely new form of violent entertainment, video games, has become a major pastime' (2011: 128). Pinker argues that attitudes to violent media have changed, however, and that their audiences are much better at immersing 'themselves in seedy cultural genres without taking any of them too seriously' (2011: 128).

REFERENCES

Anderson, Craig A., and Brad J. Bushman. 2001. 'Effects of Violent Video Games on Aggressive Behavior, Aggressive Cognition, Aggressive Affect, Physiological Arousal, and Prosocial Behavior: A Meta-analytic Review of the Scientific Literature.' *Psychological Science* 12: 353–9.

Anderson, Craig A., Douglas A. Gentile, and Katherine E. Buckley. 2007. *Violent Video Game Effects on Children and Adolescents: Theory, Research, and Public Policy*. Oxford: Oxford University Press.

Bartel, Christopher. 2015. 'Free Will and Moral Responsibility in Video Games.' *Ethics and Information Technology* 17: 285–93.

Bourdieu, Pierre. 1984. *Distinction: A Social Critique of the Judgment of Taste*, translated by Richard Nice. Cambridge, MA: Harvard University Press.

Briggle, Adam. 2012. 'The Ethics of Computer Games: A Character Approach.' In *The Philosophy of Computer Games*, edited by John Richard Sageng, Hallvard Fossheim, and Tarjei Mandt Larsen, 159–74. Dordrecht: Springer.

Brown v. Entertainment Merchants Association. 2011. 564 U.S. 768.

Burns, Ronald, and Charles Crawford. 1999. 'School Shootings, the Media, and Public Fear: Ingredients for a Moral Panic.' *Crime, Law and Social Change* 32: 147–68.

Cardwell, Paul. 1994. 'The Attacks on Role-Playing Games.' *Skeptical Inquirer* 18.2: 157–65.

Carr, Nicholas. 2008. 'Is Google Making Us Stupid?' *The Atlantic*, 15 August. <https://www.theatlantic.com/magazine/archive/2008/07/is-google-making-us-stupid/306868/> (last accessed 22 March 2021).

Carroll, Noël. 1998. *A Philosophy of Mass Art*. Oxford: Clarendon Press.

Carter, Gregg L. 1996. *The Gun Control Movement*. New York: Twayne.

Cohen, Stanley. 2002. *Folk Devils and Moral Panics*. 3rd edition. Oxford: Routledge.

Cooper, Hollander. 2012. 'Where Do 2012's Presidential Candidates Stand on Video Games?' *Gameradar*, 1 November. <https://www.gamesradar.com/au/where-do-2012s-presidential-candidates-stand-videogames/> (last accessed 30 August 2019).

Draper, Kevin. 2019. 'Video Games Aren't Why Shootings Happen. Politicians Still Blame Them.' *New York Times*, 5 August. <https://nytimes.com/2019/08/05/sports/trump-violent-video-games-studies.html> (last accessed 30 January 2020).

Ebert, Roger. 2010. 'Videogames Can Never Be Art.' *Roger Ebert* blog, 16 April. <https://rogerebert.com/rogers-journal/video-games-can-never-be-art> (last accessed 30 August 2019).

FBI. 2012. 'Crime in the United States 2011.' *Uniform Crime Reports*. <http://fbi.gov/about-us/cjis/ucr/crime-in-the-u.s/2011/crime-in-the-u.s.-2011> (last accessed 19 January 2013).

Ferguson, Christopher J. 2008. 'The School Shooting/Violent Videogame Link: Causal Link or Moral Panic?' *Journal of Investigative Psychology and Offender Profiling* 5: 25–37.

Ferguson, Christopher J. 2010. 'Media Violence Effects and Violent Crime: Good Science or Moral Panic?' In *Violent Crime: Clinical and Social Implications*, edited by Christopher J. Ferguson, 37–56. Los Angeles: SAGE.

Ferguson, Christopher J., and John Kilburn. 2009. 'The Public Health Risks of Media Violence: A Meta-analytic Review.' *Journal of Pediatrics* 154: 759–63.

Gerbner, George. 2002. *Against the Mainstream: The Selected Works of George Gerbner*, edited by Michael Morgan. New York: Peter Lang.

Goode, Erich, and Nachman Ben-Yehuda. 1994. *Moral Panics: The Social Construction of Deviance*. Malden, MA: Blackwell.

Grimes, Tom, James A. Anderson, and Lori Bergen. 2008. *Media Violence and Aggression: Science and Ideology*. Los Angeles: SAGE.

Grossman, Dave, and Gloria DeGaetano. 1999. *Stop Teaching Our Kids to Kill: A Call to Action against TV, Movie, and Video Game Violence*. New York: Crown.

Kellermann, Arthur L., Frederick P. Rivara, Norman B. Rushforth, Joyce G. Banton, Donald T. Reay, Jerry T. Francisco, Ana B. Locci, Janice Prodzinski, Bela B. Hackman, and Grant Somes. 1993. 'Gun Ownership as a Risk Factor for Homicide in the Home.' *New England Journal of Medicine* 329: 1084–91.

Kutner, Lawrence, and Cheryl Olson. 2008. *Grand Theft Childhood: The Surprising Truth about Videogames and What Parents Can Do*. New York: Simon and Schuster.

Lapierre, Wayne. 2012. 'Full Statement by Wayne LaPierre in Response to Newtown Shootings.' *The Guardian*, 22 December. <https://theguardian.com/world/2012/dec/21/nra-full-statement-lapierre-newtown> (last accessed 30 August 2019).

Mackie, Hamish. 2009. *I Want To Ride My Bike: Overcoming Barriers to Cycling to Intermediate Schools*. NZ Transport Agency Research Report. <http://nzta.govt.nz/resources/research/reports/380/docs/380.pdf> (last accessed 21 May 2012).

Mackie, John Leslie. 1977. *Ethics: Inventing Right and Wrong*. London: Pelican Books.

Mill, John Stuart. [1859] 1974. *On Liberty*. London: Penguin Classics.

Newcomb, Alyssa. 2013. 'Kindergartner Suspended over Bubble Gun Threat.' *ABC News*, 20 January. <http://abcnews.go.com/blogs/headlines/2013/01/kindergartner-suspended-over-bubble-gun-threat/> (last accessed 22 March 2021).

Nickerson, Raymond. 1998. 'Confirmation Bias: A Ubiquitous Phenomenon in Many Guises.' *Review of General Psychology* 2.2: 175–220.

Noonan, Peggy. 2012. 'Newton.' *The Wall Street Journal*, 17 December. <http://blogs.wsj.com/peggynoonan/2012/12/17/newtown/> (last accessed 15 January 2013).

NY Daily News. 2012. 'Anders Behring Breivik Trained for Mass Killing with Video Games "Call of Duty," "World of Warcraft".' *New York Daily News*, 19 April. <https://nydailynews.com/news/world/anders-behring-breivik-wanted-bomb-royal-palace-article-1.1064074> (last accessed 30 January 2020).

Obama, Barack. 2010. Speech to the Graduating Class at Hampton University, Virginia, 9 May.

Patridge, Stephanie. 2011. 'The Incorrigible Social Meaning of Video Game Imagery.' *Ethics of Information Technology* 13: 303–12.

Pinker, Steven. 2011. *The Better Angels of Our Nature: Decline of Violence in History and Its Causes*. London: Allen Lane.

Pontes, Halley M., Bruno Schivinski, Cornelia Sindermann, Mei Li, Benjamin Becker, Min Zhou, and Christian Montag. 2021. 'Measurement and Conceptualization of Gaming Disorder According to the World Health Organization Framework: The Development of the Gaming Disorder Test.' *International Journal of Mental Health and Addiction* 19: 508–28. <https://doi.org/10.1007/s11469-019-00088-z> (last accessed 22 March 2021).

Popper, Karl. 1963. *Conjectures and Refutations*. London. Routledge and Kegan Paul.

Roth, Zachary. 2013. 'Blackout: How the NRA Suppressed Gun Violence Research.' *MSNBC*, 14 January. <http://tv.msnbc.com/2013/01/14/blackout-how-the-nra-suppressed-gun-violence-research/> (last accessed 19 January 2013).

Rozin, Paul. 1999. 'The Process of Moralization.' *Psychological Science* 10.3: 218–21.

Shapiro, Ari and Douglas Gentile. 2018. 'What Research Says about Video Games and Violence in Children.' *NPR*, 8 March. <https://npr.org/2018/03/08/592046294/what-research-says-about-video-games-andviolence-in-children> (last accessed 30 January 2020).

Sternheimer, Karen. 2007. 'Do Video Games Kill?' *Contexts* 6.1: 13–17.

Tavinor, Grant. 2009. *The Art of Videogames*. Malden, MA: Wiley-Blackwell.

Tavinor, Grant. 2017. 'Fictionalism and Videogame Aggression.' In *DiGRA 2017 – Proceedings of the DiGRA 2017 International Conference*, Swinburne University of Technology, Melbourne, June. <http://www.digra.org/digital-library/publications/fictionalism-and-videogame-aggression/> (last accessed 22 March 2021).

Tavinor, Grant. 2018. 'Harm and Entertainment.' In *Communication and Media Ethics*, edited by Patrick Lee Plaisance, 251–72. Boston: De Gruyter.

Tversky, Amos, and Daniel Kahneman. 1973. 'Availability: A Heuristic for Judging Frequency and Probability.' *Cognitive Psychology* 5.1: 207–33.

Vitka, William. 2005. 'Senator Clinton on Violent Games.' *CBS News*, 2 August. <http://www.cbsnews.com/stories/2005/08/02/tech/gamecore/main713544.shtml> (last accessed 30 August 2019).

Ward, Michael R. 2011. 'Video Games and Crime.' *Contemporary Economic Policy* 29.2: 261–73.

10. RE-READING *PERSONAL INFLUENCE* IN AN AGE OF SOCIAL MEDIA

Tom O'Regan*

INTRODUCTION

When I put into my university library search engine 'Paul Lazarsfeld and Facebook', I got back 204 results. One, from *The Economist* in 2007, noted that Mark Zuckerberg's discussion of Facebook and social media was 'strikingly similar' to that of Elihu Katz and Paul Lazarsfeld in their pioneering work in communication and media studies, *Personal Influence* – making it both 'radically new' and 'reassuringly old'. Katz and Lazarsfeld published *Personal Influence* in 1955. It is one of the most cited and lauded studies in the field (see Carter 1955; Broderson 1956; Riley 1956; Roshwalb 1956). It was notable for focusing attention on the 'role of people' in communication. Lazarsfeld, a research methodologist, in conjunction with Katz, a communications specialist, improvised a set of research methodologies to disclose the role of people in communication. Their foundational move and one that is relevant to studies in social media today is that they treated interpersonal communication as a medium of mass communication:

> Behind the design of this study was the *idea that persons, and especially opinion leaders, could be looked upon as **another medium of mass communication**, similar to magazines, newspapers and radio.* We could study their 'coverage,' their effect, and, in a way, their content. [. . .] The individual person, must be studied in the setting of the primary group within which he [sic] lives. (Katz and Lazarsfeld [1955] 1964: 11–12; emphasis added)

For many years of intermittently dipping into *Personal Influence* I paid no regard to the first sentence of this passage stressing their treatment of interpersonal communication as **another medium** of mass communication. Interpersonal communication had some of the central characteristics of a medium – there was coverage, effect, and content. But, unlike the more fully-fledged mass media of newspapers, magazines, radio, and television, interpersonal communication was not professionally produced, publicly available beyond the small group, or its content readily accessible. Interpersonal communication was unprofessional, informal, and largely invisible outside an individual's own personal social networks. The central achievement of *Personal Influence* was to make visible, in its general contours, the nature, character, and defining importance of interpersonal communication in making media and the social worlds to which it referred accessible and legible. A little over fifty years later the achievement of Facebook was to turn this domain of interpersonal communication into a fully-fledged and highly visible medium in its own right. Personal influence, if you like, had become re-mediated in social media.

I am not aware of any evidence directly linking Zuckerberg with Katz and Lazarsfeld. Yet Facebook did focus on and seek to remedy what Katz and Lazarsfeld had identified as a structural deficit of the twentieth-century media system. Through their work media professionals and scholars alike recognised the central importance of people and social networks. They knew that the 'word of mouth' of influencers and their small informal groups were shaping the uptake of media campaigns and programming. They understood that communication was always media in two (and, most often, more) steps. But there was a problem. As Katz and Fialkoff (2017: 86–7) would later observe, there were few available mechanisms for advertisers, marketers, and media impresarios to activate, shape, and intervene in these interpersonal networks. Media networks, and advertising and marketing firms alike found these informal groups and influencers within them hard to reach and identify. Due to the limited scope and reach of these interpersonal networks, they would need to wait on the development of social media where such groups would be placed at the centre of the communication effort.

Social media then addressed each of the structural deficits of the traditional media and marketing system with respect to the 'role of people in communication'. It identified informal groups and their membership, rendering them visible and open to targeting. It provided marketers and media providers with access to the influencers, transmitters, and opinion leaders. It gave media providers and marketers a mechanism by which they could locate and influence word of mouth. It provided additional tools to guide media uptake in user recommendations.

Re-reading *Personal Influence* in the light of Facebook demonstrates its unexpected importance for making sense of social media's rapid rise to centrality in our commercial, advertiser-supported media. Katz and Lazarsfeld's conception of interpersonal communication seeded the idea and hope for a more developed medium that could lay bare these interpersonal networks, identify both the relevant influencers and other network members and in so doing shape by word of mouth. *Personal Influence* was simultaneously identifying the 'deficits' of traditional media and paving the way for a more fully developed social media. In an uncanny fashion, Katz and Lazarsfeld not only predicted the rise of social media but also mounted a primer for its development.

In this chapter, I want to explore the many parallels – but also discontinuities – between the interpersonal communication medium and research enterprise pursued by Katz and Lazarsfeld and the social media agenda and associated research enterprise of Facebook and Instagram. To better understand the concept of personal influence I will begin with a discussion of it as it was first developed in the 1950s, outlining its historical context and initial limited application. This discussion will show how key concepts of *Personal Influence* can be seen as having been applied and embedded in the very fabric of social media itself. I will then consider how social media takes on a distinct media form. This form is both continuous with Katz and Lazarsfeld's interpersonal medium and a distinct departure from it. Facebook represents a significant departure both from Katz and Lazarsfeld's research agenda and from the market research and information regime of traditional media. Katz and Lazarsfeld's audience research work of 1955 was avowedly public and transparent in its commitments. They were providing a market research product for advertising agencies, advertisers, and media providers to repurpose. In contrast, Zuckerberg's Facebook is private, proprietorial, and opaque in its research provision. Facebook combines, under one roof, the roles of *market research provider*, *media provider*, and *advertising agency*. By prioritising the collection and analysis of individual user profiles, Facebook has created a media enterprise that seamlessly integrates user-generated content, data collection, analysis, strategy, media provision, and associated advertising machinery.

The Centrality of Personal Influence

Katz and Lazarsfeld argued that it was people, *through* their interpersonal networks, that played the crucial role in media uptake. They based their analysis on a combined desk review of a decade or more of prior research findings on informal groups and interpersonal communication and a re-examination of an extensive research probe consisting of 800 interviews of women conducted in Decatur, Illinois, a decade earlier. As members of informal groups, people shaped public opinion and voting patterns; they governed the uptake of both media programmes and advertising alike. Media audiences consumed media in the context of many informal groups and it was within these groups that particular members would be 'called on to lead' (Katz and Lazarsfeld [1955] 1964: 101).

Variously called 'influentials', 'influencers', 'initiators', 'most popular', 'transmitters', 'gatekeepers', and 'opinion leaders' – depending on the nature of the activity involved within these small informal groups – 'leaders' played a larger role in shaping the uptake of media than did other group members (Katz and Lazarsfeld [1955] 1964: 98–9, 118–19). They exercised this influence by a combination of imitation and explicit recommendation. 'Behavioural contagion' is the term Katz and Lazarsfeld use to describe cases in which an influencer or another group member is 'imitated, though he [sic] does not attempt to transmit influence'; 'direct influence' characterises situations in which an 'influence-attempt' is 'made manifest, either by ordering, suggesting or requesting' ([1955] 1964: 104).

Katz and Lazarsfeld concluded that the media audience needed to be studied 'within the *context* of group or groups to which they belong or which they have in mind'. It was in this group context that 'influence' occurred – that opinions and attitudes were formed. The 'rejection or acceptance of mass media influence-attempts' occurred in these small informal group settings (Katz and Lazarsfeld [1955] 1964: 131). Interpersonal communication was immensely powerful. Word of mouth shaped media and message uptake and therefore media development through the related social activities of liking and disliking, endorsing and recommending, dis-endorsing and denigrating. 'Influence-attempts' by media were dependent upon members of informal interpersonal networks and particularly the 'influencers' who helped shape uptake of media content and messages by members.

This work of leading, shaping, and moulding opinion and media uptake was extensive. It was the case whether it was decisions about going to a movie or buying a book; the taking up of journalistic coverage or the selecting of various goods and services to purchase; the making of fashion choices or voting for political candidates. Styles and kinds of personal influence varied depending on context, medium, and message. It was different for movies than it was for fashion; for political campaigns than it was for advertising brands. Influencers were pivotal to the uptake of media whether that was in the form of media programming, advertising and marketing campaigns, or political messaging. Katz and Lazarsfeld were adamant that media efforts could be arrested in their tracks if 'the appropriate gatekeeper' did not 'relay it', if an 'influential' did not 'endorse it', or if the attempt at influence was 'perceived as going counter to norms shared with others' ([1955] 1964: 130).[1]

Personal Influence was avowedly 'industry' research. The parties funding the research were concerned with gauging the 'effectiveness of mass media influence-attempts' (Katz and Lazarsfeld [1955]1964: 130). Like Katz and Lazarsfeld, they were concerned with identifying the role personal influence played in media influence-attempts more generally. The 'media industry' was interested in the uptake of programmes, advertisers and ad agencies in the effectiveness of sales pitches to audiences, and foundations in the shape of political communication in circumstances where informal groups played consequential roles. All those who used the media as their conduit and relay were variously interested in interpersonal relations.

While *Personal Influence* could be – and often was – read as a marketing treatise, it also mattered more generally for what it had to say about how informal groups shaped public understandings of their social, economic, political, and social class/occupational worlds (Lazarsfeld 1959). *Personal Influence* provided guidance to media users in undertaking media consumption, buying goods and services, and voting. The informal group made not only media but wider social worlds accessible and legible to participants. They could reinforce 'a mass media campaign'; they could offer a 'relay between people who are exposed to mass media influence and others who are not' (Katz and Lazarsfeld [1955] 1964: 116). They were, above all, in the guidance, recommendation, relaying, and reinforcing business.

Personal influence, however, was just *one* mechanism for making media and our social worlds accessible and legible to audiences in circumstances where the media choices available to audiences greatly exceeded a person's capacity to consume the media on offer. The other mechanism consisted of media efforts themselves through newspapers, magazines, radio, and TV. These media each gave audiences similar levels of consumer guidance and political and social intelligence by way of film reviews, TV and radio guides, motoring and travel columns, news and information, and general social, political, and cultural intelligence. Katz and Lazarsfeld stressed the close interconnection between personal influence and media influence. In the case of movie going, for instance, they noted the 'fact feeding' role of the newspaper and the especial importance of the magazine – 'first in a series of influences' ([1955] 1964: 193).[2]

The research vehicle for Katz and Lazarsfeld's illumination of personal influence was a combination of literature review, social survey, interviews, and observations – all to be undertaken intermittently by the new communication specialist they represented. Like the broadcast ratings and opinion pollster, this specialist required a *bespoke research apparatus* improvised for the purpose of monitoring and providing specific feedback on the personal uptake of media services, campaigns, and other public messaging. Online media would later provide an automated return path of information generated by users' very transactions with their services. Without this return path, Katz and Lazarsfeld needed to set up a separate non-transaction-based research inquiry specifically designed for the task of illuminating personal influence.

In this way Katz and Lazarsfeld's work contributed to the prominence and prestige of third-party independent audience measurement instruments in a variety of contexts. A marker of its impact was that by 1983 each research director of the three major US TV networks of the period – NBC, CBS, and ABC – were former students of Lazarsfeld's (Sills 1987: 259). Together with Lazarsfeld's earlier co-authored volume *The People's Choice* (Lazarsfeld et al. [1948] 1968), the lessons of *Personal Influence* also changed the conduct of political election campaigns. Campaigning became more election-booth focused and targeted to community networks. Katz and Lazarsfeld's work also changed the ways business thought of advertising, facilitating the rise of a more broadly conceived notion of marketing. They provided a proof of concept for social science survey methods that would become taken for granted in market research companies (and academic research centres) over subsequent decades.

Like their survey counterparts in market research, public opinion polling, audience measurement, and cognate academic research centres, Katz and Lazarsfeld's research enterprise was built on surveys conducted among populations who were guaranteed anonymity and whose informed consent was necessary (see Converse [1987] 2009). These research subjects needed to be actively recruited, maintained, and refreshed. Insofar as these research methods required the cooperation of unpaid subjects, often over lengthy intervals of time, the subjects' anonymity and privacy had to be respected. Furthermore, no direct targeting of survey respondents by advertisers and marketers was permissible so as not to contaminate research results.

So, while this research provided much desired granular results, it did not provide the advertiser, marketer, political party, or programme producer with a direct targeting instrument. Informal groups could be illuminated by research conducted by communication specialists who could identify and describe the general nature and character of different styles of personal influence. But this could not provide the actionable detail sought by advertisers and marketers. While the development of the 'cookie' facilitated the tracking of individual users across the web (Turow 2013), the informal social networks remained largely invisible to advertisers, marketers, and media companies until the mid-2000s.

Personal Influence built a pent-up desire on the part of marketing and advertising for an instrument which could identify groups, directly address interpersonal networks, and exploit their word-of-mouth dynamics. The marketing dream was to move from knowing about the relation to direct activation of that relation. For the better part of fifty years this was a tantalising prospect shared across generations of market research specialists.

Personal Influence and Social Media

There are remarkable continuities of thinking connecting Katz and Lazarsfeld to Zuckerberg. *Personal Influence* provided a compelling argument for the role of people in the uptake of media messages. But, as we have seen, it required new instruments and new media forms for that insight to become actionable. *Personal*

Influence mapped a 'world' of informal groups, constantly assembling and reassembling themselves. Social media platforms succeeded in thoroughly *mediatising* personal influence. Social media built, organised, calibrated, and recalibrated personal networks *on their own terms*, and incentivised people to conduct aspects of their interpersonal and social interactions within the platform. In doing so these networks and the everyday communication they supported were made visible and available to registration and calculation. If Katz and Lazarsfeld had identified a yawning gap between media on the one hand and informal groups on the other hand, social media bridged this chasm by folding the informal group into the media provision system itself.

Social media were concerned above all with the *diffusion* of influence. Like Katz and Lazarsfeld, Facebook not only studied the individual 'within the context of group or groups to which they belong or which they have in mind' but facilitated their influencing and interconnection, aligning in their 'formulation of opinions, attitudes or decisions, and in their rejection or acceptance of mass media in influence-attempts' (Katz and Lazarsfeld [1955] 1964: 131). As in *Personal Influence*, the social media user plays a key role in determining whether or not a message will be circulated and favourably received. The user, whether an ordinary user or an 'influential', may not endorse it. The message may be perceived as going counter to norms that are shared with valued others, identified and reinforced through Facebook. We can see too how Facebook can be readily mobilised to block influence-attempts stemming from the mainstream mass media or public communication campaigns of agencies directed at the individual. Facebook promised not only the identification of influencers, opinion leaders, and gatekeepers but more importantly the composition of the informal group itself.

What had remained so doggedly invisible was now fully visible, its reach extending beyond the previous limitation imposed by proximate, often geographically defined, interpersonal networks. Whereas Katz and Lazarsfeld noted 'behavioural contagion' ([1955] 1964: 104) within informal groups, Facebook sought to enact and facilitate contagion at various scales. Small informal group mechanisms make up the majority of Facebook messaging with most user-generated content consisting of messages, forwarded stories, and photographs circulated to small groups of people in that person's immediate circle. However, Facebook also facilitates 'behavioural contagion' among overlapping groups as it seeks the involved interactive attention of its users connecting interpersonal communication into lengthier and more networked forms of communication. In this way posts can become national and even global in their reach. In these circumstances, interpersonal, intragroup communication becomes akin to broadcast and print media in terms of its reach and broadcast scale. Lazarsfeld's 'opinion leaders' became the influencers, creators, and micro-celebrities of Facebook, Instagram, and YouTube (Senft 2013; Abidin 2018). Platforms tuned their feeds to reward users who generated attention with more attention. This created the conditions for influencers to emerge as key intermediaries between marketers and the attention economy of platforms. Over time, platforms developed techniques for formalising and controlling the place of influencers in their engagement and advertising models.

Unlike Katz and Lazarsfeld, social media companies did not have to create a snapshot of personal influence through surveys. Platforms are a system for the continuous registration of networks of influence. Consequently, it has become possible to shape influence-attempts in real time through feedback loops made possible by platforms' algorithm models. To paraphrase Luciano Floridi, social media were not just 'enhancing' or 'augmenting' interpersonal communication. They were forces for change in interpersonal communication itself as Facebook created and re-engineered 'whole realities that the user is then enabled to inhabit'. Its friendly, digital interfaces now acted as friendly 'gateways' (Floridi 2014: 71).[3] Social media platforms are built on calculating, serving, building, shaping, and above all facilitating personal influence among social groups. Platforms turn personal influence into a new medium – social media.

Social Media and Other Media

Social media content is based on exchange within personal networks and is thus only partially 'produced' on any industrial or professional scale; in this regard it is unlike traditional media industries. Regardless of whether social media users create their own content or share professionally produced content, though, their practices of sharing create and render visible personal networks. The general lack of professional practice in the creating and sharing of user-generated content ensured the integrity of the informal group – or in Zuckerberg's phrasing, its 'communities' (2017). However, Facebook's orientation towards user-generated content is made possible by the professional production practices of the platform itself, facilitating the uploading and generation of content by ordinary and professional users and developing interfaces that continue to attract the attention of its user base.

Facebook also provides a vehicle for another kind of professionally produced content on the platform – that of advertising and marketing messages targeting users and encouraging their activation of these messages. Whereas traditional media always had two parallel streams of professionally produced content – the 'media content' used to attract the audience and the 'advertising content' used to pay for that attention – Facebook and other social media consist of unprofessional user-generated content sitting alongside professionally produced 'advertising and marketing' content. Professionally produced advertising and user-generated content now intermingle in new configurations. This includes audience activations where users take up and 're-broadcast' brand

messages, often resulting in an eclipse of hard-won separations between adver-
torial and editorial.

Inasmuch as social media turned to advertising to realise the value of its
media operations, it was just like its commercial media counterparts. But it
had intrinsic advantages over traditional print and broadcast media. Its unit
of analysis was not that of the de-identified sample of ratings research; it was
the individual user profile. Furthermore, there were no restrictions on what
supplementary information Facebook could obtain about users as long as this
detail was kept internal to the social media firm itself. In this way Facebook
turned the activities, including content generation activities of people on social
media, into a commodity and a market. It then sold its users' social media use
to whoever was interested in buying the audience commodity – advertisers,
governments, market research firms, and media providers alike.

Like commercial television, radio, and the press before it, Facebook and
the other social media companies promoted their use, their responsiveness,
and their accountability to their audiences and the social licence this provided.
They likewise did not trumpet that they were at base advertiser-supported
media trading in audiences as commodities. They downplayed the extent to
which they were caught in the same dual-product logic of traditional print
and broadcast media – at once communicating with users, building a 'brand
relationship' with those users, while simultaneously selling those users, their
attention, and their audiences to a motley assembly of interested actors
(see Napoli 2003, 2011).

However, for all the many similarities between Facebook (and Instagram)
and its traditional media counterparts, these social media companies sought
the audience commodity in a new way. They effectively combined operations
that the traditional media system had kept separate. They sold audience attention in ways analogous to the selling of spot advertising on radio and TV
and display and classified advertising in newspapers. They provided a market information metric based on de-identified user and audience measurement
data much in the manner of audience measurement firms like A. C. Nielsen.
And finally, they offered an advertising agency service which, while retaining
confidentiality by not disclosing user identity to advertising clients, allowed
the placement of advertising based on Facebook and Instagram's own user-
identifying metrics.

LAZARSFELD VERSUS ZUCKERBERG: PUBLIC AND PROPRIETORIAL RESEARCH PRIORITIES

For all the productive insights we can glean from *Personal Influence* to
understand the mediatisation of the informal group that became Facebook,
Instagram, and other social media platforms, there are some fundamental and

important differences between Katz and Lazarsfeld's research enterprise and that of Zuckerberg's Facebook. *Personal Influence* had avowedly public priorities of transparency and replicability whereas Zuckerberg's Facebook pursued private, proprietorial, and opaque research priorities. By illuminating these differences, we can get at the heart of the sea-change in the nature of media provision and media research that has accompanied the rise of social media. Both *Personal Influence* and Facebook have at their centre a focus on understanding and mobilising media users and have a substantial research apparatus at their very heart. Yet they each land in very different places with important consequences for media, its consumption, and research.

Both Zuckerberg and Katz and Lazarsfeld saw the public as essential partners in their respective research enterprises. For Katz and Lazarsfeld, enlisting the public provided the fine-grained research detail that could tease out the nature and character of personal influence. For Zuckerberg, Facebook's partnership with the public ensured his social media system was sufficiently fine-grained and robust not only to attract uptake by existing informal groups but also to encourage the formation of new groups. Facebook built an unheard-of research dataset amounting now to some 2.6 billion users. If both intensified the public's role as research partners, they did so in different ways. Katz and Lazarsfeld built a representative sample for research while Zuckerberg built a media system populated by individuals participating in overlapping informal groups and measured through new market information regimes and metrics based around the individual user and their personal networks.

Unlike Zuckerberg, Lazarsfeld had no aspirations to run a media company monetising media user attention. His focus on users was conducted under the aegis of university research centres (Converse [1987] 2009: 382). The research funding for *Personal Influence* came from a mix of foundations and industry contracts. Unlike his private sector counterparts such as Nielsen, Gallup, and Crossley, Lazarsfeld was not offering ongoing panel research in broadcast ratings or opinion polling as his principal project, nor was he offering 'art of opinion-management' services to corporate clients (Pooley 2006: 225). Instead, his methodologically focused research opened up a dialogue among scholarly research, marketing, and media producers.

The links between Lazarsfeld and his private sector counterparts were deep. Each pursued their audience metrics by creating a *separate* research sphere of operations external to that of the media provider. Their practice was one of creating parallel research institutions. They created their own panels. In doing so each had to identify, recruit, and persuade their research subjects to commit and remain committed to their participation. They needed to tutor their informants on their research involvement and to monitor their ongoing involvement. Ongoing panels, like the broadcast ratings, needed to be continuously adjusted and refreshed over time.

Research subjects had to self-report their media behaviours, their views, and their conduct and do so without payment. Respondents appreciated the broader social and public value of the research and their important role within it. They developed a sense of shared responsibility for the making of reliable survey instruments whether in the bespoke survey or regular ratings or opinion polling data.

External to the media industry, research was seen to be impartial and accurate. The 'guarantee' of the integrity of the Lazarsfeld project, the Gallup polls, and the Nielsen audimeters lay in the exercise of a particular office, that of the survey research intellectual. Lazarsfeld and the wider circle he connected with through the American Association of Public Opinion Research (AAPOR, founded in 1948) and *Public Opinion Quarterly* (founded in 1937) promoted a culture of the independent public audit. This was both an ethical priority and a matter of practical consideration. The intellectual circle formed around both entities consisted of academics, marketing, advertising and media industry researchers, public relations counsellors, research service providers like Nielsen and Gallup as well as governmental research, census bureaux, and agency representatives. Research was here an eminently public process providing proof of concept for research methods while encouraging their further interrogation and uptake. Lazarsfeld was working in a space in which his research efforts contributed to market information as public information and a resource for industry and for scholarly fields including most notably sociology, statistics, and social psychology.

The authority of this research enterprise was guaranteed by its structural independence from its clients, its ethical, transparent, and auditable processes, and its commitment to a third-party research methodology development that was not materially 'interested' in the transactions and issues being surveyed and evaluated. Reviews of *Personal Influence* praised its methodological openness and invitation to scrutiny, noting that it was 'pointing the way toward improvement of future research design' (Carter 1955: 383). Conducted as it was separately and away from the media itself, this 'survey' expertise and specialist competence in its analysis was what Lazarsfeld and his academic and commercial research counterparts were essentially 'selling' to industry and government. For Mark Andrejevic and Mark Burdon (2015: 19) this research enterprise was 'targeted, purposeful, and [relied on] discrete forms of information collection' in an avowedly publicly accountable research agenda.

Facebook has very different institutional commitments. Operating in an audience market, Facebook has a dual focus. On the one hand, it creates valuable audience commodities that it can sell to advertiser and marketer clients seeking to either reach finely targeted audiences or to purchase data and information about those audiences. Here Facebook is both a media provider and a market information provider. On the other hand, Facebook works with its users to continuously innovate its social media 'product', building its communities, facilitating interpersonal connections, and fine-tuning user recommendations – all with the aim of retaining and building user attention and interest in the Facebook platform.

For Zuckerberg, the focus was upon users and facilitating their interaction with each other, with the platform, and with the advertisers and marketers targeting those users. He achieved this by improvising a social media vehicle that provided continuous audience monitoring in real time, and in building tracking mechanisms which allowed the prediction of audience behaviours. This monitoring vehicle was 'institutional data' in that it was built on user transactions within the platform but it was also built – like Katz and Lazarsfeld's research before it – with the express purpose of data collection and analysis. But unlike Katz and Lazarsfeld, the data his social media generated, and the methodologies he used to develop, track, harvest, and monitor user activity, were proprietorial and not publicly available. His novel methodologies were, however, central to the organisation and practice of Facebook and the associated social media with which it is connected. Such proprietorial methodologies formed the basis of Facebook's business model and were confidential to it. Feedback and monitoring were used not to open up the relation between the media audience and media user, and between the media audience researcher and media companies to public scrutiny. Instead, its metrics were used to run a media service with limited capacity for public interest scrutiny and audit.

Facebook internalised its audience metrics. Its media provision model eliminated the need for third-party monitoring and feedback by independent market information providers. It turned the monitoring and feedback stage of the media provision cycle from a public to a quasi-private transaction. Production, distribution, display/exhibition, consumption, and feedback and monitoring of this consumption were now internal Facebook operations.

Facebook was able to place itself, if not outside of independent audience metrics and measurement provisions altogether, then certainly outside the kind of independent audit advertisers and marketers and competition regulators – like the Australian Consumer Commission (ACCC 2019: 149) – were seeking. Facebook's market power placed it in a position to resist calls by large advertisers and bodies such as the Australian ACCC and occasionally AAPOR for greater scrutiny of its methodologies and associated algorithms.

Facebook argued that it did not need an independent audience research service. It was not reporting, as did Nielsen, on radio and TV stations and their relative competitive performance with respect to each other. Instead it was reporting its own performance as a platform and then selling this internally generated market information to media buyers on the terms it set. This was unlike the terms hammered out by, for instance, the various parties to the ratings conventions (media companies, ratings providers, and advertisers and advertising agencies). While advertisers and marketers and media providers grumbled about the absence of third-party auditing, those using the Facebook system had very little leverage once the scope and scale of Facebook made advertising and being on the platform essential first steps in advertising and marketing campaigns (Herrman and Maheshwari 2016).

As a consequence, Facebook's public disclosures and reporting on itself and its activities typically fall short of what 'government officials, activists and academics have long pushed the social network to disclose' (Frenkel 2018). Instead Facebook seeks control over its various levers, typically lifting the curtain on its operation only so far. It prefers to 'black box' its activities in ways that emphasise the media provider and media audience relation and dismiss calls for audit and review as calls to disclose trade secrets and intellectual property.

Facebook has also stressed how its data collection on individual users helps them receive a more tailored, useful, and convenient service. Data was certainly used to fine-tune the service, enhance its recommendation and guide functions, calibrate the service more closely to its users, and involve users as active co-creators of the service. Facebook was making adjustments, conducted as engineering data science experiments on behalf of users. In this way Facebook was building and crafting a service that would later permit predictive modelling based on user historical data.

Like its commercial media predecessors, Facebook was Janus-faced. It not only used the extraordinary opportunity such extensive monitoring and feedback provided for user benefit but it also used it to create an advertising vehicle and an associated promotional culture of considerable scope, reach, and power (Ingram 2017). Compared with traditional print and broadcast media, Facebook's audience commodity offer was particularly compelling. Advertisers and marketers could buy finely calibrated audiences based on aggregations of individual user profiles. These user profiles had the added advantage of being built from Facebook's own user data, that of others in their personal networks, and from the detailed profiles of these users available from commercial datasets covering other aspects of users' lives (see Dewey 2016). In this way Facebook was offering unprecedented levels of precision in direct targeting (Ingram 2017).

This 'face' of Facebook was writ large in the platform's courting of advertising and marketing clients but downplayed in its general messaging to users. There the platform's advertiser-supported base was cast as a benign by-play facilitating the formation of community in a new kind of service. In getting this information they were not acting like a media company but like a technology company seeking a more calibrated and useful service. But like every other advertiser-supported media player, Facebook has needed to settle on a balance between the demands of providing a valuable user experience and providing an effective advertising vehicle delivering audience commodities for its advertising, marketing, social, and political party clients.

Zuckerberg then constructed a data research enterprise almost the antithesis of that which Katz and Lazarsfeld promoted. Zuckerberg's Facebook instituted its own data collection, storage, and analysis behemoth. It wound its data collection and analysis tightly around its production work of mounting its own and others' content (from both users and corporate clients) and its advertising and marketing offer to clients. This same data collection and analysis then informed user distribution of Facebook posts and the ways in which content was exhibited through Facebook apps and web portals. In this way Zuckerberg merged the survey research enterprise of institutional market information with media provision and advertising and marketing sales.

Zuckerberg is involved in the development of a digital data *collection*, *analysis*, and *intervention* device whose functions are performed internally and simultaneously with that of media provision itself. For Facebook cycles of production, distribution, exhibition, and feedback and monitoring are occurring at one and the same time as are the research probes. Consumption, feedback, and monitoring once seen as necessarily constituting so many spheres independent of the media provision cycle were now internal to what José van Dijck, Thomas Poell, and Martijn de Wall call the Facebook 'ecosystem' (2018: 12–16). This marks an important shift in information collection and analysis. As Andrejevic and Burdon would have it, this is 'a shift [. . .] to always-on, ubiquitous, opportunistic ever-expanding forms of data capture' (2015: 19). We have moved from the temporally discrete to the continuous.

The Zuckerberg world – and that of other media platforms such as Google and Amazon – is a world of whole populations: 'entire systems of records, so that the aggregate is not as important as the individual profile' (Savage et al. 2010: 12). When 'everyone and every transaction can be scanned, monitored, and subject to analysis and intervention' (Savage et al. 2010: 12) those who analyse such data can insist on its value at a granular level. We are likewise moving from the individual datasets of the ratings to the now joined up datasets. With datasets being joined the priority becomes the amalgamation of databases which in turn 'allow ever more granular, unique, specification' (Savage et al. 2010: 12).

With data generated as a by-product of everyday media transactions and with Facebook and other social media applications further increasing their scope of data collections through exploiting the various affordances of the mobile phone such as its portability, geo-locational mapping, camera/video capturing, and quick response (QR) code reading, the mode of 'institutional' data collection now has a decided edge over the non-transactional, bespoke methods Lazarsfeld championed (1958: 99–104). In these circumstances the independent survey expert and their bespoke survey data collection methods are no longer useful. Fine-grained knowledge of media use and uptake lay in the company's datasets ideally calibrated to not only understand individual and group behaviour but facilitate 'personalised advertising in real time' based on the 'precision instruments offered by data analytics' (van Dijck et al. 2018: 11). Zuckerberg has re-established institutional data collection, analysis, and actions based on that data and its analysis at the very centre of the media market information regime and business model. As van Dijck et al. put it, Facebook and the rest of the 'big five' (Amazon, Apple, Google, and Microsoft) are now the online gatekeepers 'through which data flows are managed, processed, stored and channelled' (2018: 13).

Conclusion

To adopt an analogy drawn from Donald MacKenzie (2006), the survey research of Katz and Lazarsfeld provided a 'camera', a representation of relations as they stood. This was subsequently used by other actors as an 'engine' to drive their actions and interventions in the form of advertising campaigns and marketing decisions, media development, scheduling, and programme evaluation. By contrast, Zuckerberg had a much larger ambition: Facebook was in the business of rendering the distinction between 'camera' and 'engine' indistinguishable. User data collection, analysis, media strategy, advertising placement, and user recommendations were all conducted within the platform creating a formidable 'engine'.

Both *Personal Influence* and Facebook were concerned about the role that people played in the trajectory of and effectiveness of media, whether to sell goods and services and media content, conduct public affairs, or to mobilise fashion's outreach. Each staged the coming into contact of the different spheres of personal networks in small group settings and that of media provision. But with *Personal Influence* the interest in interpersonal relations was for what it could do for media and for the aims of those who used media for influence. It explicitly addressed itself to those media, advertising and marketing firms who used these media as their conduit and relay – fashion houses, political classes, marketers of all kinds, and media content producers/TV networks. In being concerned with the 'effectiveness of *mass media influence-attempts*' (Katz and Lazarsfeld [1955] 1964: 130; emphasis added) their task was to bring together distinct media and non-media worlds.

Facebook was, by contrast, making its offer to its media, advertiser and marketer, and media buyer and seller clients in circumstances where the social media platform had brought together these two complementary worlds in the one media service. They were being offered access to the social media platform's command of a mediatised version of interpersonal communication in which influencers were known, informal groups were identified, and users were pinpointed based on substantive user profiles. This not only permitted superior forms of direct targeting but put Facebook in the box seat in its dealings with marketers and advertisers. Those advertisers and marketers who had been using print and broadcast media and their online variants now had an alternative media outlet promising direct targeting, greater responsiveness to user inquiry, more effective word-of-mouth and user recommendation and guidance systems.

The comparison between social media and traditional media was stark. Traditional media competitors were stuck with an interrupted advertising model of spot and display advertising and audiences that could only be identified in limited ways through randomly sampled panels. In the language of *Personal Influence*, Facebook was dedicated to showing how, as a service built on personal networks and personal profiles, it was more 'effective' in terms of 'mass media influence-attempts' than any other media. Courtesy of their size, scope, and reach, social media increasingly dominated national advertising expenditures. They drew attention and audiences away from traditional media outlets and led the development of digital first advertising and marketing campaigns as evidenced by digital advertising's command of new dollars spent on advertising (Cohen 2017: 142; ACCC 2019: 75–99). Evaluation strategies were now principally centred on the effectiveness of direct targeting efforts through social media and search's tracking mechanisms as these media increasingly took over the role of providing access and legibility to our social, political, and economic worlds (Cohen 2017: 137–40).

In this new media ecology Facebook and Instagram, like Google and YouTube, offered advertisers and marketers opportunities to analyse, guide, recommend, and relay word of mouth in ways that gave them more access to and influence over the 'message'. The concern for the transmission of media influence had mutated from a concern to manage the role that interpersonal communication played in guiding people, to the business of building guidance media systems shaped in various ways by the interpersonal relations systems of the platform. To be sure, interpersonal relationships still offered prospects for the 'relay between people who are exposed to mass media influence and others who are not' (Katz and Lazarsfeld [1955] 1964: 116); they still offered prospects of 'reinforc[ing] a mass media campaign' ([1955] 1964: 116); but this relaying and reinforcing was now embedded in individual media platforms themselves of considerable scope, reach, amplification, and power.

It seems especially ironic that *Personal Influence*, which had done so much to advance the view of a media system encompassing a media world and a parallel audience and user world, should also be the text that provides a basis for navigating and illuminating social media as vehicles that bring into being new configurations of media provision, media metrics, and media users. Paradoxically, Katz and Lazarsfeld's exposition of the role of interpersonal relations in communication provides us with the script for a social media system built on top of interpersonal communication. For many years after its first publication *Personal Influence* has been the poster child for the argument that media have little effects or intrinsic power (Curran et al. 1982: 13–16), yet with social media we have a media form built on the very apparatus that mediated, filtered, and was proclaimed as uniquely powerful in shaping media consumption. The very argument against media effects mutates before our eyes into an argument for media effects, particularly as they relate to social media.

With Facebook and Instagram the small informal group and personal networks are now thoroughly mapped and mediatised, shaped by users, the social media platforms, and advertisers and marketers. There is here no 'research subject' invisibility, no difficulty in targetting. Yet there is every incentive for the user to become involved in advertiser and marketer activations. *Personal Influence* provided communication studies with a theory of the centrality of interpersonal relations to the uptake not only of media but also of ideas. Social media reformed interpersonal communication. In its application to social media this theory has given rise to a new kind of media system built on these interpersonal relations. For Natascha Just and Michael Latzer, it is a media system characterised by increasing levels of 'individualisation', 'commercialisation', and in its mixing of geographical scales favouring viral spreading of posts 'deterritorialisation' (2017: 238). It is also a media system in which there is a decreasing sense of 'transparency, controllability, and predictability' (Just and Latzer 2017: 238). These are all aspects of Facebook that *Personal Influence* has helped illuminate. Far from it being time to jettison *Personal Influence* and its central concepts, it is time to critically update the concept of personal influence and its diffusion in social media platforms. It is time to recognise the enduring legacy of its conceptualisations and approaches to media, marketing, research, and market information and scholarship.

* Sadly, Tom O'Regan passed away before he had finished editing this essay. The editors would like to express our thanks to Nicholas Carah for his assistance in preparing the essay for publication. Although Tom wrote this paper for the present volume, a version of it was published previously in a 2021 special issue of the journal he co-founded, *Continuum: Journal of Media and Cultural Studies*, dedicated to his memory and scholarship.

NOTES

1. Elihu Katz has recently issued a guarded repudiation of core concepts of *Personal Influence*: that of 'two step flow of communication' where communication is mediated by an informal group(s) and 'opinion leaders'. In his work with Yonatan Fialkoff (2017) he has urged their 'retirement'. The two-step model was inaccurate as 'it involves more than two steps; it takes a network'; while the 'opinion leader' was an inaccurate fit for the 'everyday influentials' characterising interpersonal group

dynamics. Ironically, at the precise moment that the vocabulary of the influencer was being repurposed to create a whole new cadre of micro-celebrities, Katz and Fialkoff were wanting to 'retire' the very concepts that were being hardwired into social media's very operations.

2. Katz and Fialkoff (2017: 87) mistakenly counterpose the relation between traditional media and personal influence as one of 'competition' rather than 'interconnection'. This is more likely an expression of the subsequent uptake of *Personal Influence* which tended to counterpose the communication and media of distinct rather than interconnected worlds.

3. One important gateway is to other media content – in particular news and information media – which are simultaneously displaced from their central place in monitoring our social worlds. Ironically, social media now provides an aggregator role – offering a guide to the news but also a substitution for that news. For Katz and Lazarsfeld, informal groups made media and our social worlds accessible and legible; since Facebook, the news and information media have a vastly reduced role as an optional source of news and information about the world.

References

Abidin, Crystal. 2018. *Internet Celebrity: Understanding Fame Online*. Bingley: Emerald Publishing.

Andrejevic, Mark, and Mark Burdon. 2015. 'Defining the Sensor Society.' *Television & New Media* 16.1: 19–36.

Australian Competition and Consumer Commission (ACCC). 2019. *Digital Platforms Inquiry: Final Report*. Canberra: ACCC.

Broderson, Avid. 1956. Review of *Personal Influence: The Part Played by People in the Flow of Mass Communications*, by Elihu Katz and Paul F. Lazarsfeld. *Social Research* 23.1: 113–15.

Carter, Roy. 1955. Review of *Personal Influence: The Part Played by People in the Flow of Mass Communications*, by Elihu Katz and Paul F. Lazarsfeld. *Social Forces* 34.4: 383.

Cohen, Julie. 2017. 'Law for the Platform Economy.' *U.C. Davis Law Review* 51: 131–204.

Converse, Jean. [1987] 2009. *Survey Research in the United States: Roots and Emergence 1890–1960*. New Brunswick, NJ: Transaction Publishers.

Curran, James, Michael Gurevitch, and Janet Woollacott. 1982. 'The Study of the Media: Theoretical Approaches.' In *Culture, Society and the Media*, edited by Michael Gurevitch, Tony Bennett, James Curran, and Janet Woollacott, 11–29. London: Methuen.

Dewey, Caitlin. 2016. '98 Personal Data Points that Facebook Uses to Target Ads to You.' *The Washington Post*, 20 August. <https://www.washingtonpost.com/news/the-intersect/wp/2016/08/19/98-personal-data-points-that-facebook-uses-to-target-ads-to-you/> (last accessed 22 March 2021).

The Economist. 2007. 'Word of Mouse; Conversational Marketing.' *The Economist*, 8 November. <https://www.economist.com/business/2007/11/08/word-of-mouse> (last accessed 10 June 2021).

Floridi, Luciano. 2014. *The Fourth Revolution: How the Infosphere is Reshaping Human Reality*. Oxford: Oxford University Press.

Frenkel, Sheera. 2018. 'Facebook Says It Deleted 865 Million Posts, Mostly Spam.' *The New York Times*, 15 May. <https://www.nytimes.com/2018/05/15/technology/facebook-removal-posts-fake-accounts.html> (last accessed 10 June 2021).

Herrman, John, and Sapna Maheshwari. 2016. 'Facebook Apologizes for Overstating Video Metrics.' *New York Times*, 23 September. <https://www.nytimes.com/2016/09/24/business/media/facebook-apologizes-for-overstating-video-metrics.html> (last accessed 22 March 2021).

Ingram, Mathew. 2017. 'How Google and Facebook Have Taken Over the Digital Ad Industry.' *Fortune*, 4 January. <https://fortune.com/2017/01/04/google-facebook-ad-industry/> (last accessed 22 March 2021).

Just, Natascha, and Michael Latzer. 2017. 'Governance by Algorithms: Reality Construction by Algorithmic Selection on the Internet.' *Media Culture and Society* 39.2: 238–58.

Katz, Elihu, and Yonatan Fialkoff. 2017. 'Six Concepts in Search of Retirement.' *Annals of the International Communication Association* 41.1: 86–91.

Katz, Elihu, and Paul Lazarsfeld. [1955] 1964. *Personal Influence: The Part Played by People in the Flow of Mass Communications*. New York: Free Press.

Lazarsfeld, Paul F. 1958. 'Evidence and Inference in Social Research.' *Daedalus* 87.4 (Fall): 99–130.

Lazarsfeld, Paul F. 1959. 'Reflections on Business.' *American Journal of Sociology* 65.1 (July): 1–31.

Lazarsfeld, Paul F., Bernard Berelson, and Hazel Gaudet. [1948] 1968. *The People's Choice: How the Voter Makes Up His Mind in a Presidential Campaign*. New York: Columbia University Press.

MacKenzie, Donald. 2006. *An Engine, Not a Camera: How Financial Models Shape Markets*. Cambridge, MA: MIT Press.

Napoli, Philip M. 2003. *Audience Economics: Media Institutions and the Audience Marketplace*. New York: Columbia University Press.

Napoli, Philip M. 2011. *Audience Evolution: New Technologies and the Transformation of Media Audiences*. New York: Columbia University Press.

Pooley, Jefferson. 2006. *An Accident of Memory: Edward Shils, Paul Lazarsfeld and the History of American Mass Communication Research*. PhD dissertation. Columbia University.

Riley, Matilda. 1956. Review of *Personal Influence: The Part Played by People in the Flow of Mass Communications*, by Elihu Katz and Paul F. Lazarsfeld. *American Journal of Sociology* 62.1: 101–3.

Roshwalb, Irving. 1956. Review of *Personal Influence: The Part Played by People in the Flow of Mass Communications*, by Elihu Katz and Paul F. Lazarsfeld. *The Journal of Marketing* 21.1: 129–30.

Savage, Mike, Evelyn Ruppert, and John Law. 2010. 'Digital Devices: Nine Theses.' *CRESC Working Paper Series*, Working Paper No. 86. Manchester: University of Manchester/CRESC, Open University.

Senft, Theresa M. 2013. 'Microcelebrity and the Branded Self.' In *A Companion to New Media Dynamics*, edited by John Hartley, Jean Burgess, and Axel Bruns, 346–54. Chichester: Wiley-Blackwell.

Sills, David. 1987. *Paul F. Lazarsfeld, 1901–1976: A Biographical Memoir*. Washington, DC: National Academy of Sciences.

Turow, Joseph. 2013. *The Daily You: How the New Advertising Industry Is Defining Your Identity and Your Worth*. New Haven, CT: Yale University Press.

van Dijck, José, Thomas Poell, and Martijn de Waal. 2018. *The Platform Society: Public Values in a Connective World*. Oxford: Oxford University Press.

Zuckerberg, Mark. 2017. 'Building Global Community.' *Facebook*, 16 February. <https://www.facebook.com/notes/markzuckerberg/building-global-community/10154544292806634> (last accessed 10 June 2021).

11. PRINCIPLES OF EXCHANGE: FREE SPEECH IN THE ERA OF FAKE NEWS

Kris Fallon

INTRODUCTION

Beginning in 2016, a series of high-profile elections and referenda produced populist results and candidates that appeared to signal a conservative, right-wards shift in many Western democratic states.[1] Even as this populist wave was unfolding, however, questions began to emerge from across the political spectrum around the part that mainstream and social media play in informing the public and stimulating debate amongst citizens, two functions at the heart of the democratic project. As the public, the US president and the mainstream press debated the meaning of 'fake news', the influence of bots, trolls, and fake accounts cast suspicion on the powerful role private tech companies play in providing platforms for connecting citizens with information and with one another. Further, emerging technology capable of easily faking and manipulating moving images raised the spectre of false and misleading visual media. The visible evidence that had long been, however dubiously, the gold standard of evidence and objectivity, was newly suspect. If technology and social media were at one time viewed as means of democratising access to information and removing the powerful institutional gatekeepers, then in 2016 they appeared to pose an imminent threat to democracy itself.

While many of these issues may seem like transitory topics for mainstream political discussion, the questions they pose connect with fundamental, abstract principles at the heart of liberal, democratic political theory including individual freedom of speech and the role of the press in holding the state to account and informing the public. At their root, these technologies pose basic but nonetheless fundamental ethical, aesthetic, and epistemological challenges to the framework of the democratic project: if we cannot trust what we see, how are we supposed to make good political choices? This chapter will consider these larger questions through the lens of the fundamental ethos behind freedom of speech in many Western democracies – what is often referred to as the 'marketplace of ideas' – and demonstrate the extent to which it pervades both the macro and micro debates shaping freedom of speech today, as well as the underlying technologies on which they are taking place. I will conclude by considering the extent to which the principles that it implies offer a workable model for freedom of speech in our current context.

The Marketplace of Ideas

The individual right to free expression and freedom of speech is widely considered to be a fundamental, core ingredient for democracy. As a democratic value, it has been explored in central philosophical texts and written into specific constitutional frameworks across Europe and the United States. It appears in the Declaration of the Rights of Man and of the Citizen, the United States Bill of Rights, the United Nations' Universal Declaration of Human Rights, and in Article 11 of the European Union's Charter of Fundamental Rights.

In the American framework, freedom of speech is set down in the First Amendment of the Bill of Rights, which prevents the government from making laws 'abridging the freedom of speech', as well as other specific forms of expression, including religion, peaceable assembly, government petition, and significantly, the press. The broad, abstract principles contained in the few phrases that constitute the Bill of Rights were later elaborated and interpreted through the myriad of cases which sought to interpret the practical application of these principles in various contexts.

The specific formulation or working model of what constitutes 'free speech' in our contemporary context derives from the defence that the influential Supreme Court Justice Oliver Wendell Holmes outlined in a pair of widely cited opinions, *Schenck v. United States* and *Abrams v. United States*. Taken together, the two opinions spell out the justification for (and the potential limits of) freedom of speech for individuals. In *Schenck*, Holmes claimed that the protections for individual freedom of speech did not constitute an absolute protection, arguing that speech which advocated for or inspired imminent violations of the law was not protected by it. In an oft-repeated example, Holmes stipulated that actions like 'falsely shouting fire in a theater and causing a panic' posed what he had earlier classified as 'a clear and present danger' to public safety.[2]

In *Abrams*, however, Holmes found himself in the minority, authoring a dissent that for many seemed to contradict the majority opinion that he had put forward in *Schenck*.[3] The *Abrams* case turned on a pamphlet circulated by two self-described socialist anarchists denouncing the war against Germany and advocating for a general strike to oppose US intervention in the Russian revolution. Using recently passed legislation, the government sought to convict the defendants for sedition and espionage. Here, Holmes held that the pamphlet was not an incitement to violence against the government or its citizens. In other words, it failed to meet the imminent threat standards set out in *Schenck*. Instead, Holmes argued, the defendants were being prosecuted for the basic ideas and beliefs that they held. In the opinion's most memorable (and cited) phrase, Holmes wrote: 'the ultimate good desired is better reached by free trade in ideas [. . .] [T]he best test of truth is the power of the thought to get itself accepted in the competition of the market.'[4]

Holmes's specific formulation here, 'the competition of the market', has become the basis for the more common metaphor 'marketplace of ideas' that now serves as the primary explication of how freedom of speech is supposed to work and the deeper justification for its protection (Baker 1992). In codifying the principle, Holmes was specifically drawing upon the defence of freedom of speech laid out in 1859 in John Stuart Mill's *On Liberty* (2003), where Mill advocates for the protection of individual thought, speech, and action regardless of the extent to which they contradict popular opinion, common sense, or even scientific fact. In the occasionally awkward marriage of utilitarian 'greatest goods' and liberal 'individual freedoms', Mill argued that unless these freedoms impacted others, they should be entirely left alone from government sanction, legal interdiction, or popular censure. For Mill, competition between ideas ensures that the best existing ideas retain their strength by being constantly tested and hence rescued from the stagnation of passively accepted dogma. The allowance for a diversity of ideas further safeguards and preserves new or unpopular ideas which may eventually prove true, rather than prematurely stifling their expression in the face of popular, if incorrect, consensus to the contrary. As Owen Fiss points out, Mill wanted to 'foster our individuality, even to the point of eccentricity' in order to push back on 'the forces that drive us to conformity' (2003: 179).

While Mill never uses the marketplace metaphor specifically, Holmes's framework accords with the larger justifications that Mill laid out for preserving the broadest possible diversity of ideas. The clear echo here between Mill's liberal political philosophy (ensuring the best ideas through competition and diversity) and a laissez-faire economic policy (giving markets the power to determine – through competition – inherent, abstract values like price) was inevitably the resonance that lead Holmes to connect the two principles in forging the *Abrams* metaphor. As Vincent Blasi (2004) demonstrates, the formative force of competition and diversity in producing specific outcomes was also further justified in another prominent nineteenth-century philosophy, namely

Darwinian evolution. Indeed, Mill's *On Liberty* and Darwin's *On the Origin of Species* were both published in 1859. For the circle of theorists and philosophers surrounding Holmes (Chauncey Wright, William James, Charles Sanders Peirce, and eventually John Dewey), the connections between Mill's liberalism, economic competition, and Darwinian evolution offered an interlocking set of self-justifying principles (Menand 2002: 236; Misak 2013: 16). The marketplace of ideas would produce good outcomes through competition, just as the competition of species produced the best fit through diversity, and diversity in the marketplace produced the best prices and products through unregulated competition. As Louis Menand puts it, in the intellectual circles in which Holmes travelled, 'the market operated like nature because they had already decided that nature operated like a market' (2002: 195).

Absent from the use of the market as metaphor for both natural selection and free, democratic exchange was any critique of the market itself in either material or abstract terms. This omission does not seem to have hindered its widespread adoption by Holmes and others in the years that followed.[5] But this set of associations offers a great deal to unpack, and different legal theorists and philosophers on both Mill and Holmes have interpreted the connections differently. For Richard Posner (2003), the libertarian philosophy at work in both Holmes and Mill provides a coherent connection between individual freedom of speech, free competition within the market, and the particular version of social Darwinism that animates some of Holmes's other, less cited, opinions. For Edwin Baker (1992), Mill's faith in speech to deliver 'best outcomes' resonated with the faith in the power of free markets that Holmes and others expressed. For Jeremy Waldron, we might attribute the influence to Mill, but the introduction of the marketplace into the discussion of free speech was Holmes's own, and the phrase 'would have never occurred to Mill' (Waldron 2010; 2003 n.9). For Vincent Blasi (2004), the connection to Darwinian evolution and its emphasis on the necessity of diversity to ensure survival is what drew Holmes to Mill and animated his wider support for individual freedoms.

Regardless of how we interpret the influence of these ideas on Holmes at the time that he rendered the *Abrams* dissent, there is no question that the marketplace of ideas has become the de facto understanding and justification for freedom of speech. One finds it cited repeatedly both directly and indirectly in discussions dealing with principles of free expression. Jillian York of the Electronic Frontier Foundation, for example, used the opinion as an epigraph to an article denouncing calls for Twitter and other social networks to censor specific users (York and Timm 2012). The European Union's Commissioner for Information and Society used the phrase to describe the EU's motivation to strengthen protection for freedom of the press (Reding 2007). And Carol Christ, the Chancellor of UC Berkeley, in an open letter to the campus addressing a series of controversial conservative speakers, used the marketplace metaphor alongside references to Mill and the historic Free Speech Movement of the 1960s (Christ 2017). Beyond these more popular applications, the phrase finds its way into innumerable legal texts on First Amendment principles by renowned legal scholars across the political spectrum from Richard Posner to Erwin Chemerinsky to Jeremy Waldron (Stone and Bollinger 2018; Waldron 2014; Chemerinsky and Gillman 2017).

The marketplace metaphor, its popularity and ubiquity notwithstanding, does have its critics. Indeed, what many of the theorists who connect Holmes and Mill (except Posner) share is the belief that our current conception/interpretation of the marketplace of ideas is either incorrectly applied or inadequate to address our contemporary situation. For Blasi (2004), the missed or misunderstood connections with evolutionary theory in Holmes's thought have privileged the free market faith in best outcomes over the preservation of a diversity of opinion for its ability to adapt. For Baker (1992), the reliance of the metaphor on a universally objective theory of truth, a unity of social priorities, and a faith in the choices of rational individuals (all outmoded ideas in one way or another) renders the model inadequate as a justification for a principle as important as freedom of speech. Jared Schroeder (2018) maintains, like Baker, that the Enlightenment-era theory of a universal truth that Holmes and Mill drew upon has given way to a more discursive understanding of truth as something that emerges through consensus and communicative interaction, hence the need to protect speakers within the marketplace more than speech itself.

What I want to suggest here is that while none of these critiques of the applicability of the marketplace of ideas metaphor is wrong, their dismissal of the model as inadequate to or misapplied in our contemporary context misses the extent to which it provides a surprisingly accurate account of our current information environment. We may disagree with the metaphor as a prescription for protecting or regulating speech in a democratic society, but we cannot deny that it offers an ideal description of the forces at work in many of our own contexts. If it seems to many commentators that freedom of speech as embodied in the marketplace of ideas model is somehow broken, it is because we have the wrong idea about how markets operate. Focusing on the error of the model or its modern irrelevance overlooks the fact that our current information environment actually works very much like a marketplace, and it does so in complete indifference to its impact on the protection of freedom of speech, or the best outcomes for the democratic citizens subject to its whims. In order to see how this is so, I would like to offer a basic description of markets, and then demonstrate the extent to which these market forces are deeply embedded into various levels of our contemporary information environment.

The description I would offer of markets is the rather uncontroversial and commonplace claim that they are arranged on competition, produce a diversity of (unequal) competitors, and are driven by the self-interest of all involved (Fiss 2003). Certainly this was part of the basic theory of markets put forward by Adam Smith, but it is one clearly reiterated by Mill himself in the final sections of *On Liberty* where he explores freedom of action and the harm that occur as a result:

> it was once held to be the duty of governments, in all cases which were considered of importance, to fix prices, and regulate the processes of manufacture. But it is now recognised, though not till after a long struggle, that both the cheapness and the good quality of commodities are most effectually provided for by leaving the producers and sellers perfectly free, under the sole check of equal freedom to the buyers for supplying themselves elsewhere. (Mill 2003: 157)

Here again, scholars may differ as to whether Mill would have applied the marketplace idea to his theory of individual freedom of speech (Gordon 1997). However, the point is not that Mill connects the two ideas or that Holmes had this specific definition of the marketplace in mind, but rather that this conjunction of the marketplace and freedom of expression quite accurately reflects our current situation. Suspending for a moment whether or not a marketplace actually produces outcomes that are beneficial for either individual citizens or a functioning democracy, let us instead consider how two different dimensions of our own information environment of free expression actually behave like a marketplace.

FakeApp: Obfuscation through Competition

Returning to the 2016 election, the marketplace of information was at this point in time overrun with the discussion around fake news and election hacking. As these stories began to ramp up, so did the appearance of news stories demonstrating advances in computer vision and deep learning artificial intelligence (AI) algorithms that make it easy to manipulate live video and audio footage. Dubbed the 'next frontier in fake news', many of these tools such as Retiming and Lyrebird seem to have replicated the crisis of confidence that still photography experienced with the advent of programs like Photoshop several decades ago (The Economist n.d.; Lomas 2017). While many were still proof of concept tools that required significant resources and fairly extensive programming knowledge to execute, a few were being actively developed into commercial products for video and audio post-production.

Late 2017 saw the appearance of a tool named 'FakeApp', which was aimed at delivering a free, consumer-facing desktop application capable of swapping the faces of two people in a piece of video footage. Around the same time, a user on Reddit, where FakeApp had been largely developed and beta-tested, began posting videos created with the tool that swapped the faces of several high-profile Hollywood actors including Natalie Portman, Emma Watson, and others into scenes from pornographic videos. The scandal the videos generated, along with the user's handle, 'DeepFakes', gave the burgeoning genre of face-swapping videos its de facto name as well as a degree of high-profile notoriety. Most of the press coverage once again sensationalised the capabilities of FakeApp (usually vastly overstating it) and pointed towards an imminent future where there would be no way to determine the truth status of any given piece of video footage (Lee 2018). It seemed as though a science fiction future had arrived that challenged the reliability of human perception. If the marketplace of ideas was intended to ensure a free flow of information in the hopes of preserving the best possible ideas for the broadest segment of the public, then deep fakes seemed to indicate that something was amiss in the market. And yet, a close look at the specific algorithms used to create these videos demonstrates that they are instead a direct product of the incorporation of marketplace concepts at the procedural level.

At a procedural level, the specific algorithms used to create deep fakes draw directly on the abstract principles of competition and optimisation at the heart of the marketplace of ideas framework. Formally, deep fakes are produced in a series of computational steps not unlike the series of steps involved in the broader process of object and facial recognition, both long-standing research areas in computer vision and AI. In simple terms, a target object, in most cases a face, is identified in a given image and then abstracted through a series of calculations that determine the relative values of pixels adjacent to one another. Quantifying the set of statistical relationships and patterns produced by an object in the world on the CCD chip of a camera provides a means for the algorithm analysing this data to identify which object the camera has seen. In different images, the same face or object will produce a similar set of value ratios within a predictable probability range. As the algorithm is trained on a series of images with the same content, it eventually learns to identify that object or person in future images.

Procedurally, creating a fake video clip is merely an extension, or a conglomeration of the object recognition process. Identifying an object within an image is, after all, a necessary first step to being able to manipulate and redefine that object. Once specific definitions have been achieved (when the training is complete), the program is then able to manipulate these images in a variety of ways. In the case of face-swapping programs like FakeApp, facial recognition algorithms are trained on two specific objects, the face in the original video and the new face that the user would like to replace it with. After it has learned the faces of both people, the final step involves mapping the new face over the old face and then refining the results.

The quality or believability of the fake image is dependent upon the quality of the real input data which the program receives, as well as the amount of time that the program is given to analyse and deconstruct its target data. The larger the data set that the program has to learn both faces combined with the time that it is given to analyse each data set determines the extent to which the substitution will be convincing. As this description makes clear, the difficult task in object recognition is the training algorithm since this traditionally involves providing a large enough data set to achieve good definitions as well as providing it with enough computing power to iteratively produce the calculations needed to define and refine the statistical relationships described above.

Over the past decade, however, AI research has accelerated in part thanks to both hardware innovations that address the computational challenge as well as new types of algorithms that simplify and minimise the quantity of training data needed.[6] Both advances were essential to delivering a relatively easy, consumer-facing application like FakeApp. On the software side, a new breed of algorithms referred to as generative adversarial networks, or GANs, were essential to producing the results that so amazed and alarmed the public in 2016 (Goodfellow et al. 2014, 2015).

In essence GANs solve the problem of creating a massive training set of images or other data in order to train the patterns of recognition that AI depends upon, and thus they play an important role in many different types of deep learning AI algorithms. These networks, as the name implies, are based on an adversarial model where two AI 'agents' are linked to directly compete against one another in a simulation of a minimax game. Drawn from game theory, the minimax framework describes a strategy intended for use in zero-sum, two-player games that seeks to minimise one's maximum possible loss at each successive point within a game like chess or checkers (Ben-El-Mechaiekh and Dimand 2011). Within the game, one agent, the generative agent, creates data that is then tested by the other agent, the discriminator agent. The discriminator is designed to distinguish between real data and fake data, or accurate/inaccurate data based on the same statistical probabilities and resemblances discussed above. After it makes a determination, it then passes this information back to the generative agent, which uses the feedback to tweak its input for the next round. Through successive iterations, the distinctions between real and fake, or in the case of images, generated and recorded, eventually approach zero.

One can immediately see that this provides a significantly useful tool for automating the task of creating fake or artificially generated images that look convincingly real. Up until about five years ago, this had been an incredibly difficult challenge for AI to achieve. It is worth noting that from a teleological standpoint, fake images or false data are a step in the process towards achieving a deeper or better trained AI for decoding real data. In other words, they use simulation and dissimulation as a means of decoding and defining, we might say understanding, what is contained in real or recorded data. Procedurally, GANs use the minimax simulation game as a way to speed up and automate the training process for data recognition and classification using a much smaller set of training data, typically one of the more labour-intensive portions of creating an artificially intelligent agent.

The echoes here of industrial capitalism and marketplace logic (efficiency, automation, and competition) are no mere coincidence. The creator of the GAN, Ian Goodfellow, has pointed out in several talks and papers that he has authored on the subject that the basic principle at work is drawn from economics and market theory (Goodfellow 2016). Indeed, the most common metaphor used to explain the simulation process at work in the GAN is counterfeit currency, where the generator agent plays the role of counterfeiter and the discriminator agent plays the role of the state or the police. The minimax game itself comes from predictive analytics and game theory models featuring two players competing for a fixed set of resources, a branch of work that found its own adversarial application in Cold War military computing research (Erickson et al. 2013: 139–42, ch. 2). In this sense, GANs exemplify the sort of digital ideological reification that scholars such as Safiya Noble, John Cheney-Lippold, Johnathan Cohn, and many others have identified at work in other spheres of digital culture (Noble 2018; Cheney-Lippold 2018; Cohn 2019; Striphas 2015). Rather than escaping or circumventing certain ideological traps that have characterised human perception at the moment they were designed (racial and gender biases, for example, or a steadfast pursuit of winner-take-all geopolitical domination), algorithms working in these domains embed or reflect these same characteristics. In this context, GANs extend marketplace principles down to the level of the code itself, manifesting an almost literal translation of the free-speech marketplace of ideas concept into digital terms: multiple parties (AI agents), exchanging and comparing ideas (data) in order to achieve desired outcomes and shared truths (highly accurate recognition algorithms).

But rather than producing 'true' ideas or information, FakeApp was instead designed to produce 'fake' information that might appear true, an inversion of the marketplace principles that the GAN methodology was modelled on. And while it might operate according to market logic or resemble the marketplace in its procedural framework, these outcomes seem antithetical to the larger justifications that Mill, Holmes, and many other defenders of free speech articulate. Something close to this debate was had on a number of sites in the wake of the original DeepFake pornographic videos themselves, prompting a number of sites including Reddit, Twitter, and Pornhub to ban the videos from their sites, all with varying degrees of success, in response to a wave of outrage from critics and legal scholars who claimed they directly violated established privacy and First Amendment law (Schwartz 2018). Shortly after this, FakeApp itself ran into legal trouble and as of the summer of 2019 had been removed from both its publicly available websites as well as various code repositories where parts of the tool had once been tested. While the direct cause for its demise remains unclear, one can surmise that being the flagship product used to defame and degrade the public image of some of Hollywood's most prominent (and profitable) public personalities might draw some pretty intense legal scrutiny. In an ironic turn, at one point during this on again/off again phase for the app, someone posted a piece of imitation software that contained malicious code designed to mine bitcoin while appearing to create deep fake videos, a 'fake' FakeApp, if you will (Boyd 2018; Chesney and Citron 2018).

Nonetheless, we can see how the various technological and ideological levels in the stack begin to replicate and reinforce one another: the neural networks that produce simulation and dissimulation through competition to create deep fakes, the discursive policy networks that held First Amendment debates around allowing or removing deep fakes from various locations, and the social networks like YouTube which circulate deep fakes amid a broader sea of uncertainty increasingly populated by real and fake material of all sorts. At each level, various entities compete with one another to determine the veracity of information traded back and forth. The stakes and motivations of the players at each level of the stack may vary, but the basic set-up appears throughout: multiple parties weighing out degrees of truth in a widening circulation of information both real and fake.

Within these wider frameworks, FakeApp and the GANs technology which it relies upon appears to both uphold and undermine different dimensions of free speech in its marketplace of information iteration. On one level, it seemed to spread the capacity and capability to create these videos, enabling more participants to enter the marketplace (this is often described as technology's 'democratising' capacity). In the brief window of time that it existed, face-swapping videos began appearing using any number of ridiculous targets, including politicians (Donald Trump swapped with Hillary Clinton), fictional characters (old Spiderman Tobey Maguire swapped with new Spiderman Tom Holland), and other celebrities besides the notorious DeepFakes (Nicolas Cage was a favourite). FakeApp's imperfect algorithms and relatively easy process provided the basis for a broader level of engagement with the cutting-edge AI technology.

This development had two important impacts. First, it enabled a new type of remix culture where users might manipulate and rework the media and political figures more typically used to manipulate them. In free speech terms, this was a version of speaking back to the dominant culture that Henry Jenkins (2006) and others associated with early social media, or what in a pre-digital period was often referred to as 'culture jamming'. And second, it circulated videos that foregrounded the power of these tools, making the concept of fake videos all the more legible to the broader public by flooding the market with gimmicky, humorous examples of the genre. In essence, they engaged audiences in a game not unlike the discriminator agent in a GAN, sitting back and deciding for each video, real or fake. This is vital given that FakeApp may have disappeared, but the broader technology behind it is still very much around, and without an impulse that asks, 'real or fake?' we place ourselves in a position to passively believe the next shocking video that surfaces. This is a lesson we should have learned a long time ago, but nonetheless one that FakeApp made painfully apparent. After all, such visible evidence may look real, but it clearly cannot be taken at 'face value'.

Midstream Media Marketplaces

Where technologies like FakeApp and others were promising future disruption and greater individual participation on the margins of the marketplace of ideas, other changes were simultaneously disrupting its centre. The 2016 US election also demonstrated the increased influence of a new type of news site, one that I am describing as the 'midstream' media outlet. Midstream media are news websites that were primarily 'born digital' rather than as an online component of an established, offline media outlet (although several were started as spinoffs of such outlets). Examples of this new breed of news outlet include *Vox*, *FiveThirtyEight*, *Breitbart*, *The Intercept*, *Quartz*, *Slate*, and *Axios*, although many more occupy specific vertical content categories.[7] They position themselves midway between mainstream news and more marginal independent bloggers and fringe news sources. Like social media, this positions them somewhere in-between the tenets of First Amendment law that govern the freedom of speech and freedom of the press. Many of them, in an effort to generate trust in readers and attract top tier talent, are connected with or headlined by veteran journalists who once worked with older mainstream media outlets. Many employ techniques which are dependent upon or critical towards the practices of traditional mainstream journalists. And several of them are independently funded by wealthy individuals as ideological or political projects. Rather than producing consensus, these various outlets instead seem to respond to the polarisation and dissensus which so characterises the environment in which they emerged. In market terms, they appear to foster a more diversified product offering, creating clear, well-defined distinctions between the approaches and opinions of various news outlets.

As an illustration of this phenomenon, we can briefly compare two midstream outlets, *Breitbart* and *The Intercept*. On the surface, both sites resemble one another and fit the midstream model described above. *The Intercept* is largely backed by Pierre Omidyar, the billionaire founder of eBay, through an umbrella media project he started called First Look Media (Ellison 2015). The founders of the site, Glenn Greenwald, Laura Poitras, and Jeremy Scahill, all came from existing careers in media and journalism, listing among their credits *Salon*, *The Guardian*, *Democracy Now*, and *The New York Times*, although Poitras was best known as an independent documentary filmmaker. Similarly, *Breitbart* was founded by veteran blogger and *Fox News* commentator Andrew Breitbart and heavily funded by the Mercer Family Foundation (Hylton 2017). After Breitbart's death in 2012, Steve Bannon became executive chair and worked on revamping and expanding both the website and the organisation itself. Ideologically, the two sites could not be further apart. Under Bannon's leadership, *Breitbart* positioned itself as a platform for the far right and 'alt-right', openly supporting extreme conservative political issues and candidates, including Donald Trump. *The Intercept*, on the other hand, is largely considered liberal or left-leaning, although it would balk at any political affiliation. Both sites position themselves as correctives to the failings of the mainstream news. For *The Intercept*, this takes the form of what it calls 'adversarial journalism' pointed at the traditional sources of power, including older, established media like *The New York Times* (Risen 2018). For *Breitbart*, it means countering what it perceives to be the liberal bias in most mainstream media.

The evolution of these midstream players and their 'adversarial' relationship with their competitors is the latest development in a longer chapter in the history of the news. Beginning in the 1990s, the rather stable landscape of mainstream journalism, comprised for decades of print media and the major broadcasting networks, was invaded by newcomers from cable, radio, and eventually the internet. But rather than extending the homogeneity of mainstream media with new but similar material, each new voice positioned itself as an essential antidote to some key deficit in the existing sources of information. Thus, CNN was the answer to the limited amount of time allotted to news by broadcast networks, Fox was the answer to the liberal bias of CNN and others, MSNBC a response to Fox's overt right-wing bias, bloggers were the answer to the class of professional journalists, and so on (Farhi 2003; Coe et al. 2008). Each new entrant to the increasingly competitive news marketplace, newly marketised itself as a result of media consolidation and shifting revenue sources within older, established norms like newspapers and broadcast networks, thus joined the mainstream by critiquing its existing framework and positioning itself as a better instrument of truth and objectivity. This market-driven sense of distrust also came amidst cogent critiques of mainstream media practices from figures like Jon Stewart, Stephen Colbert, and even The Onion, attracting large audiences while delivering well-justified outlines of mainstream media's shortcomings.

This reaches something of a crescendo in the emergence of midstream media. All of these new entrants to the news marketplace position themselves in some way as the antidote to what is wrong or what is lacking in the existing voices of mainstream media. *FiveThirtyEight* prides itself on its data-driven journalism, and the manner in which objective data might counter the affective, subjective voices of individual reporters that comprise traditional journalism. *Vox*, with its tagline 'Understand the News', positions itself as the explainer news source, filling out details that other sources take for granted. *Breitbart* and *The Intercept* are both independently funded, hence not reliant on traditional advertising revenue. Each of these outlets competes for market share by offering not just an additional source of information, but a 'better' source of information. There is not necessarily anything wrong with a broader variety of voices. Media consolidation (that is, fewer unique voices) has long been a primary concern amongst scholars and media watchdog groups (Noam 2009). But this greater heterogeneity does provide an outlet, or perhaps an alibi, for those seeking to dismiss information that conflicts with their own opinions, a move implicitly or explicitly encouraged in an adversarial environment haunted by the spectre of 'fake news'. The marketplace of ideas logic that drives the circulation of ideas and information within a democracy dictates that more ideas, more voices, are ultimately better for the individuals who make political choices based on this data. But the market logic which drives news outlets to compete for audience through product differentiation based on the critique and dismissal of one's competitors seems to produce the opposite effect. As Yochai Benkler and his collaborators demonstrated, followers on both sides of the political spectrum in the 2016 US election were consuming a diet of media that came from across the political spectrum, but were consuming that information differently. Framed, reframed, and shared to one's network on Twitter and Facebook, these stories simply amplified or reinforced the opinions and input that one already possessed (Benkler et al. 2017). A broader diversity of media sources like the one provided by the midstream outlets, built on the premise that something is lacking in the news more generally, seems to produce dissensus and suspicion rather than consensus and trust in the media.

This broader diversity of media outlets also makes brand recognition more difficult. Consider, for example, beyond the relatively larger midstream choices discussed so far, the broad array of choices and sources that confront users of digital news aggregators like Instapaper, Flipboard, Google News, and Apple News and on the feeds of the platforms like Facebook. These apps enable users to choose from and curate a broad diversity of sources, potentially enabling them to explore a variety of voices from across the increasingly politicised news spectrum (Stanyer 2010). Several studies have further demonstrated that these apps are also beneficial for news providers, bringing in additional readers who might not have been part of the existing audience (Anderson 2013). While the experience of browsing such aggregators seems intended to remediate the experience of browsing of titles at a newsstand in the analogue era (itself an emblematic 'marketplace of ideas'), the digital form dissolves any of the material indicators that might be used to judge the quality of a source's content. When getting something into print or even into a professionally produced website required vast resources, the mere presence of a news source spoke to some level of investment and commitment. This is no longer the case, and rather than a few trusted sources that one has tested over and over through years of consideration, these apps instead offer an endless sea of choices and newcomers. This makes for a deeper level of confusion about what is real or fake, trustworthy or unreliable. Unlike the shoddy series of videos that FakeApp made prominent for a brief time, the slick and polished news providers that appear in these news aggregators offer few clues as to their reliability.

This sort of imitation in the context of information density is also what enabled the alleged disinformation campaigns that appeared on social media sites including Facebook, Twitter, and Instagram. In the midst of investigating potential Russian interference in the US election, the social media platforms Twitter and Facebook provided a Congressional committee with examples of the various propaganda (Shane 2017). Of what was purported to be thousands of advertisements purchased by these groups and paid for in roubles, fourteen examples were provided as a representative sample. As a whole, the aesthetics of these ads are fairly consistent, working to seed and spread the sort of viral, meme-driven media that already readily circulate in political channels across the web. Most seem to provide an alibi for their informal, unpolished look by pretending to be the work of amateurs and small, grass-roots organisations. To borrow Paul Arthur's term (1993), this sloppy aesthetic is part of their 'rhetoric of authenticity', much in the way that shaky, handheld camera work connotes a type of amateur, documentary production. Ideologically, they are all over the map, espousing contradictory and in some cases incomprehensible political positions, but all benefiting from the sort of oppositional, adversarial environment that predominates in this same mediascape. While the larger strategy behind these ads can only be guessed at, the flashy, provocative graphics and extreme positions they espouse seem designed to fuel a kind of viral, populist polarisation. As their metadata indicate, none of them were seen by that many people, but most were shared forward multiple times beyond their original placement, making any assessment of their audience, and hence their impact, a near impossibility.

These advertisements thus offer a sort of stand-in or emblem of the larger environment of misinformation and disinformation, paranoia and suspicion that pervades the modern marketplace of ideas. Hidden within a much larger environment of media heterogeneity that feeds on critique and suspicion, they offer a marked contrast with the efforts at mass persuasion and propaganda at work in prior historical moments, representing instead the diffusion of free speech principles within a networked, mediated space. Purchased for small amounts of money, they seem to have slipped in unnoticed amongst everyone else on the back of a platform whose only logic is the exchange and monetisation of content created by others. It was only much later that anyone thought to ask after these ads, real or fake?

Ironically, the emergence of all of these imitators, both real and fake, satirical and earnest, seems to have produced a positive outcome for the mainstream, traditional targets of their attack. Since the election and Donald Trump's one-man war on the media, many of these older news outlets have been asking for, and in many cases receiving, direct support from their readers in the form of subscriptions, donations, and other revenue streams which might replace the declining advertising revenue from their print and broadcast properties (Chatterjee 2018). Almost in the way that the media critic Jean Baudrillard (1994) once claimed that Disneyland, with its simulations of Main Street USA and other fantastical, nostalgic spaces provided an alibi or sense of reassurance that the real world outside the park still existed, these fake news websites and the paranoia and suspicion that they have engendered seems to have given traditional media a new aura of authenticity and importance. Newspapers, the most hard hit of mainstream news providers, seem to have benefited from the fake news brouhaha, with many including *The New York Times*, *The Wall Street Journal*, and Tribune Publishing, the publisher of the *Chicago Tribune*, posting record subscriber growth in the wake of Trump's election. *The Washington Post* and *The New York Times* both advertised aggressively using savvy 'post-truth' era slogans like the *Times*' 'The truth is more important now than ever' and the *Post*'s adoption of its dramatic new masthead 'Democracy Dies in Darkness'.

CONCLUSION

What disruptive technologies like GANs and FakeApp demonstrate alongside alterations in the landscape of competitive news media is the extent to which market principles dominate the channels of exchange where freedom of expression takes place as well as the nature and creation of those forms of expression themselves. The result is something of a mixed bag for the practice this is supposed to protect (freedom of speech and the press) as well as the larger enterprise this is intended to support (democracy and individual rights). While tools like FakeApp reify the power of a competitive version of AI to streamline and democratise the ability to manipulate various forms of media, they also remind us of the deeper plasticity of the media we rely upon to inform us about the world. This can serve as an important warning to question what appears to be true, but it can also activate a general scepticism towards visible evidence and legitimise the easy dismissal of information and opinions that may run counter to our own. This scepticism would find further support in an increasingly diversified and polarised news landscape where emergent midstream players compete for audience in part by critiquing the broader media itself. Hence, competition within these markets might foster a greater diversity of opinion even as it undermines any kind of faith in the process or places of exchange.

Considered together, these individual and institutional marketplaces also demonstrate the emergent centrality of social media to both freedom of speech (usually focused on the individual) and freedom of the press. Indeed, a platform like Facebook or Twitter begins to dissolve the differences between these categories, forcing everyone into a centralised, competitive melee where 'likes', links, and retweets are both the currency of attentional exchange as well as the desired end in themselves (van Dijck et al. 2018). This provides a more level playing field, on the one hand, providing individual citizens with an outlet to express and exchange their ideas. On the other hand, it also moves the burden for regulating speech away from the government over to powerful, private corporations that may be less transparent and accountable to individuals and outside forces. While corporatising governance and monetising individual citizens fits within a neoliberal framework quite nicely, it is perhaps less amenable to the traditional democratic framework that the marketplace of ideas was intended to support.

And finally, what appears to be the most difficult dimension for reconciling the competition of the marketplace of ideas in its current form with the ideals of a democratic framework is its perceived impact on free speech and free expression itself. In the context of the 2016/17 elections that I began with, both the right and left issued dire warnings about the future of free expression and individual liberty in the current political environment. For the left, these values were under attack by the perceived rise of authoritarianism on the right through its attack on the mainstream press seeking to hold it accountable. For the right, the chief threat to individual liberty and freedom of expression was the censorious force of political correctness and identity politics espoused by the left. The debate itself might be evidence of a healthy marketplace of diverse ideas, but the shared alarm potentially points to troublesome underlying fundamentals in the marketplace itself. To put this issue in market parlance, we might say that in spite of the broad array of products on offer and a diversity of consumer tastes and desires, there appears to be a universal lack of customer satisfaction. Taking the marketplace metaphor at face value once more, we may conclude that this portends a very dismal outlook for democracy itself.

NOTES

1. Here I am thinking of the Brexit vote in the UK in the summer of 2016, as well as the election of Donald Trump in the United States and the surprising showing of right-wing figures such as Geert Wilders, Marine LePen, and Nigel Farage. For an extended discussion of the economic underpinnings of these developments, see Norris and Inglehart (2019).

2. *Schenck* v. *United States*, 249 U.S. 47 (1919) (Holmes et al affirming).
3. For a more detailed discussion of the specific events and potential influences surrounding both opinions and their surprising about face, see Healy (2014).
4. *Abrams* v. *United States*, 250 U.S. 616 (1919).
5. A more complete critique of the market would be published in the same year, 1859, in Marx's *Contribution to the Critique of Political Economy* where he lays out his early iteration of the theory of materialist history and directly discusses the market theories of both David Ricardo and Adam Smith. See Marx (1904: 265–304).
6. The hardware innovation I am referring to here is the utilisation of chips designed for graphics processing (GPUs) to process the massive number of computations required for deep learning. See Raina et al. (2009).
7. Examples of more focused midstream outlets can be found in categories like politics (*Politico*), food (*Eater*), and style (*The Cut*) and many others.

References

Abrams v. *United States*. 1919. 250 U.S. 616. <https://supreme.justia.com/cases/federal/us/250/616/> (last accessed 22 March 2021).

Anderson, Christopher W. 2013. 'What Aggregators Do: Towards a Networked Concept of Journalistic Expertise in the Digital Age.' *Journalism* 14.8: 1008–23.

Arthur, Paul. 1993. 'Jargons of Authenticity: Three American Moments.' In *Theorizing Documentary*, edited by Michael Renov, 108–35. New York: Routledge.

Baker, C. Edwin. 1992. *Human Liberty and Freedom of Speech*. Oxford: Oxford University Press.

Baudrillard, Jean. 1994. *Simulacra and Simulation*. Ann Arbor: University of Michigan Press.

Ben-El-Mechaiekh, Hichem, and Robert W. Dimand. 2011. 'A Simpler Proof of the Von Neumann Minimax Theorem.' *American Mathematical Monthly* 118.7: 636–41.

Benkler, Yochai, Ethan Zuckerman, Robert Farris, and Hal Roberts. 2017. 'Study: Breitbart-Led Right-Wing Media Ecosystem Altered Broader Media Agenda.' *Columbia Journalism Review*, 3 March. <https://www.cjr.org/analysis/breitbart-media-trump-harvard-study.php> (last accessed 22 March 2021).

Blasi, Vincent. 2004. 'Holmes and the Marketplace of Ideas.' *The Supreme Court Review* (January): 1–46. <https://doi.org/10.1086/scr.2004.3536967> (last accessed 22 March 2021).

Boyd, Christopher. 2018. 'Deepfakes FakeApp Tool (Briefly) Includes Cryptominer.' *Malwarebytes Labs* blog, 23 February. <https://blog.malwarebytes.com/security-world/2018/02/deepfakes-fakeapp-tool-briefly-includes-cryptominer/> (last accessed 22 March 2021).

Chatterjee, Laharee. 2018. 'New York Times Beats as Digital Subscriptions Surge, Shares Rise.' *Reuters*, 8 February. <https://www.reuters.com/article/us-new-york-times-results/new-york-times-posts-quarterly-loss-as-costs-rise-idUSKBN1FS249> (last accessed 22 March 2021).

Chemerinsky, Erwin, and Howard Gillman. 2017. *Free Speech on Campus*. New Haven, CT, London: Yale University Press.

Cheney-Lippold, John. 2018. *We Are Data: Algorithms and the Making of Our Digital Selves*. New York: New York University Press.

Chesney, Robert, and Danielle Citron. 2018. 'Deep Fakes: A Looming Crisis for National Security, Democracy and Privacy?' *Lawfare* blog, 21 February. <https://www.lawfareblog.com/deep-fakes-looming-crisis-national-security-democracy-and-privacy> (last accessed 22 March 2021).

Christ, Carol. 2017. 'Chancellor Christ: Free Speech Is Who We Are.' *Berkeley News* blog, 23 August. <https://news.berkeley.edu/2017/08/23/chancellor-christ-free-speech-is-who-we-are/> (last accessed 22 March 2021).

Coe, Kevin, David Tewksbury, Bradley J. Bond, Kristin L. Drogos, Robert W. Porter, Ashley Yahn, and Yuanyuan Zhang. 2008. 'Hostile News: Partisan Use and Perceptions of Cable News Programming.' *Journal of Communication* 58.2: 201–19. <https://doi.org/10.1111/j.1460-2466.2008.00381.x> (last accessed 22 March 2021).

Cohn, Jonathan. 2019. *The Burden of Choice: Recommendations, Subversion, and Algorithmic Culture*. New Brunswick, NJ: Rutgers University Press.

Ellison, Sarah. 2015. 'Can First Look Media Make Headlines That Aren't about Itself?' *The Hive – Vanity Fair* blog, January. <https://www.vanityfair.com/news/2015/01/first-look-media-pierre-omidyar> (last accessed 22 March 2021).

Erickson, Paul, Judy L. Klein, Lorraine Daston, Rebecca Lemov, Thomas Sturm, and Michael D. Gordin. 2013. *How Reason Almost Lost Its Mind: The Strange Career of Cold War Rationality*. Chicago: University of Chicago Press.

Farhi, Paul. 2003. 'Everybody Wins: Fox News Channel and CNN Are Often Depicted as Desperate Rivals Locked in a Death Match. In Fact, the Cable Networks Aren't Even Playing the Same Game. There's No Reason They Both Can't Flourish.' *American Journalism Review* (April). <https://www.lehigh.edu/~jl0d/J246-06/everybody-wins.html> (last accessed 22 March 2021).

Fiss, Owen. 2003. 'A Freedom Both Personal and Political.' In John Stuart Mill, *On Liberty*. New edition, edited by David Bromwich and George Kateb, 179–96. New Haven, CT: Yale University Press.

Goodfellow, Ian. 2016. 'NIPS 2016 – Generative Adversarial Networks – Ian Goodfellow.' *YouTube*. <https://www.youtube.com/watch?v=AJVyzd0rqdc> (last accessed 22 March 2021).

Goodfellow, Ian J., Jean Pouget-Abadie, Mehdi Mirza, Bing Xu, David Warde-Farley, Sherjil Ozair, Aaron Courville, and Yoshua Bengio. 2014. 'Generative Adversarial Nets.' In *Advances in Neural Information Processing Systems 27*, edited by Z. Ghahramani, M. Welling, C. Cortes, N. D. Lawrence, and K. Q. Weinberger, 2672–80. Boston: Curran Associates. <http://papers.nips.cc/paper/5423-generative-adversarial-nets.pdf> (last accessed 22 March 2021).

Goodfellow, Ian J., Jonathon Shlens, and Christian Szegedy. 2015. 'Explaining and Harnessing Adversarial Examples.' *ArXiv:1412.6572 [Cs, Stat]*, March. <http://arxiv.org/abs/1412.6572> (last accessed 22 March 2021).

Gordon, Jill. 1997. 'John Stuart Mill and the "Marketplace of Ideas".' *Social Theory and Practice* 23.2: 235–49.

Healy, Thomas. 2014. *The Great Dissent: How Oliver Wendell Holmes Changed His Mind – and Changed the History of Free Speech in America*. New York: Picador.

Hylton, Wil S. 2017. 'Down the Breitbart Hole.' *The New York Times Magazine*, 16 August. <https://www.nytimes.com/2017/08/16/magazine/breitbart-alt-right-steve-bannon.html> (last accessed 22 March 2021).

Jenkins, Henry. 2006. *Convergence Culture*. New York: New York University Press.

Lee, Dave. 2018. 'Deepfakes Porn Has Serious Consequences.' *BBC News*, 3 February. <https://www.bbc.com/news/technology-42912529> (last accessed 22 March 2021).

Lomas, Natasha. 2017. 'Lyrebird Is a Voice Mimic for the Fake News Era.' *TechCrunch* blog, 25 April. <https://social.techcrunch.com/2017/04/25/lyrebird-is-a-voice-mimic-for-the-fake-news-era/> (last accessed 22 March 2021).

Marx, Karl. 1904. *A Contribution to the Critique of Political Economy*. Chicago: Charles H. Kerr.

Menand, Louis. 2002. *The Metaphysical Club*. London: Flamingo.

Mill, John Stuart. 2003. *On Liberty*, edited by David Bromwich and George Kateb. New edition. New Haven, CT: Yale University Press.

Misak, Cheryl. 2013. *The American Pragmatists*. Oxford: Oxford University Press.

Noam, Eli. 2009. *Media Ownership and Concentration in America*. Oxford: Oxford University Press.

Noble, Safiya Umoja. 2018. *Algorithms of Oppression: How Search Engines Reinforce Racism*. New York: New York University Press.

Norris, Pippa, and Ronald Inglehart. 2019. *Cultural Backlash: Trump, Brexit, and Authoritarian Populism*. Cambridge: Cambridge University Press.

Posner, Richard. 2003. 'On Liberty: A Revaluation.' In John Stuart Mill, *On Liberty*, edited by David Bromwich and George Kateb. New edition, 197–207. New Haven, CT: Yale University Press.

Raina, Rajat, Anand Madhavan, and Andrew Y. Ng. 2009. 'Large-Scale Deep Unsu-pervised Learning Using Graphics Processors.' In *Proceedings of the 26th Annual International Conference on Machine Learning*, 873–80. ICML '09. New York: ACM. <https://doi.org/10.1145/1553374.1553486> (last accessed 22 March 2021).

Reding, Viviane. 2007. 'The Importance of Freedom of Expression for Democratic Societies in the Enlarged European Union.' Speech presented at the EU Press Conference, Brussels, 9 July. <http://europa.eu/rapid/press-release_SPEECH-07-478_en.htm?locale=en> (last accessed 22 March 2021).

Risen, James. 2018. 'The Biggest Secret: My Life as a New York Times Reporter in the Shadow of the War on Terror.' *The Intercept* blog, 3 January. <https://theintercept.com/2018/01/03/my-life-as-a-new-york-times-reporter-in-the-shadow-of-the-war-on-terror/> (last accessed 22 March 2021).

Schenck v. United States. 1919. 249 U.S. 47. <https://supreme.justia.com/cases/federal/us/249/47/> (last accessed 22 March 2021).

Schroeder, Jared. 2018. 'Toward a Discursive Marketplace of Ideas: Reimaging the Marketplace Metaphor in the Era of Social Media, Fake News, and Artificial Intel-ligence.' *First Amendment Studies* 52.1–2: 38–60. <https://doi.org/10.1080/21689725.2018.1460215> (last accessed 22 March 2021).

Schwartz, Oscar. 2018. 'You Thought Fake News Was Bad? Deep Fakes Are Where Truth Goes to Die.' *The Guardian*, 12 November. <https://www.theguardian.com/technology/2018/nov/12/deep-fakes-fake-news-truth> (last accessed 22 March 2021).

Shane, Scott. 2017. 'These Are the Ads Russia Bought on Facebook in 2016.' *The New York Times*, 1 November. <https://www.nytimes.com/2017/11/01/us/politics/russia-2016-election-facebook.html> (last accessed 22 March 2021).

Stanyer, James. 2009. 'Web 2.0 and the Transformation of News and Journalism.' In *Routledge Handbook of Internet Politics*, edited by Andrew Chadwick and Philip N. Howard, 201–13. London: Routledge.

Stone, Geoffrey R., and Lee C. Bollinger (eds). 2018. *The Free Speech Century*. New York: Oxford University Press.

Striphas, Ted. 2015. 'Algorithmic Culture.' *European Journal of Cultural Studies* 18.4–5: 395–412.

The Economist. n.d. 'The Next Frontier in Fake News – The Economist: Editor's Picks (Podcast).' *PlayerFM*. <https://player.fm/series/the-economist-editors-picks-1464638/the-next-frontier-in-fake-news> (last accessed 9 August 2017).

van Dijck, José, Thomas Poell, and Martijn de Waal. 2018. *The Platform Society: Public Values in a Connective World*. Oxford: Oxford University Press.

Waldron, Jeremy. 2003. 'Mill as a Critic of Culture and Society.' In John Stuart Mill, *On Liberty*, edited by David Bromwich and George Kateb. New edition, 224–45. New Haven, CT: Yale University Press.

Waldron, Jeremy. 2010. 'Mill and Multiculturalism.' In *Mill's* On Liberty: *A Critical Guide*, edited by C. L. Ten. Reissue edition, 165–84. Cambridge: Cambridge University Press.

Waldron, Jeremy. [2012]. 2014. *The Harm in Hate Speech*. Reprint. Cambridge, MA: Harvard University Press.

York, Jillian C., and Trevor Timm. 2012. 'U.S. Government Threatens Free Speech with Calls for Twitter Censorship.' *Electronic Frontier Foundation*, 6 January. <https://www.eff.org/deeplinks/2012/01/us-government-calls-censor-twitter-threaten-free-speech> (last accessed 22 March 2021).

INDEX